Twayne's English Authors Series

Sylvia E. Bowman, *Editor*

INDIANA UNIVERSITY

Norman Douglas

Norman Douglas

by RALPH D. LINDEMAN

Gettysburg College

Twayne Publishers, Inc. :: New York

To Toni

Preface

NORMAN DOUGLAS will probably never find a place in the
first rank of English writers. His output was not great, and
its quality was not always the best of which he was capable.
Moreover, his imaginative powers were limited; and his ability
to construct a plot, no small part of the stock-in-trade of most
successful novelists, was comparatively slight. Yet it seems certain that several of his books—*Siren Land* and *Old Calabria*
among the travel books and *South Wind* among the novels—will
be with us for a long time. Among readers devoted to the literature descriptive of lands and peoples, Douglas' name ranks with
those of Borrow, Doughty, and T. E. Lawrence. And although
the Italian lands and seas have been taken as subject by such
established literary figures as Gissing and D. H. Lawrence,
Douglas' books, with their casual wit and erudition, remain the
favorites of many.

Douglas wrote only three novels, and of those *South Wind*
alone has found its way into literary histories. This strange
book, which virtually created a genre of its own, is as singular
among Douglas' writings as it was among the novels of its day.
When it appeared in 1917, during World War I, when serious
people were reading serious writers like Bennett, Wells, and
Galsworthy, *South Wind* achieved immediate popularity. Its sunny, windswept vistas and its atmosphere of playful hedonism
appealed to a younger generation in revolt against the values of
its parents. Although it has retained some of the popularity
it had in the 1920's *South Wind* now seems less significant than
it once seemed and a good deal less original. Its method had
precedents in Peacock's conversational novels, and many of its attitudes were ones that had been popular in the 1890's. Nevertheless, to the "bright young people" of the 1920's it was a
breath of fresh air; and Aldous Huxley, Rose Macaulay, and
Compton MacKenzie were among those who wrote novels in
Douglas' manner. Graham Greene has written, "My generation was brought up on *South Wind* . . ."[1]

Douglas produced no other novel comparable to *South Wind,* and his imitators sometimes surpassed him in literary artistry. But at least one of his claims to distinction has seldom been challenged—his power of description. An apprenticeship in the writing of scientific papers and Foreign Office reports helped him develop a prose style of such clarity and precision that it has been praised by almost every critic and reviewer who has written of it. In addition to the distinction of an admirable style and that of having written a "Minor classic," Douglas also exerts the appeal of an unusual personality and one that is everywhere reflected in his writings. Since his death in 1952 there have appeared several booklength studies, a number of new editions of his books, and a convenient book of selections. It is probably still too early to make predictions about his future reputation, but there is little reason to doubt that it will remain modest but secure.

The present study is intended as a consideration of Norman Douglas as a man of letters. I endeavor to discuss his thought, materials, methods, and style, drawing upon what criticism is available and illustrating with rather copius quotations from his books, because many of these are unknown or are not readily available to the general reader. The first chapter, intended as a background to the critical study, includes the principal facts of Douglas' life and a description of his personality. If I have given more attention to these matters than is customary in a study of this sort, it is because the life and personality of the author play a larger role in the kinds of books that Douglas wrote than in other types and hence have greater relevance for the critic. Brief descriptions of his books are included, to facilitate subsequent reference.

The second chapter attempts to survey Douglas' thought. Here and elsewhere the numerous quotations are intended not only to illustrate various attitudes and concepts but also to give an impression of Douglas' tone, which is inseparable from the ideas expressed. In this chapter, I have placed emphasis upon *Good-bye to Western Culture.* Though it is by no means the best of Douglas' books, it provides a clear exposition of his views concerning society. And I have given consideration to the reviews of this book as a convenient way of noting contemporary reaction to Douglas' thought.

The remaining chapters undertake to discuss critically Douglas' method and style. This task is made difficult by the diversity of subject matter and literary types, and I have simplified it somewhat by giving only passing notice to the early scientific writings, which can be considered outside the province of literary criticism. I have found it convenient to treat the three novels in a separate chapter, though much of the material could have been dealt with elsewhere. This choice left the emphasis of the chapter on method to fall upon the travel writings, which form the largest group. The chapter on style naturally cuts across all types. The principle employed in distinguishing method from style was simply to take *method* as the handling of larger elements and *style* as the arrangement of words, phrases, imagery, and other details. Some decisions had, of course, to be arbitrary. In the concluding chapter I have attempted to establish the main lines of Douglas' contribution to the various areas of English letters and to generalize circumspectly concerning his place in the history of the novel, of travel writing, and of English humor.

Douglas' bibliography is a tangled affair, mainly because of his practices of reusing material and incorporating published articles into books. Readers who want more bibliographical information than I have provided should consult the excellent bibliography by Cecil Woolf. The various editions of Douglas' books contain minor textual variations; but, since these do not reflect significant changes in the author's thought or style, I have used whatever edition came most readily to hand. The editions referred to by the page numbers cited in the text and in the notes are identified either in the list of abbreviations prefixed to the notes or in the first note referring to the particular book.

I should like to express my thanks to Professor Frederick Mayer, who supervised my doctoral dissertation on Norman Douglas at the University of Pittsburgh, and Professor Sylvia E. Bowman for her careful reading and editing of my manuscript. Special thanks go also to my wife, whose patient checking of references saved me many hours of tedious work.

RALPH D. LINDEMAN

Gettysburg, Pennsylvania
September, 1964

Acknowledgments

Acknowledgment is gratefully made to the following organizations and individuals for their kindness in permitting quotation from works to which they control publishing rights:

To Martin Secker and Warburg, Ltd., for permission to quote from *Fountains in the Sand* (1912), *Old Calabria* (1915), *South Wind* (1917), and *Siren Land* (1923), all by Norman Douglas.

To Chatto and Windus, Ltd., for permission to quote from *Alone* (1921), *Together* (1923), *How About Europe?* (1930), *Experiments* (1932), and *Looking Back* (1933), all by Norman Douglas.

To Dodd, Mead and Co., Inc., for permission to quote from *Fountains in the Sand* (reprinted by permission of Dodd, Mead and Co. from *Fountains in the Sand* by Norman Douglas.) and *They Went* (reprinted from *They Went* by Norman Douglas. Copyright, 1921, by Dodd, Mead and Co.).

To E. P. Dutton and Co., Inc., for permission to quote from *Siren Land* (1911). (Selections from *Siren Land* by Norman Douglas reprinted by permission of the publishers, E. P. Dutton and Co., Inc.).

To Harper and Row, Publishers, for permission to quote from *Good-bye to Western Culture* by Norman Douglas (Harper and Brothers, 1930).

To Ernest Benn, Ltd., for permission to quote from *Late Harvest* by Norman Douglas (Lindsay Drummond, 1946).

To The Society of Authors (London) for permission to quote from *They Went* by Norman Douglas.

To Mr. Richard Aldington for permission to quote from *Pinorman* by Richard Aldington (William Heinemann, 1954).

Contents

Chronology

1868   Norman Douglas born, December 8, in the Austrian Tyrol, at Falkenhorst, Thuringen.

1874   Father killed in a fall while chamois hunting.

1878   In school in England, Yarlet Hall, Staffordshire.

1879   In school at Mowsley Rectory, Leicestershire.

1881   In school at Uppingham.

1883-
1888   In school at Karlsruhe.

1886   First publication, "Variation of Plumage in the Corvidae," the *Zoologist*.

1888   First visit to Capri.

1889   In Paris, studying French. Trips to Ireland and the Hebrides.

1890   In London, preparing for diplomatic service.

1892   First visit to Greece.

1893   Passed civil service examination. Served in British Foreign Office. Visits to Italy and Greece.

1894   Third Secretary of the British Embassy at St. Petersburg.

1895   *On the Darwinian Hypothesis of Sexual Selection. Report on the Pumice Stone Industry of the Lipari Islands.*

1896   Left the Foreign Service under mysterious circumstances. To Italy.

1897   Inherited part of his father's property. Purchased Villa Maya on the Posilipo.

1898   Married Elsa Fitzgibbon. Visited India.

1899   First son, Archie, born. First visit to Tunisia.

1900   Son Robin born. Visit to Ceylon.

1901   *Unprofessional Tales,* under pseudonym "Normyx," in collaboration with his wife.

1903   Working on Capri materials. Divorced.

1904-
1907   Built Villa Daphne on Capri. *Capri: Materials for a Description of the Island.*

1907   First visit to Calabria.

1909 Walking tour of southern Italy and visit to Tunisia (described in *Fountains in the Sand*). Article on Edgar Allan Poe in *Putnam's*.

1910 To London.

1911 *Siren Land.*

1912 *Fountains in the Sand.*

1912- Assistant editor of the *English Review,* first under Ford
1916 Madox Ford, then under Austin Harrison.

1915 *Old Calabria.*

1916 *London Street Games.* Visit to Italy (described in *Alone*). *South Wind* finished on Capri.

1917 *South Wind* published. Left London. To Paris, then to Italy.

1920 *They Went.* Visit to Greece (described in *One Day*).

1921 *Alone.*

1922 Settled in Florence. Began association with Orioli.

1923 *Together.*

1924 *A Plea for Better Manners.*

1925 *Experiments.*

1927 *In the Beginning. Birds and Beasts of the Greek Anthology.*

1929 *How about Europe?* (American title *Good-bye to Western Culture*). *One Day.*

1930 *Three of Them. Paneros.*

1931 *Summer Islands.*

1933 *Looking Back.*

1937 Left Florence.

1937- In South of France, at Vence and Antibes.
1940

1940 In Lisbon.

1941 In London. *An Almanac.*

1946 Back at Capri. *Late Harvest.*

1952 *Venus in the Kitchen.* Died at Capri. *Footnote on Capri.*

CHAPTER 1

The Man

THE person who undertakes a definitive biography of Norman Douglas will not have an easy task. He will be faced with a subject of many and paradoxical facets—Douglas the scientist, the topographer, the novelist, the aristocrat, the humanist, the bohemian, the Epicurean, the cynic, the satanist, and so on—and the problem of balancing these aspects will be difficult. As John Davenport has put it, "Everybody got the Norman Douglas he deserved."[1] Among those who have chosen to write about Douglas—and they have usually been acquaintances, friendly or otherwise—the views differ widely. Richard Aldington, who apparently did not deserve a very pleasant Norman Douglas, depicts a "well-bred cad."[2] Other, such as Nancy Cunard and Douglas' relative Constantine Fitzgibbon describe a figure of greater personal and literary stature than the facts warrant. The truth, almost certainly, lies somewhere between these extremes.

As to Douglas' own autobiographical passages, these too are clearly chosen and presented in such a way as to produce a particular impression—Norman Douglas as he wished to be known to his readers, full of frank common sense, unsentimental to the point of brutality, learned but scornful of pretense and affectation. It is this view, Douglas' own, which is pursued here, not to the exclusion of those of others, but somewhat at their expense. The reason for this choice is not that Douglas' own image of himself is necessarily the whole truth, but rather that it represents the Douglas of the books, the Douglas who ought to interest the reader and the critic.

I *Childhood in the Tyrol*

George Norman Douglas was born at Falkenhorst, Thuringen, in the Vorarlberg of Austria, on December 8, 1868. He was the third son of John Sholto Douglas of Tilquhillie, Deeside, Scotland. His paternal grandfather had settled in Austria to operate cotton mills at Bregenz. Douglas' mother was only half Scottish: her mother was a daughter of the seventeenth Lord Forbes; her father was Baron Ernst Von Poelnitz, who lived at Bregenz, although his family was originally at Schloss Frankenstein in Franconia. Thus the household in which Norman Douglas was reared was aristocratic and bilingual.

Douglas was proud of his father, who died in a hunting accident when the boy was six years old. John Douglas had been a mountain climber, a hunter, and an amateur geologist and archeologist; and Norman Douglas' penchant for out-of-the-way-research and curious facts was influenced by memories of his father. In *Together* he writes of his father's contributions to the journal of the Alpine Club and of his two monographs—one an archeological study of his excavation of a Celtic hill fort and the other a study of the Roman occupation of the Vorarlberg. The latter work Norman Douglas describes as:

an exhaustive and conscientiously written memoir, full of ripe speculations of his own, enriched with copious footnotes and citations from those authorities, ancient or modern, who had hitherto touched upon these matters; and defining all remains of antiquity excavated here up to that day. . . . It has given me a feeling difficult to describe, to go through this paper again; I seem to be reading my own lucubrations, for at the same time of life I was writing in the same style of subjects of the same kind. (151)

Even though Douglas' relationship with his father was brief, it was important. In *Looking Back* he records that as early as 1879, when only eleven years old, he was reading basic books on geology and collecting rocks; he adds nostalgically, "My father was devoted to this study and would have brought me forward, if he had lived (384)." When Douglas discusses his father, telling of the respect which his name commanded in the vicinity and of how hunters kept a cross perennially in repair at the place of his death, he comes close to the sentimentality which he usually eschews.

Douglas' early youth was spent in the Alpine surroundings of his native Austria, close to nature and to the peasantry; and many of his tastes and beliefs were formed by this region or by his memories of it. He retained all his life a love for the Tyrol and a belief that the sort of childhood he had known there was the best sort: ". . . these are the surroundings in which children ought to grow up. At home, domestic beasts of every kind, and gardens and orchards; further afield, flowery meadows and forests; the glittering snow of winter and cloudless summer skies; rock and rivulet; a smiling patriarchal peasantry all about; these are the surroundings. Keep them off the street-pavement."[3]

In such surroundings the young Douglas nourished an awakening interest in natural history and made early versions of the expeditions which would later take him to more distant lands. "... I scoured those upper regions over field and forest and rock, covering immeasurable distances and never following a path unless obliged to do so, up to the snow-line and down again, sleeping in hay-huts or remote villages. . . ."[4] He was already the indefatigable hiker, the patient observer of topography and people, the thorough searcher for curious facts.

II *School Years*

In 1878 Douglas was sent, at the insistence of his Scottish aunts, to the preparatory school Yarlet Hall in Staffordshire. He hated the school itself, as well as the bullying of the "fag" system; and he was moved at his own urging first to Mowsley Rectory, Leicestershire, and later to Uppingham. But by the age of fifteen he had rebelled completely against the English schools—"That everlasting 'chapel' with its murky Gothic ritual—and before breakfast too: what a fearsome way of beginning the morning!"[5] His threats to get himself expelled—he was already aggressive and strong willed—finally secured his removal to Germany, where he attended the gymnasium at Karlsruhe from October, 1883, to July, 1889. A passage in *Together* expresses his retrospective view of English education in the late nineteenth century:

Men in general are brought up so differently nowadays that they cannot realize what a disheartening trial it was for some of us youngsters at that particular age and in that particular environment, where you could heave a Liddel and Scott at your form-master's head and only get a caning for it like anybody else, whereas, if you were suspected of doubting the miracle of the barren fig-tree, you were forthwith quarantined, isolated, despatched into a kind of leper-colony, all by yourself . . . . What I think is that a grown-up man would be a poor fellow, unless he felt fairly comfortable in any leper-colony into which these gentle ghost-worshipers may care to relegate him . . . . (58)

Despite the element of exaggeration and sarcasm characteristic of Douglas' reminiscences, it seems clear that even at fifteen he was repelled by restraint and also by religious ritual. His lifelong antagonism to Christianity and to middle-class values had its beginning in the "noisome atmosphere of medieval ecclesiasticum" to which his pious aunts condemned him.

The years at Karlsruhe, on the other hand, were by his own testimony happy ones; they were marked by a pronounced freedom and by a remarkable amount of activity, intellectual and otherwise. The schools of imperial Germany had high standards, and Douglas received a sound education in the Classical languages and literatures and did a good deal of desultory reading, especially in out-of-the-way travel writings and various antiquities. Here also he began the study of Italian and Russian with a private tutor.

To his earlier hobby of geology he had added interests in ornithology and herpetology. Christmas holidays were spent in the Vorarlberg, "chiefly to secure certain Alpine birds, such as the citril finch, Alpine accentor, yellow-beaked choughs, wall creeper and others which descend from their heights only at this wintry season."[6] There were also field trips by bicycle and on foot to places in the neighborhood of Karlsruhe to search for bird's eggs, rocks, or plants. And there were correspondences with ornithologists and a trip to Wurzburg to discuss cell formation with a Professor Leydig, a famous physiologist.

The new-found release from surveillance also resulted in unrestrained social activities which took the form of a reaction against the sternness of the English schools. If we are to believe the boastful stories in *Looking Back*, Douglas had as many as three mistresses simultaneously during the Karlsruhe period, although he was scarcely more than a boy. He described this aspect of his school career as "A sound education for boys eighteen to twenty. If some of my young English friends could enjoy its advantages, they would not grow up to be the flabby nincompoops they are, in the matter of sex! (41)" And, in addition, he claimed to have found time to learn Greek, Latin, French, Italian, and Russian, and to become a competent pianist.

Douglas's first published works were scientific articles. "The Variation of Plumage in the Corvidae" appeared in a monthly journal the *Zoologist* (February, 1886) when Douglas was only seventeen. It recorded the observation of two carrion crows, one

with a single white wing tip and one with two white wing tips.
It reached the conclusion that "albinous or part-coloured specimens of this bird are of less frequent occurrence than those of
the jackdaw or rock."[7] Two more contributions were made to
the *Zoologist* in 1886, "Variation of Colour in the European Squir-
rils" in November and "The Present Distribution of the Beaver
in Europe" in December. And several years later, in July, 1889,
there appeared "Der Moorfrosch, Rana Arvalis, bei Karlsruhe"
in German in *Der Zoologische Garten*. These early articles were
published under the name G. Norman Douglass.

Douglas' first visit to Italy was made in 1888, during his school
career. At that time he visited Capri in search of the famous blue
lizard of the Faraglione Rocks. This trip marked the beginning
of his love for the bay of Naples; the Sorrentine Peninsula, which
he was to write about under the name "Siren Land"; and the
island, then thinly populated and free from tourists, on which
he was to spend many of the happiest years of his life—Capri.
Love of the classic lands and literature now took root in soil
that was well prepared. Douglas' temperament and point of
view might have been described as pagan and Mediterranean
from the beginning. In any case, his scientific studies, his rejection of dogmas, and his intense interest in the physical world
made him amenable to the values of the ancient Greeks; and
he was quick to recognize his "spiritual home" under the clear
skies of Magna Graecia. The greater part of the remainder of
his long life was to be spent in Italy.

III *Dandy and Diplomat*

Douglas left Karlsruhe in July of 1889, when he was about
twenty years old; and he spent the subsequent four years mainly in London, with frequent trips to the Continent. His goal
was a position in the British Foreign Office; and, unwilling to
attend Oxford or Cambridge, he "crammed" for nearly two
years with a Mr. Scoones, who was well known for such tutorial
service. In the notorious London of the 1890's—the London of
Wilde and Whistler and Henry James—Douglas lived in rooms
at the Walsingham House, a haunt of various young aesthetes,
and cut a dashing figure. Richard Aldington describes the Douglas of this period as "... a handsome young Scotsman about
town who, as he was fond of repeating, spent most of his youth
and early manhood 'consumed with a passion for a seemingly
endless series of young women.'"[8]

Some months of 1889 were spent in Paris, where the aspiring diplomat went, at the invitation of a friend, to perfect his French and to study political economy and constitutional history. In 1890 he returned to the neighborhood of Karlsruhe to "geologize," and in 1891 he visited the Shetlands and Orkneys in search of specimens. His first visit to Greece occurred in 1892, when it was necessary for him to "escape" from an affair with a girl named Cora who sold hats in a London shop.[9] Other trips were to Vulcano in 1891 in search of reptiles and to Santorin in 1892 to study its fauna. The latter trip produced the article "Zur Fauna Santorins" in the *Zoologischer Anzeiger* of December 12, 1892, forty or fifty copies of which were published separately. This article, like the later studies of the Duchy of Baden, was produced because the young scientist saw a gap in the available printed knowledge of the area. He seems always to have investigated the scientific literature concerning the regions he visited, and he was always disturbed to find that the flora or fauna of the area had not been cataloged.

Douglas entered the Foreign Office by examination in March, 1893. He was sent first to Whitehall, and then, in March, 1894, to St. Petersburg, where he served for two and a half years, as third secretary of the British Embassy. During 1894 and 1895 there were a trip to Finland and a tour of the Middle East. Several more scientific articles were published, based on observations made in Germany in 1889. *On the Herpetology of the Grand Duchy of Baden* was reprinted from the *Zoologist,* with the introductory remarks that "the following notes . . . may perhaps induce others visiting this part of Germany to take up the same branch."[10] *Contributions to an Avifauna of Baden,* also reprinted in 1894, Douglas described as "little more than a catalogue of the commoner birds to be met with in the neighborhood of the capital." He hoped it would induce some resident to take up the study, "if only in order to keep the country up to the level of most other German states in this respect."[11]

In 1895 appeared a long paper *On the Darwinian Hypothesis of Sexual Selection,* the most interesting of Douglas' scientific monographs and one that he referred to as his "only valuable contribution to scientific thought." Its thesis was that characteristics such as decorative coloration and habits such as nuptial dances and exhibitions of prowess are not explainable as efforts to please the female but are rather products of excessive vitality. This theory is related to Douglas' belief that leisure is the key to all creative activity and to all civilized practice. It was in this light that he favored an aristocratic culture and preferred the Mediterranean lands, where it is not necessary for man to consume the major part of his time and energy in a struggle against the elements.[12]

One other publication appeared during Douglas' diplomatic career. This was the *Report on the Pumice Stone Industry of the Lipari Islands* (1895), an official report to both houses of Parliament, later reprinted, and regarded by its author as an act of social service. The result of a visit to Lipari, it comprised a detailed "exposé" of the British-owned and foreign-operated industry there. In the notes that Douglas supplied for Mc-Donald's bibliography, he said: "The trade in London was annoyed with me for publishing what was then the true price, which I ascertained with a good deal of difficulty. . . . An inspector was sent down in consequence of what I said on the subject of child labour, and the 'mechanical means of transport' has now been realized (33)."

In 1896 Douglas left the Foreign Office, going voluntarily *en disponibilité,* a kind of inactive duty. The situation which brought about this move is somewhat obscure. The story Douglas told Adlington and others was that there had been an affair with a Russian noblewoman and that an open scandal would have meant death for both parties. He escaped—"evaporated" was the word Douglas liked for this sort of thing—crossing the border just ahead of the secret police. In Berlin he received a telegram in a language that neither he nor any of his friends could decipher. Persumably it was from his mistress, with a plan for a meeting. Thirty years later he discovered that the language of the telegram had actually been "Siamese, transliterated," but he refrained from translating it in order to avoid further regrets. It is an amusing and an incredible story; but, whatever the truth of the matter, Douglas' diplomatic career was over and an important turning point in his life had been reached.[13]

IV *Marriage and Early Literary Efforts*

Douglas had apparently been receiving a sizeable income from his share of the proceeds of the Bregenz cotton mills. He had no need of the Foreign Office position and probably had no intention of returning to it. In 1896 and 1897 he traveled, visiting London, Paris, Capri, and the Vorarlberg, and purchased a villa, the Villa Maya, on the Posilipo. In 1898 he married an Austrian-Irish first cousin, Elsa Fitzgibbon, and they made their home at the Villa Maya between tours. With her he visited India in 1898, Tunis in 1899, and Ceylon in 1900. Two sons were born of the marriage—Archie, born at Posilipo in 1899; and Robin, in the Vorarlberg in 1900.

The collection of short stories published as *Unprofessional Tales* (1901) under the pseudonym "Normyx," was a collaboration between Douglas and his wife, and, from all reports and evidence, was mainly her work. It contained seven short stories, one long story, and a poem. In his note to McDonald, Douglas said, ". . . only one of the stories and the little Anacreontic are entirely by myself." He called the stories "badly constructed and poorly executed in detail . . . immature and derivative apprentice work."[14] Douglas' most recent bibliographer, Cecil Woolf, says of the collaboration: "she providing the plots and ideas, he giving them form and expression."[15] But, on the basis of internal evidence, it is difficult to believe that Douglas' share in the project went even this far. The style is not at all that of his later books; little, if any of his descriptive power is in evidence; and the atmospheres, which are usually macabre, are not of his usual sort. The themes are reminiscent of Maupassant and Poe, some depending on surprise endings, others truncated somewhat in the manner of Chekhov. None is of much literary value or even shows much promise of better things from their author. Eight copies of *Unprofessional Tales* were sold, the remainder were pulped, and the book is now a curiosity.

Despite his low opinion of these stories, Douglas made use of them in the frugal fashion in which he was to handle all his work. The longest of them, *Nerinda,* was revised and printed separately in 1929 and also appeared in *Three of Them* in 1930. It is about a sensitive young man who, while traveling in Italy with his sister, falls in love with a statue of a girl in the museum at Naples. He grows to believe that the statue is alive and ultimately murders the museum keeper in an effort to kidnap it. Douglas was proud that an eminent psychiatrist had approved *Nerinda* as valid depiction of the paranoid mind. The descriptions of Italian scenery are in a style which perhaps anticipates that of his mature work but is somewhat more lavish. In *Late Harvest,* looking back over fifty years, Douglas called the book "sloppily written (56)."

The other stories in *Unprofessional Tales* were also eventually

turned to profit, for Douglas published them under pseudonyms
in various periodicals during the next twenty-five years. Some
of these stories appeared, along with the Anacreontic, which is
Douglas' only poem aside from his limericks, in the strangely
titled *Experiments* (1925).

The marriage was short lived. Douglas told Muriel Draper
that he had loved his wife deeply for about two years—had
"followed her about all over the place."[16] But the divorce, which
took place in 1903, seems to have left a deep resentment. Fitzgibbon says that in later years Douglas referred to his ex-wife
with some bitterness (19). Aldington, on the other hand, denies
that Douglas ever spoke unkindly of her but admits that "his
utterances about her usually started with the formula, 'Give the
devil her due . . . !' and ended up with a sardonic 'Ha!'" Aldington also records a story received from Orioli, Douglas' friend
and associate of the 1920's, that for two days before the separation he would not answer her except with 'mew!' The remainder
of Douglas' confidences concerning the marriage and divorce
Aldington describes as "hardly publishable."[17] After the separation, Douglas moved to Capri and began to write seriously
about the subjects nearest his heart—the natural history and antiquities of the Neopolitan region. His sexual interests were
henceforth directed predominantly toward his own sex.

There is much that is obscure about this period of Douglas'
life. One feels that those who might know the details have
chosen, probably correctly, to maintain silence. Davenport
writes: "The divorce, the removal to Capri from the mainland,
the recurrence of an old illness, the change in sexual direction,
the beginning of serious writing—all of these are interrelated
and of essential importance to any understanding of that complex
personality—"[18] Fitzgibbon's comments on this crisis contain
the same hint of something beneath the surface, and he is in
agreement in regard to the importance of the period to Douglas' career: "The end of this first decade of the century was a
critical period in Norman Douglas's life. . . . It was at this time
that he developed a certain recklessness towards the more
generally accepted social conventions, which was to involve him
in trouble both in England and in Italy, which later lost him
the affection of several friends, among them Joseph Conrad,
and which made him the object of much gossip (21)."

During this same crucial period Douglas suffered the financial
reverses which caused him to turn to writing as a livelihood.

His brother had sold the Austrian property at a poor price, and Douglas' share of the estate was not commensurate to what he had been receiving as income. Both he and his wife had apparently been extravagant, and his capital, which had been limited, was not sufficient for the sort of life he had been living. The Villa Maya had to be sold, along with the new villa which was being constructed on Capri. Of the latter he wrote: "To part with this place, the apple of my eye, was a wrench, one of the worst of many. It had to be done."[19]

V The Scholar of Capri

Between 1904 and 1907 Douglas made Capri his headquarters. These were lean years, and some of the loans which his charm and apparent lack of conscience in such matters enabled him to extract from acquaintances and tourists probably date from this period. Much of his time, during these years, was spent in study. His interests had moved in the direction of archeology and antiquities, and in this three-year period he produced a number of short studies concerning the history and literature of Capri. Originally published privately, they were later collected under the title *Capri: Materials for a Description of the Island.* They were heavily documented papers based on research in the Naples library, the archives of Capri, and the author's own collection, which numbered almost a hundred items—rare documents and prints.

The first of these studies was *The Blue Grotto and Its Literature* (1904), which discusses the famous tourist attraction of Capri its ancient history, and its rediscovery in modern times. This was followed by *The Forestal Conditions of Capri* (1904), which has an admonitory tone (afforestation was always a "cause" with Douglas). He discusses the condition of the forests in Roman and medieval times, digresses on the "benignant moral influence" of forests, and makes his recommendations, usually with a certain disdain rather than with any hope of their being accepted.

Fabio Giordano's Relation of Capri (1906), is a heavily annotated text of the five pages devoted to Capri in Fabio's *Historia Neapolitano. Three Monographs* (1906) consists of *The Lost Literature of Capri*, notes on thirty-six writers who are known to have lived on Capri but whose work is not extant; *Tiberius*, a discursive apology and vindication of the Roman emperor whose orgies on Capri are a matter of history; and

Saracens and Corsairs in Capri, which discusses the various incursions of pirates and their influence on the town, the populace,
the morals, and the literature.

The Life of the Venerable Suor Serafina di Dio (1907) followed the next year. It relates the saint's life with some cynicism
but also with a touch of admiration for the strength of her will,
and it includes a point-by-point comparison of the lives of Serafina and St. Teresa to prove a theory Douglas held that saints'
lives follow a precedented pattern. In the same year came *Some
Antiquarian Notes* (1907), an extended collection of commen-
taries on diverse matters, mostly geological and archeological. A
partial list of the contents gives an impression of the nature and
range of the things which interested Douglas at this time:
"Brick stamps," "Caves with Roman Cement," "Cicerone Archeology," "Citrella," "Destructiveness," "Etymologicals," "The
Faraglione Group," "Inscriptions," "Marble and Building Materials," "Monticello Vase," "Phallus Worship," "Post-Tiberian
Occupations," "Prehistoric Archeology," "Public Museums," "Sirens," "Some Works of Ancient Art," "Treasure Legends." The
remainder of the materials which made up the Capri collection
included the random comments entitled *Disiecta Membra* and
the *Index,* which were first published in 1915, although probably completed about 1907.

Douglas seems to have intended to write more books on
Capri, or perhaps to organize what he had already completed
and to fill in the gaps. He wrote in *Disiecta Membra* that at one
time he had seen no reason why he "should not browse a life-
time among such literature as might be expected to deal with
the island, producing every now and then some fresh monograph illustrative of its historical or other curiosities (265)."
But he was discouraged by the loss of his library, which had to
be sold for fifty pounds to an American lady who was probably
less interested in owning the collection than in helping a handsome and aristocratic bohemian. He held back ten or fifteen of
the choicest specimens. "What expert would not do the same?"[20]

Aldington has suggested that further work concerning Capri
was forestalled by the publication in 1905 of Harold Trower's
Book of Capri. Aldington writes: "It is true that this [Trower's]
book has small literary merit and lacks that flavour of abstruse
erudition which Norman hit off so well, but in its modest way
Trower's book covers most of the possible Capri topics, which,
anyway, were already very hackneyed by then, and he includes

Douglas on the *Blue Grotto*. Incidentally Norman developed a furious vendetta against this man Trower and satirised him virulently in *South Wind*. . . ."[21]

During the latter part of the first decade of the century, Douglas was writing the material which was to make up *Siren Land*, his first significant book. It was begun near Nerano in 1908 in a house called the "Casa degli Spiriti" on a road that runs under the cliffs of San Costanzo hill and has a view toward Amalfi.[22] Douglas wrote nostalgically about this period, and about the house boy who woke him each morning with orchids.[23]

He was able to get a few things published, beginning in 1909. "Another Source of Paradise Lost" appeared in the *Atlantic Monthly* in November of that year, and an article on Edgar Allan Poe in *Putnam's* in January. At the age of forty-one he was earning his first literary pay. The Poe article, which was sold with the help of an American girl, praised Poe for his aestheticism. The Milton article was an attempt to prove that *Paradise Lost* was influenced by the *Adamo Caduto* of Serafino della Salandro. It contains praise of Milton's style and its effect on the language. Both articles later appeared in books in keeping with Douglas' practice of wasting nothing. Some of the short stories from *Unprofessional Tales* were reworked and also sold, and by 1910 Douglas' travel pieces were appearing with some regularity in the *Cornhill Magazine* and in the *English Review*.

VI *The London Years*

In 1910 Douglas removed, somewhat reluctantly, to London, probably because it had become necessary for him to find some steady occupation or to find a publisher for the book which he had put together of materials from the Capri pamphlets and travel sketches of southern Italy. This book, *Siren Land*, was "hawked about for more than a year without success."[24] But it was finally sold with the help of Joseph Conrad and Richard Garnett to J. M. Dent and Sons, who published it in 1911. An American edition by Dutton appeared in the same year. Parts of *Siren Land* were from the Capri materials—mainly the chapters on the Blue Grotto, on Tiberius, and on Sister Serafina. Several of the other chapters had already appeared in the *English Review*. The publishers cut seven of the original twenty chapters, as lacking in reader interest; but the thrifty Douglas later managed to get them included in *Old Calabria*.[25] The reviews of *Siren Land* were complimentary, praising the author's erudition, his clear style, and his "fine scornfulness." But only six hundred copies were sold of the fifteen hundred printed, and the royalties totaled only about sixty dollars. In 1927 first editions of this book sold for fifty dollars.[26]

During the early part of 1910 Douglas had spent three months in Tunisia, mostly at Gafsa, Tozeur, and Nefta, collecting materials for a book which he hoped would have more success than *Siren Land* had then had. In London this book was put into final form and published by Martin Secker in 1912 as *Fountains in the Sand*. Douglas said that it "originally had a story running through it: a kind of romance. I showed the thing in this form to Joseph Conrad, who read it carefully and then said: 'What is that woman doing here? Take her out!' Out she went, with all that belonged to her, and the book became what it is now."[27] The scenery of North Africa, with its bareness and cleanness of line, held an appeal for Douglas, and this book contains some of his finest descriptive passages.

Another region which held great attraction for Douglas, although it was unknown to tourists in his day, was the southernmost part of Italy. This district is the subject of *Old Calabria* (1915), often considered his best travel book. The circumstances of its writing were described in *Late Harvest* as an "acute financial depression which preceded my appointment as assistant editor of the *English Review;* whereafter my affairs began to straighten themselves out again (47)." Long and rich in the number and variety of places and subjects treated, this book contains the leisurely erudition and the condiment of cynicism which came to form so much of the appeal of Douglas' work. The many memories of the ancient Greeks which present themselves to the traveler in Magna Graecia provided material attractive to his tastes and learning. Collecting saints' lives was always a hobby with him, and one of the best-known chapters in this book is the delightful sketch of the life of St. Joseph of Copertino, the flying monk.

Douglas' position as assistant editor of the *English Review* was secured with the help of Joseph Conrad, an old friend, who introduced him to the editor, Ford Madox Hueffer (later Ford Madox Ford). Conrad, who claimed to value Douglas' literary judgment above all others,[28] had once written to H. G. Wells, "Douglas can not only think but write."[29]

From 1913 to 1916 Douglas wrote a number of articles and reviews for this comparatively young magazine, work which he did not find particularly pleasant. His reviews were often amusing and frequently sarcastic; they were seldom of much value as literary criticism. His favorite prejudices are always in evidence in these reviews, usually too noticeably so. He reviewed a great many travel books and was prone to discuss the places rather than the books. Among books which he reviewed favorably were Robert Frost's *A Boy's Will,* H. M. Tomlinson's *The Sea and the Jungle,* and some of D. H. Lawrence's earliest short stories.

During this period Douglas lived in an apartment at 63 Albany Mansions and ate at Gennaro's in Compton Street with such friends as Conrad, Sabatini, Mavrogordato, and Austin Harrison; he frequently visited Muriel Draper, who wrote about Douglas and his friends in *Music at Midnight* (1929). He also saw a good deal of his son Robin, who ordinarily heard nothing from his father except "luridly-colored post cards" with such admonitions as "Brush your teeth!" and "Use a nailbrush—never a nailfile!"[30] Among varied activities, Douglas founded and helped manage a "cut-rate London niteclub,"[31] and also served as British representative for a plan to drain the Pontine marshes to control malaria.

The years 1910 to 1915 comprised a busy period for Douglas. In addition to preparing *Old Calabria* and *Fountains in the Sand,* and performing his duties on the *English Review,* he was spending a great deal of time gathering materials for *London Street Games.* Douglas showed this strange little book to five or six publishers before the St. Catherine Press accepted and published it in 1916. Over a period of years he had collected the rules of hundreds of street games, as described by children of London's East End. The difficulty of inducing the shy children to take him into their confidence gave him trouble as well as pleasure. The book itself is an unbroken listing of these descriptions—usually in the exact words of the children or in an imitation of their speech—which Douglas called a "breathless catalogue."[32] The intention was to demonstrate the inventiveness of these children and to deprecate the standardizing influence of organized games.

In 1916 Douglas' fortunes fell. He was dissatisfied with the management of the *English Review* by its new editor Austin Harrison; he fell out with Conrad; and he was advised by the government to leave England. In 1911 he had become ill while on an excursion and had managed to get to Conrad's house, which was nearby. His illness proved to be jaundice, and he had to be nursed by Conrad's wife. The situation became difficult when, after several weeks, Conrad became concerned about the strain on his wife's health and the danger to his household. In a letter to Galsworthy, Conrad said, "Should he die, I shall have to bury him I suppose."[33] It was years later that the letter came to Douglas' attention and angered him, playing a large part in the split between the friends. Fitzgibbon suggests, however, that Conrad was also disturbed by Douglas' sexual activities, which seem to have become common knowledge about this time (21).

In 1916 Douglas was looking desperately for some sort of war work and meeting with repeated refusals from various government agencies. These difficulties are amusingly described in the introduction to *Alone,* where he relates a particular refusal by "a plump though not ill-looking, young Hebrew . . ., Mr. W." According to Aldington this was Humbert Wolfe, who described the circumstances in his *Portraits by Inference* (1934), saying that he knew and admired Norman Douglas but that "It had been indicated . . . that at that particular moment in England he would not be a success." Aldington writes: "The irony of restraint in that last sentence is crushing, for to those who asked him Humbert Wolfe would explain that the reason he could not get Norman Douglas a job was that Wolfe had received a very disagreeable commission from his superiors, namely, to tell Norman that he had the alternative of getting out of England at once or of facing arrest on a certain charge. It was just about the time he published *London Street Games.*"[34]

VII *Productive Years in Italy*

Douglas' career as a writer had had a late start. He had been in his mid-thirties when financial reverses changed him from an amateur scientist to a genteel but impecunious man of letters. He had been in his mid-forties when he accepted the position on the *English Review.* In October, 1916, nearly fifty years old, he found himself in Paris virtually destitute, living "from hand to mouth" and begging tobacco from soldiers.[35]

The year 1917 was probably the darkest of Douglas' life, and yet it was the year of the publication of *South Wind,* his brightest and most successful novel. *South Wind,* planned and begun in London, had been finished on Capri in 1916. The bright hedonistic and amoral atmosphere found immediate success with a war-weary public. Its mythical island, Nepenthe, owed a great deal to Capri; but in later years Capri was also to owe a debt to Nepenthe. Its characters—the cheerful cynic, Mr. Keith; the swindling Classicist, Count Caloveglia; the innocuous scholar, Mr. Eames; and the lovable dipsomanic, Miss Wilberforce—were all in some way facets of Douglas, and their learned and amusing conversation was his also. The theme was one dear to Douglas' heart—the subtle ability of the sunny Mediterranean atmosphere to "open the moral pores" —in this case those of an amenable but stuffy Anglican bishop. The "bright young people" of the 1920's loved and lived the characters and the ideas of *South Wind,* and Douglas became a sort of symbol of the free and pleasure-seeking personality in revolt against Victorian moral standards.

A rumor which persisted until recent years had it that the copyright of *South Wind* was sold for fifty pounds. Douglas seems to have fostered this story; it helped give rise to a popular conception of him as an eccentric bohemian who sold his books for a pittance and squandered the money on debauchery. The truth seems to be that Douglas received a fair royalty from Martin Secker. There was, however, during the 1930's, difficulty about the American royalties; and, as a result, Douglas was deprived of a source of income which might have made the remainder of his life more comfortable.[36]

After the Armistice Douglas left Paris to winter badly at St. Malo and Mentone and in 1919 reached Italy again. For the next twenty years his base of operations was Florence. His friend Edward Hutten had begun a journal called the *Anglo-Italian Review.* It was a short-lived publication, but in its two volumes, which appeared between May 1918 and December 1919, there appeared four travel pieces by Douglas, the sale of which was no doubt a partial alleviation of his economic problems. All of these later became chapters of *Alone,* another travel book about Italy, published in 1921. It treated Rome and Florence, as well as the usual varied subjects, in a style more conversational than that of *Siren Land* and *Old Calabria,* and was Douglas' favorite. He wrote in *Late Harvest*:

Were I forced to spend the remaining years of life on some desert island with no companion save one of my own books—unenviable fate! —I should choose *Alone.* A nostalgic and multi-herbal fragrance hangs about those pages. They conjure up a legion of friendly phantoms—

memories that are fading away, towns and villages never to be revisited, voices that I cannot well hope to hear again. This book is too short for my taste; I would have it longer. One craves to savour more keenly the delights of those hours, and to discover yet more details, however insignificant, of what befell during those months when, at the age of fifty, I exhaled the last breaths of an inconstant youth by the wayside of a beaten track in Italy. (37)

At about this time also Douglas published an odd little book of fiction which some critics have preferred to *South Wind*. This was *They Went* (1920), a bizarre tale of the legendary city of Ys on the coast of Britanny during the waning years of the Roman Empire. A lovely young princess, cruel but in love with beauty in all forms, is aided in her plans to rebuild the ugly city by a Mephistophelian creature named Theophilus. *They Went* is a kind of allegory of beauty versus betterment; in it the forces of incipient Christianity, duped by their belief that the ruler of the universe cares about them, foil the forces of beauty. When the city is destroyed by a flood, Theophilus takes the princess off to his own world where, he promises, "goodness" will be non-existent and beauty will be everywhere.

In the Beginning, which appeared in 1927, was somewhat similar in tone. It is a kind of fanciful history of religion. The scene is set in a distant pseudomythological past, and the earth and heavens are peopled with races of gods and heroes. Man is made by the frivolous "Great Father" out of the dung of a "loathesome fowl" and does well enough cavorting with nymphomaniac goddesses until he falls victim of a dread disease, "goodness." He refuses to take advice from the last remaining members of the great race of satyrs and ultimately destroys himself. Aroudi, "haunter of outskirts," then reclaims the world from reformers and improvers and changes it back to desert.

These books are somewhat different from the remainder of Douglas' work and were not so well received. *In the Beginning* especially annoyed many readers because of the lascivious scenes presented, to a good degree, for their own sake. The themes are, of course, characteristic of Douglas and represent ideas which he seems to have held seriously, even though the treatment of them in these books is somewhat whimsical.

Another important travel book of the 1920's was *Together* (1923), the result of a tour of Douglas' native Vorarlberg with a young Italian friend, René. In the informal style of *Alone*, it contains more autobiographical material than any of the other travel books and is marked by a note of nostalgia which creeps into descriptions of scenes familiar to the author's childhood.

The 1920's and 1930's were a prolific and crowded period for Douglas. In addition to producing more than a dozen books, he took trips to many parts of Italy and to Africa, Syria, and Greece with such friends as Edward Hutten, Nancy Cunard, and Giuseppi Orioli. Between tours there was time for the leisure which Douglas considered the key to life and art, and for the wine which he loved to drink in quiet cafes. He was a familiar figure on the streets of Florence during the 1920's and at almost any time on Capri. He was described as "tall, burly, a bit slouched, with straight white hair and plenty of it, a florid complexion, a nose as long and quite as quizzical as Francis the First's, and deep-set, very blue eyes which sparkled so with humour and malice you had to look twice to perceive the warm sympathy and kindliness there."[37]

He was always neatly dressed and dignified, if at times a little threadbare; and his manners were those of a nineteenth-century gentleman. Jessie Conrad describes, in her charming Victorian tone, an incident that took place early in the century in a villa on Capri: "Some remarks made by that extraordinary man [Frank Harris], who must have forgotten he was in an English drawing room, brought Norman Douglas to his feet with a bound. But consummate gentleman that he always was, in his dealings with a woman, he merely offered me his arm and led me to the door."[38]

Douglas knew a number of writers—Richard Garnett, Compton MacKenzie, Scott Moncrieff, Rupert Brook, W. H. Hudson, Charles Doughty, Harold Acton, Ronald Firbank, Michael Arlen, and others—but he seldom discussed literature and was virtually uninterested in the work of his contemporaries. He did not like to meet strangers and was notoriously adept at making quick disappearances when the situation became uncomfortable. He preferred to talk with children: "From them you may learn what their elders, having forgotten it, can nevermore teach you. New horizons unroll themselves; you are treading untrodden ground. Talk to a simple creature, farmer or fisherman—well, there is always that touch of common humanity, that sense of eternal needs, to fashion a link of conversation."[39] His reputation as a conversationalist seems to have been widespread, and Fitzgibbon says of his personality:

. . . he had an effect upon his friends which may be comparable in

its nature, though in little else, to that which Dr. Johnson exercised
on the people about him. Men and women of all classes and many
nationalities would travel far out of their way to spend a few hours
in his company. The loyalty and affection that he inspired, often in
the most unlikely people, was extraordinary. He had the rare and delightful quality of being able to understand without any desire to
interfere. His wit was of an infectious variety, so that only the
dullest of dogs did not seem more amusing when he was about. His
detection of humbug was instantaneous and he blew it away with a
joyful boisterousness. His rare laughter will surely never be forgotten.
. . . (34-35)

Aldington's description of Douglas' conversation verifies this:

My general impression of his talk was of its good sense, its contempt
for sham and sentimentalities ("Cinquecento" as he called them),
and range of knowledge of a rather obsolescent kind. He seemed to
me not to want to monopolise the talk. . . . What Lawrence called
his "wicked whimsicality" was not very obvious either, though I
suspect he enjoyed giving an appearance of devil-may-care cynicism
and disillusion—in his youth people had still been Byronic. But he
most certainly had a gift for caricature in speech, with humorous
exaggeration which you might call whimsical.[40]

Douglas was well known as a gourmet who delighted in harry-
ing waiters and restaurant owners. His tastes in food were as
individualistic as his ideas on other subjects, and he was always
ready to employ his wide knowledge of Italian dialects, including the Florentine oaths and invectives of which he once made
a collection, to see that dishes were prepared exactly as he
wanted them. Although he undoubtedly enjoyed playing the role
of the fussy old aristocrat and connoisseur, he seems to have
taken genuine pleasure in eating, drinking, talking, and traveling, as well as in leisure, solitude, and the fair places of the
earth.

VIII *Orioli and the Lungarno Series*

It was also in the early 1920's that Douglas' long and close
association with Giuseppi Orioli began. This irrepressible little
Italian seems to have been liked by everyone who knew him,
but he was himself inseparably attached to his admired friend
and associate Norman. Douglas' attitude toward him was pos-
sessive and somewhat condescending, and yet there seems to
have been love as well. Orioli was some twenty years younger

than his friend and in some respects took the place of the sons Douglas seldom saw.

Orioli, a collector and seller of rare books, made his head-quarters in a flat below the one which Douglas had purchased in Florence and was within easy reach by means of a speaking tube. The two were constant companions, taking most of their meals together and making a number of trips to various parts of Italy. When Orioli decided to embark on a publishing venture, he asked Douglas for something with which to begin and received a revision of *Nerinda*. He printed several hundred copies in attractive bindings and was soon sold out. Thus began the Lungarno Series, in which Douglas was virtually a partner with his friend. In its short but stormy history the company published not only many of Douglas' books but also the work of Maugham, Aldington, Lawrence, and others, giving these writers a "chance," as Orioli put it, "to say what they wanted to say, and of seeing their writing produced in an appetizing form."[41]

Douglas formed an unusual arrangement for marketing his writings. He would first have Orioli print a limited number of copies in a superior format. These the partners would sell by subscription to people who were willing to pay premium prices for a rarity. When this market was exhausted, Douglas would sell the copyright to a commercial publisher. The proceeds were put into annuities, which at the time of his death, were bringing him a yearly income of more than a thousand pounds. Fitzgibbon says of the system and its results: "It is not a great income for so outstanding a writer; it is safe to say that if he had been dependent on royalties it would have been considerably less. He was perhaps not a brilliant businessman—he would have regarded the effort needed to make a fortune a waste of time that could be more pleasantly spent—but he was certainly not a financial fool. Indeed he despised that sort of fool as much as he did all other varieties of the species (27).

Among the first of the books Douglas published during this period was a pamphlet called *D. H. Lawrence and Maurice Magnus: A Plea for Better Manners* (1924). It was one of the central documents in the feud between Douglas and Lawrence which lasted until the latter's death and after. Maurice Magnus was an American journalist whom Douglas had met on Capri in 1909. He had escaped from the Foreign Legion and carried about with him the manuscript of his memoirs, in which Douglas later claimed to have collaborated. The two lived together for a time; and according to Lawrence, who visited them, Douglas exploited the effeminate Magnus. Some years after the Douglas-Magnus association, Lawrence met Magnus when the latter was without money and desperately trying to escape arrest. Magnus begged Lawrence for help, and Lawrence paid his hotel bill and his fare to Malta—only to be horrified at the extravagant fashion in which Magnus traveled and in which he set himself up on Malta. Magnus, who despite Lawrence's version of him must have had some attractive aspects, was able to borrow more money on Malta; but when he was unable to sell his articles he found himself again in difficulty. This time his appeal to Lawrence was unsuccessful, and he eventually committed suicide.

After Magnus' death, his manuscript, *Memoirs of the Foreign Legion*, fell into the hands of Lawrence (despite the fact that Douglas had been made literary executor); and Lawrence decided to publish it, ostensibly in order to pay the Maltese debtors, although these men appear to have retained less ill-feeling about the whole matter than he. Lawrence supplied the memoirs with a long introduction which was the least elegiac of introductions to posthumous works but one of his best literary efforts. He called Magnus, among other things, a "scamp," a "Judas," a "treacherous little devil," a "traitor," and "human rot,"; and he depicted Douglas (disguised only by the use of the initial—the correct initial) as a selfish and ungrateful old blusterer who had allowed himself to be "kept" by the other man. Douglas was described as "...decidedly shabby and a gentleman, with his wicked red face and tufted eyebrows . . . with his grandiose air—now a bit shabby, but still courtly."[42] Lawrence said that Magnus "ran around and arranged D-'s affairs and settled his little bills, and was so benevolent, and so impatient and nettled at the ungrateful way in which the benevolence was accepted." In answer to accusations of ingratitude, Douglas had said: "Seems to be smitten with me, somehow or other. All the better for me—ha-ha!—if he *likes* to run round for me. My dear fellow, I wouldn't prevent him, if it amuses him. Not for worlds."[43] Lawrence confessed in so many words that he was not sorry for having refused to lend Magnus the money that would have saved his life.

Douglas' answer, *A Plea for Better Manners*, which was first published by Orioli and then included in *Experiments* (1925), is less invective than it is subtly condescending. Alexander Woollcott described its tone as "elaborately good-humored and with a 'come, come, little man' note."[44] The pamphlet was written in Syracuse in eight or ten days during which the evenings were spent in a certain cellar cafe. Douglas later wrote: "Those were evenings of grateful contemplation for me, down in that dim recess, generating a fresh dose of venom for tomorrow's task."[45]

The essay contains an exposition of Douglas' favorite complaint about modern novelists: they are busybodies who are unable to achieve impersonality and who put their friends into their novels in an unmannerly fashion. Aldington claims that Douglas' anger was actually caused mainly by Lawrence's depiction of him as Argyl in *Aaron's Rod*.[46] Referring to this portrait of himself, Douglas wrote in the *Plea*: "'The same high-handed old swaggerer, rather unsteady on his legs, and giving utterance to opinions which are quite in harmony with this romantic figure but which, as a matter of fact, have never yet entered my head."[47] He claimed that Magnus had been far more "civilized, intelligent, and multifaceted" than Lawrence had presented him and that he had lived far more economically than Lawrence had reported. Moreover, Douglas claimed to have applied several times for the literary remains, which were rightfully his, but to have received no answer.

In 1926 Lawrence wrote a letter to *The New Statesman* concerning the *Plea*, which had appeared while he was in New Mexico. He said he was "weary of being slandered" and included a letter to him from Norman Douglas (December 26, 1921) giving him permission to publish the memoirs, to keep the money, and to put him into the introduction if he liked.[48]

Douglas included in *Looking Back* (1933) incidents which illustrated Lawrence's stinginess and his libelous methods. In *Late Harvest* (1946) Douglas fired a last salvo, denying the claim that had been made by Aldington in the *Atlantic* that Douglas had been paid a hundred pounds by an unnamed woman to write the pamphlet.[49] "My own biliary secretion was amply sufficient for that particular essay, though a hundred pounds might go a little way toward the production of a second one." He also laughed off Aldington's suggestion that he had been angry about *Aaron's Rod*: "I am far too tough to care Tuppence what anybody thinks or says or writes about me. To hell with them! (52)"

A Plea for Better Manners was included in the volume called *Experiments* in 1925. This was a potpourri selection including some of the stories from *Unprofessional Tales,* as well as a number of reviews and articles from the *English Review.* One reviewer said, with a good deal of justice, that there was "no powerful reason for the publication of the book itself, and some-one should have advised author and publisher of this fact."[50]

In 1927 Douglas published *Birds and Beasts of the Greek Anthology,* a listing, with comments and digressions, of all the animals mentioned by the Greek poets. In 1930 the Capri materials were collected and reprinted. Douglas said the idea of publishing these monographs was "a sporting one on the part of Orioli." It was the largest English-language volume ever printed in Italy. The friends agreed to share the profits equally and sold the edition by subscription at three to five guineas a copy. Douglas later referred to this edition with pride, calling it "a reference book" and adding, "Whoever glances into it may realise that the labour expended on its composing was sufficient occupation for an ordinary writer's life-time—almost."[51]

In 1929 appeared *One Day,* a brief book about Greece which had first been an article in *Travel* magazine. In 1920 Douglas had been offered three hundred pounds by a Greek prince to write a book on that country in the manner of *Old Calabria.* He accepted the money and made a trip but found the book an impossibility. There was too much material in the Athens library to be assimilated in the time which he could afford to give to the project, and the language, which he had "chattered" in 1892, was no longer with him—six or eight Greek lessons showed him that it was too late to learn. Thus the Greeks did not get their *Old Hellas,* but got instead *One Day,* fifty pages of discursive comments about the Athens vicinity along with some brief but valuable remarks on the Greek poets and on the ancient Greek world view.

In *Late Harvest* Douglas rationalized his failure to fulfill the agreement by calculating that *One Day* cost the Greek people less than a cent a head: "Nine million men have therefore contributed a fraction of a farthing each (if my arithematic is not at fault) towards the production of a book not imposing perhaps as to bulk, but crammed with shrewd and suggestive observations, exhaling a candid love of their race and fatherland and a reverence for its traditions; a book written by a countryman of their national hero, Byron, and in a style, moreover, which no critic will call displeasing: all this for the fraction of a farthing! (56)"

The controversial *Good-bye to Western Culture* (English title *How About Europe?*), a severe indictment of English middle-class values, was also published in 1929. It was suggested to Douglas by his reading of Katherine Mayo's *Mother India*—in fact, he called it an expansion of "observations . . . scrawled on the margin" of that book.[52] *Good-bye to Western Culture* contains Douglas' most ill-humored writing, and its reviews were generally unfavorable. Everyone seems to have recognized that sociology and politics were subjects about which Douglas was not particularly well informed; he had, in fact, boasted of his indifference to them. One reviewer wrote: ". . . the real revolutionary social critic must have a knowledge of the history, struggles, and theories of his subject . . ., a philosophy of values, and the courage to get into trouble with the philistines of the values he attacks. Dissidence without an outlook is mere personal maladjustment."[53]

Paneros (1930) is a collection and discussion of purported aphrodisiacs. It is presented with antiquarian erudition and written in a pseudo-archaic style. Its tone has a note of the nostalgia of a sensualist whom age has robbed of his pleasures.

Douglas again made use of old material in *Three of Them* (1930), which included *On the Herpetology of the Grand Duchy of Baden* (1891), *Nerinda* (1901), and *One Day* (1920). *Summer Islands* (1931) was a travel piece written many years before. His last really creative effort was *Looking Back* (1933), a volume of reminiscences that is rich in biographical information and amusing anecdotes about friends and acquaintances— some famous, some obscure, and most long dead. It is cast in a strange form. Douglas supposedly chose, at random, calling cards which he had allowed to gather over the years in an old vase, then wrote of the memories evoked by each one. Although the book is almost certainly more systematic than it pretends to be, it does create an effect of informal, spontaneous conversation.

IX *The Last Years*

In the 1930's the Lungarno Series got into trouble with the Italian government. Such books as *Lady Chatterley's Lover* had shocked the narrowminded. An attack on one of the publications by Aldington in *The Referee* did not help matters, and soon complaints were being made to the Home Office in London. The Home Secretary, Joynson Hicks, was waging a campaign against what seemed to him to be indecent English language books published abroad. But one such case had already been thrown out of the French courts, and now the Italian courts threw out a similar case against Orioli. The next book scheduled to be assailed was *Some Limericks,* collected by Norman Douglas, supplied with witty and learned footnotes, and published in the series in 1928. Defending it as literature before the self-righteous Fascists would not have been easy. Douglas left for Vence in the south of France. It was impossible for him to return to his adopted homeland without facing immediate prosecution, and he was unable to visit Italy or even to discover the status of his apartment in Florence until 1946. Orioli, who was in danger of prosecution for English sympathies and connections, later escaped also and died in Portugal in the 1940's.

During World War II Douglas was reported missing, but he eventually turned up in Lisbon, where he remained for some time awaiting an opportunity to get to England. While in Portugal and in serious financial straits, he collected apothegms from his books, choosing one for each day of the year, and published them under the title *An Almanac* in 1941. He was old, tired, and apparently incapable of any greater creative effort.

He reached London in 1941, having been away for twenty-five years, and spent the remainder of the war years there. But the Norman Douglas of those years, as he is described by Nancy Cunard, was a worn and disheartened figure who prowled with slow steps the blacked-out streets. Nearly all his friends were gone, and he held little hope of living to see the end of the war and the possibility of return to the sunny lands. He was awaiting death with a "half-mocking, half-melancholy dignity."[54] In answer to questions concerning his health, he was accustomed to mutter that he was "putrefying" as gracefully as possible. The drop in his spirits had not been sudden; Aldington describes him as he was during the 1930's: ". . . he had spells of dreadful ennui. He let drop the fact that at times he spent much of his morning, sitting down with his eyes closed and his head leaning against the wall because there was nothing he wanted to do. At another time, more hopefully, he was suggesting that if somebody would stand him half a bottle of vintage champagne every morning about eleven, he might be able to do some writing."[55]

Douglas did live to return to Italy in 1946, and he resided on Capri at the villa of an old friend, Kenneth Macpherson, for six years until his death. His bent figure, haunting the favorite cafés, was an object of interest to tourists. He led a quiet life, even submitting to a diet; drank very little; and took little interest in things. He occasionally read the *Times Literary Supplement* or the *News of the World*. "Nothing in either, I'm sorry to say. Nothing of any interest whatsoever," was his usual verdict. But he still complained about the food, and he still tried to shock people with his frank language and his iconoclastic opinions.[56]

He put together in *Late Harvest* (1946) some personal comments on his own books. And some photos by his friend Islay Lyons induced him to attempt one more small book about Capri, which was published posthumously as *Footnote on Capri* (1952). This book proved to be mostly things he had already published, sometimes in exactly the same words. He deplored the influx of tourists, the cars and trucks, the modern music; but a comment on the new forms of bathing apparel demonstrates that not all things modern were subject to Douglas' disapproval: "Now Capri is not the place for moralizing, and even old-fashioned folk like myself will sooner or later be driven to confess that living human thighs and arms and breasts and backs, not to mention certain voluptuous posteriors that would do credit to a Hottentot Venus, are a surprising and delectable sight and one that may presently—who knows?—eclipse the fame of mere terrestrial objects like the Blue Grotto (41-42)."

Douglas died in February, 1952, on a day for which the entry in *An Almanac* reads "Why prolong life save to prolong pleasure?" He is buried on a Capri hillside which overlooks Siren Land. Since his death, his friends have written eulogies, and his enemies have attacked his memory. He was able to make one thrust from beyond the grave in the introduction to the posthumously published collection of aphrodisiac recipes called *Venus in the Kitchen*:

Not many years ago I met in the South of France a Mr. D. H. Lawrence, an English painter, whom I interested in the subject, and who certainly looked as if his health would have been improved by such recipes as I had gathered together. He became so enthusiastic that he drew for me the frontispiece which adorns this book. I repro-

duce it because I understand that many of his admirers will be glad
to see a new example of his art. For my own part, I must confess
that this picture of a fat naked woman pushing a loaf into an oven
is not at all my notion of "Venus in the Kitchen." I think such a
creature would scare a good many people out of the kitchen, and
perhaps out of the house. (xii)

CHAPTER 2

Attitudes And Values

NORMAN DOUGLAS lived and wrote according to a set of values less complex than those of many modern thinkers. With the temper of the empiricist, he believed only in what was observable or demonstrable and in what he had been taught by his own experience and by the experience of the race as he had found it recorded in the history and literature of western Europe. He was an indefatigable and, within limits, a systematic observer of nature—of plants, animals, and topography—as well as of the behavior and customs of men. He found nature and man alike to be self-seeking, cruel when necessary, frequently beautiful, and always interesting. This pattern of things he described in his books, and to it he tried to adjust his life and his thought. He was accordingly unsentimental, egotistical, and curious. But his acceptance of the world about him—the evil and the ugly along with the good and the beautiful—led also to such warmer traits as a tolerance for individual foibles, a hatred of tyrannies which would thwart the individual's rights to the natural pleasures of life, and an insistence upon temperance, moderation, and such practices as conduce to physical and intellectual health.[1] Douglas seems to have adopted these values as a youth and to have changed them very little during his long life, though in his later years these values may have tended, as some of his critics maintain, to harden and to assume the nature of a pose.

I *The Dilettante Scientist*

Most of Douglas' thought and writing is informed by his "scientific" curiosity concerning the physical world. He was a respecter of nature and of thorough investigation of it. This attitude Douglas called "the humility of the true artist,"[2] and he was right to the extent that the ideal artist, like the ideal scientist, is honest and humble before his material. One of the aphorisms in *Almanac* is "Everything is interesting," a point of view which is reflected in the diverse subject matter of Douglas' early scientific writings, as well as in the wide-ranging digressions which mark his more mature travel books. Once the youthful Douglas had decided to pursue a particular topic, he was tireless in his direct observations and in his perusal of available literature. Such early monographs as *On the Herpetology of the Grand Duchy of Baden* (1891) and *Variation of Plumage in the Corvidae* (1886) testify to his thoroughness; and the Capri volumes are remarkable for their coverage of hundreds of aspects of the island's history and topography.

Some of the early expeditions were searches for particular specimens or efforts to prove some biological or geological point. He sought and found toads on Lipari because Darwin had said there were none on volcanic islands. On the Greek island of Stympolis he discovered a frog which should not have been there. There were slugs to be tracked down on Santorin, the Asterolepis and the Great Skua in the Shetlands and Orkneys, and a rare fresh water seal in the lake of Saima in Finland.[3]

Sometimes the stimulus for these projects came from reading, which from the Karlsruhe days include a great deal of natural history—especially rare, specialized studies of specific localities. In *Looking Back* he recalls the origins of several trips made about the turn of the century: "It was not Tennent that sent me to Ceylon, nor yet those earlier writers like Percival and Jean-Christophe Wolf, but something still older, an account of the island by some English adventurer which I had read, as a boy, in a collection of travels. The 'Relation,' as it may have been called, inflamed me. One of these days, I thought, I'm going there (82)."

In the early years of the century, when the failure of Douglas' income necessitated his recourse to writing as a livelihood, the amateur scientist had perforce to become the commercial writer, but the compromise was by no means complete. The passing years also had their mellowing effect, and the researcher whom no discomfort or danger could deter from the necessary investigations grew to prefer a more leisurely approach, a more passive reception of nature's displays. There were still tours to be taken and observations to be made, but these were to be a more desultory sort of wandering, and the books which they produced were more discursive and riper reportings. Yet, the "scientific temper" was always present, influencing the writer's choice of subject matter, underlying his methods and style, and forming his outlook.

There is a distinction to be made between the sort of passion for unusual researches which Douglas had and what might be called professional scholarship. Despite his desire for knowledge and his insistence upon verification and documentation, his scholarship had its limitations; and he sometimes displayed an ironic awareness of them. D. M. Low, who has made the necessary qualifications in respect to this aspect of Douglas' reputation, writes: "In fairness to Douglas's true reputation and to the meaning of terms, it has been a mistake to eulogise his scholarship overmuch, and it must not seem ungracious to say so. Although he was fond of alluding playfully to his 'professorial moods', he made the distinction between himself and scholars perfectly clear."

Low points to certain speeches of that omnivorous but desultory scholar Mr. Keith of *South Wind* as providing an insight into Douglas' own practices:

'I am nearly done with psychology now. It was the Greek philosophers before then. When I take up a subject, this is what I do. I don't ask what are Aristotle's teachings or relations to his age or to humanity. That would lead me too far. I ask myself: what has this fellow got to say to me? To me, you understand. To me.'

'That must simplify matters.'

'It does,' replied Keith, quite unaware of the faint tinge of College irony in the other's words.[4]

It is always dangerous to read too much of the author into the speeches of his characters, and it must be admitted that the thoroughness of some of Douglas' researches belies the kind of cursory approach that Mr. Keith described; and yet the point that Douglas' approach was not actually that of the professional scholar is well taken.

In *Late Harvest* the octogenarian Douglas reviewed his attitude toward the kind of scholarly and detailed study that he had produced in *Birds and Beasts of the Greek Anthology:* "Monographs of this kind, to my way of thinking, have a charm of their own, and become more appetising in proportion as the field of inquiry is limited (26)." He also suggested several topics which had recently occurred to him and which he would have liked to undertake had he felt that sufficient time remained to him: "The Flora and Fauna of Canterbury Cathedral"; "The Flora of Bombed Areas"; "The Evolution from Early days of our Building Materials, their kinds, their places of origin and modes of application (26)." These were the projects which Douglas preferred and the types to which he could lend his peculiar erudition. There is here less of the genuine scientist, with his inexorable drive toward the embracing generalization, than of the leisured dilettante.

But the penchant for scholarly and patient investigation was more than a whim with Norman Douglas; it was an attitude toward reality. Scientific discipline taught him to trust only facts dispassionately considered; to fear and distrust abstract reasoning; and to feel only contempt for metaphysical conjecture and idealisms, which seemed to him not only useless dreamings but dangerous superstitions. To lose sight of facts was to lose objectivity: "What strange creatures we are, placing more faith in deductions than in facts—why? God created the facts and they may take care of themselves, but the deductions are our own, to be clung to with parental attachment."[5]

II *The Naturalist*

Douglas' view of reality is one that is clearly connected with the scientific attitudes that held so much appeal for him. He considered the things of this world as sufficient, and he scorned conjecture concerning anything beyond nature. He refused to consider problems of creation, believing that the universe had always existed and would always exist and that God was not the inventor of the world but was the invention of man. The question of the relationship between such views—often called by the generic term "naturalism"—and the discoveries and assumptions of modern science is a complex one, but obviously a close relationship exists. Douglas' scientific attitudes were those of nineteenth-century science, a science to which biology was central; and they led him to a naturalistic and materialistic interpretation of reality. His beliefs, in all areas, were compatible with what were, to him, the scientific explanations of phenomena. A self-assured and self-sufficient viewpoint, sceptical and hard, yet it was on the whole cheerful and optimistic. Through Mr. Keith of *South Wind* he says, "I find everything useful and nothing indispensable. I find everything wonderful and nothing miraculous. I reverence the body. I avoid first causes like the plague (164)."

Despite his closeness to nature, Douglas did not conceive it as capable of offering or of receiving the sympathy of man. There was in his thought no "primitive animism," no pantheism, and none of the so-called "pathetic fallacy." In *Birds and Beasts of the Greek Anthology,* he scoffed at the ancient belief that certain creatures—the dolphin, the nightingale, the swallow—have "a certain kindheartedness and man-loving propensity." He pointed out that "the dolphin cares no more about us than cares the haddock," and "the swallow profits by our hospitality solely in order to satisfy its personal nesting instincts; and long may it do so."[6]

Douglas professed not to have felt the needs which have driven men to seek explanation and consolation beyond the natural, and he ordinarily treated such needs and their manifestations with considerable scorn.

And what is it—this want, this great unrest. I cannot tell, having never felt it. I have no want that cannot be gratified with a little pertinacity. Perhaps that is because I am not conscious of possessing an eternal soul which "vexes" itself and craves for strange meats. When anything goes wrong, I know that either I have done something I ought not to have done or—more commonly—that my friends have left undone those things which they ought to have done (for me). My desires are of this planet.[7]

Although he is frequently and with some justification called a Humanist, Douglas was no more illusioned about the infinite possibilities of man than were earlier Humanists such as Montaigne. He was always ready to hurl his contempt at the human weakness which produced the kind of thought he considered to be superstition. He attacked the "hermaphroditic yearnings of mysticism and idealism" and found them derived from "firm-fixed bodily imperfections which prevent us from adapting ourselves perfectly to our surroundings and leading the true cosmic life." Although couched in the terms of nineteenth-century science, this is as a clear a recognition of human frailty as is that of orthodox Christianity. But Douglas' response takes the form neither of faith nor of *Weltschmerz.* It is resigned, tough, stoical; and it contemptuously rejects "metaphysical palliatives": ". . . this setting up of non-truths as ideals to be pursued because of their utility as soporifics, is amateurish and oblique. . . . Whoever endures real grief of heart soon learns to dispense with this kind of philosophy or religion."[8]

In the autobiographical *Together* Douglas described the beginning of his atheism:

We visited, yesterday, the very spot where, at the callow age of seven, I formulated and was promptly appalled by its import, a far-reaching aphorism: There is no God. For some obscure reason (perhaps to test the consequences) those awful words were spoken aloud. Nothing happened. Who can tell what previous internal broodings had led to this explosive utterance! None at all, very likely. The phenomenon may have been as natural and easy of birth as the flowering of a plant, the cutting of a wisdom tooth. . . . There is was: the thing had been said. . . . the periodical relapses into credulity, into a kind of funk, rather, occurred for the next few years. After that, my intellect ceased to be clouded by anthropomorphic interpretations of the universe. Let each think as he pleases. To me, even as a boy, it was misery to profess credence in any of this Mumbo-Jumbo or to conform to any of its rites. (56-57)

Throughout Douglas' writings appear the attacks on religion. Christianity is the principal target; but Islam, Hinduism, and even the Greek mystery cults come in for their share. Sometimes the attacks are subtle and telling; at other times, and all too frequently, they are shrill in tone and unreasoned in attitude, full of emotion-loaded words like "vulgar," "stupid," and "mephitic." He blamed the Christian religion for everything that he found personally distasteful, from its usurpation of pagan mythology to the English legal code. In that broadside against modern values called *Good-bye to Western Culture*, perhaps the most ill-considered and offensively expressed of all of his books, he places the blame for the antifeminist tradition on Christianity, especially on St. Paul and on St. Augustine (41). In *Late Harvest* he pronounced the source of both Hitlerism and Bolshevism to be the Bible. The Chosen People and Pure Race ideas are from the Old Testament (Ezra and Nehemiah) and were "eagerly sucked up by those passionate Bible-readers, the Germans (40)." Socialism, he wrote, is rooted in the envy of the rich and in that glorification of the proletariat "which crops up repeatedly in the New Testament . . . (41)."

As might be expected, the aspect of the Christian tradition which drew Douglas' finest scorn is the emphasis upon abstemiousness and mortification of the flesh, as it appears in ascetic medieval Catholicism and in northern Puritanism. He hated to see people throwing away the good things in life and inducing others to do so, all for the sake of intangible and to him incredible returns. He discussed the Christianity of St. Theresa in *Siren Land:*

Too indolent to scale the heights of doubt or dogmatic specula-

tion, it avoids those fruitful sources of dissension and finds content-
ment in phlegmatic submission to authority; too selfish to expend its
energies in altruistic schemes, it silently disregards, while professing
loudly, the perilous and irksome doctrine of neighbourly love; too
sensual to desire or conceive an impersonal deity, it throws the
impetus of its misguided sexual yearnings into a sub-carnal passion
for the Son of God who, by a presumption unique and degrading,
is supposed to appreciate and actually to reciprocate such sentiments:
the whole edifice, if it deserves that name, being interpenetrated
and enlivened by mysticism, the convenient refuge of all who can
feel, but not reason. (166)

One of the clearest contradictions in Douglas' attitudes lay in
the fact that he could in one breath condemn the more extravagant forms of Christianity and in the next prefer these to more
rationalized theologies. Although he ordinarily condemned anthropomorphism, he also despised the more sophisticated and
impersonalized conceptions of deity. He often expressed a preference for the fantastic saint-worship of southern Italy over
the colder dogmas of Anglicanism: "Fully to appreciate their
attitude as opposed to ours, we must also remember that the
south Italian does not trouble himself about the objective truth
of any miracle whatever; his senses may be perverted, but his
intelligence remains outside the sphere of infection." Although
the Englishman may sneer at the absurd beliefs of the Italian
peasant, he will himself profess belief in metaphysical conceptions such as the Trinity which seem to Douglas just as absurd.
Moreover, he will allow these beliefs to influence his life. In
other words, he will take them seriously—the worst absurdity
of all. "It is the old story: Gothic intensity and Latin spacious-
ness."[9]

Douglas approved a thoroughgoing polytheism as expedient
for the peasantry. He recognized that the problem of evil—the
contradiction between the presence of evil and that of an
omnipotent and just God—grew with the monotheistic emphasis:
"If we must have gods, let us have them by the score—it is
the only way out of the difficulty. . . . Then we shall know on
whom to fix the blame, when anything disagreeable happens
to us. At present, God being good, we are up a tree."[10] The
God who is omnipotent, transcendent, and personal strikes him
as inevitably a Puritan and a spy, designed to relieve the weak
of individual moral responsibility: "A great Being who sets the
Cosmos in order and then goes to sleep; that will pass. One

who remains awake and responsible for all that happens on earth is a monster. Even with the help of the Devil to explain away the worst of his tricks, he cuts an indifferent figure. Monotheism, a graceless and unreasonable belief, has its origin in laziness. A single God is an absurdity and a bore."[11]

Douglas' affinity for the attitudes of the early (pre-Periclean) Greeks is apparent in many aspects of his thought, and it is reflected in his paradoxical attitude toward various kinds of polytheism. The southern Italians, whom he considered more sane than northerners, were like the Greeks: they were able to leave their religion in the temple and to live with their reason and their senses. The patron saint is called upon only in emergencies and is not permitted to affect everyday life, to override common sense, or to obscure those virtues which are universally human. In fact, Douglas' position seems to be that the more absurd the beliefs, the less likely they are to be taken seriously and the more likely they are to produce a healthy reaction. The Russian Orthodox Church, for instance, is described as

. . . an establishment after my own heart. It fosters blandly those virtues which every sensible man cannot help practicing even without its authority or approval; its art forms, frozen to immobility, appeal to the lover of things obsolete. Its fetishistic ceremonials beguile the senses; for the rest—a veritable nightmare, a repository of apocalyptic nonsense of the right kind, the uncompromising kind; and in so far affording a better springboard into a clean element of thought than the incurable Catholicism of the Poles, or our own Church whose *demi-vierge* concessions to modernism offer seductive resting places for the intellectually weak-kneed.[12]

The saints are "downstairs gods," like the impulsive and often rascally members of the Homeric Pantheon. They will foster rather than discourage the enjoyment of physical pleasures (ascetic saints such as Teresa or Serafina are, of course, exceptions) and will not interfere with the individual's healthy tendency to look out for himself: "Every one of the heavenly host may be cheated at a bargain; the Virgin and her infant Son—the adult Jesus is practically unknown here—are adored with feasts and flowers; they are *tanto belli;* but to endeavour to imitate either of them would be deemed a most unprofitable speculation. A Greek fashion of regarding the gods."[13] In pointing out the pagan nature of these practices, Douglas is, of course, granting his highest order of approbation.

Douglas thought of Christianity as imported from the East

by the Greeks, "who ought to have known better"; and he was particularly harsh on Plato, whose ideas he correctly considered germinal to much that he disliked in Western thought. Plato, that hater of facts, is mere "food for adolescents." He may possibly have a value also for the aged: "For questioning moods grow burdensome with years; after a strain of virile doubt, we are glad to acquiesce once more—to relapse into Platonic animism, the logic of valetudinarians. The dog to his vomit."[14] Douglas considered Plato's influence to have lain in his ability, through the magic of language, to make the reader think he knows more than he does. Plato is hence the father of wishful dreams and comfortable lies. To Douglas the poet and the metaphysician are virtually the same: obscure dreamers who soften the fibers of humanity. Their kind of truth is not for him.

Pythagoras is another Greek who does not fare well at the hands of this apostle of reason and hard facts. To Pythagoras he attributes ". . . that oriental introspectiveness which culminated in the idly-splendid yearnings of Plato, paved the way for the quaint Alexandrian tutti-fruitti known as Christianity, and tainted the well-springs of honest research for two thousand years."[15]

The more modern and sophisticated idealisms do not slip past this thorough skeptic. He is quick to recognize his old enemy in whatever guise; to him, modern pantheistic philosophies, if less crude than old-fashioned anthropomorphism, are little better, for they lack its picturesqueness and simplicity. World Souls and Gods-in-Nature are merely products of the human phantasy at a more advanced stage of its evolution. Pragmatism, which one suspects Douglas never completely understood or even cared to understand, is "the last ditch in the metaphysico-sentimental steeplechase." It was conjured up by Professor James out of the "rubbish-heaps of Königsberg and Athens" and is only a systematization of those "disordered flashes of intelligence that animate the savage or the child." Such philosophies are no more than yearnings for the unreal, for "consolation from the bewildering stress of phenomena . . . *The horror of a fact.* . . ."[16]

Douglas was not an optimistic skeptic anticipating a utopia of noble pagan clarity. Completely aware of human fallibility, he recognized that the kind of thought he deplored is natural to man and shows no promise of disappearing. One critic has noted that Anatole France, with whom Douglas is often compared, seems to imply that if others would share his skepticism concerning moral and religious values, all would be well; whereas, as far as Douglas is concerned, we will all be lucky if things do not get a good deal worse.[17] Douglas frequently professed his indifference to the fate of his neighbor, and his jibes were not as a rule so much preachings as scornful sport. He usually avoided the pitfall of allowing his skepticism to become a religion. With the coming of old age, however, he became considerably more irritable and was given to venting his eloquent but not especially convincing spleen on every convenient occasion. *Good-bye to Western Culture* represented an unhappy culmination of this tendency. Perhaps the increased cantankerousness was a part of the pose necessary for the reputation of the writer who had become a symbol of the rejection of Victorian attitudes to an entire generation.

III *The Touch of Brutality*

George Santayana's description of the ethical temper of the naturalist can serve as an introduction to Douglas' ethical views. So well do Santayana's words describe Douglas' attitudes that they might have been written about him:

. . . primarily an observer . . . he will probably be such in ethics also; that is, he will have no ethics, except the emotion produced upon him by the march of the world. If he is an *esprit fort* and really disinterested, he will love life; as we all love perfect vitality, or what strikes us as such, in gulls or porpoises. This, I think, is the ethical sentiment psychologically consonant with a vigorous materialism: sympathy with the movement of things, interest in the rising wave, delight at the foam it bursts into, before it sinks again. Nature does not distinguish the better from the worse, but the lover of nature does. He calls better what, being analogous to his own life, enhances his vitality and probably possesses some vitality of its own. This is the ethical feeling of Spinoza, the greatest of modern naturalists in philosophy. . . . Pity and repentence, Spinoza said, were vain and evil; what increased a man's power and his joy increased his goodness also. The naturalist will believe in a certain hardness, as Nietzsche did; he will incline to a certain scorn, as the laughter of Democritus was scornful. He will not count too scrupulously the loss of what he achieves; he will be an imperialist, rapt in the joy of achieving something. In a word, the moral hue of materialism in a formative age, or in an aggressive mind, would be aristocratic and imaginative.[18]

Douglas was "disinterested" in the sense in which Santayana

uses the word, and his ethical values have the Nietzschean hardness, the admiration for vitality, the aristocratic bent, and, above all, the scornful amusement of Democritus.

The only general guide to human conduct to be gleaned from Douglas' numerous discussions of this subject is a rather vague and changing standard set by the most refined and most agreeable practice of the best and healthiest elements of the society into which one has been born.[19] One's conduct should always be governed by the circumstances rather than by any preconceived code and should have as its end the achievement of refined pleasure and the avoidance of discomfort, ugliness, or purposeless cruelty. Certain habits of kindliness, politeness, temperance, moderation, and taste he seems to consider familiar and agreeable to all; but even these would vary with time, place, and circumstances. Although Douglas would probably have denied that any action or practice could be in itself either good or bad, he nevertheless often made judgments according to a kind of fixed criterion. This was a general standard characteristic of his own particular personality and viewpoint. Certain human failings—superstition, prudery, slovenly thinking, weakness, and submissiveness—almost always drew his condemnation wherever or whenever they were found. His *summum bonum* was a state of self-contained placidness, a freedom from perturbation and intrusion similar to that sought by the Greek philosophers; he seems to have considered ethical superiority as born of hereditary taste and intelligence, as well as learned by worldly experience. This is an egotistical and aristocratic morality in which virtue is described as "conduct which conduces to the actor's welfare."

Douglas had, of course, no use for moralities based on divine sanction: "We can be trusted, I hope, to hack out a decent code of conduct for ourselves without assistance from any other quarter."[20] Most distasteful of all was the morality of the New Testament: "that doctrine of loving and forgiving one's enemies is based on sheer funk; our pity for others is dangerously akin to self-pity, most odious of vices."[21] The insistence upon the relativity of morals is central to much of Douglas' thought; in fact, it forms the theme of his best-known novel, *South Wind*. His recognition of the ever-changing nature of our ideas of right and wrong led him to his professed nihilism. He described himself as one who, "convinced of the eternal fluidity of all mundane matters, and how that our most sacred institutions are merely conventionalities of time and place, conforms to only one rule of life—to be guided by no principle whatever."[22]

Douglas' egocentric view, which he believed to be based on a recognition of the facts of life as they are reflected in nature and in honest men, sometimes displayed a streak of cruelty or unfeelingness. Of course, he considered this attitude to be merely a freedom from sentimentality and bourgeois values. But the reader unavoidably notes the almost gleeful tone with which Douglas sometimes describes instances of cruelty. For example, one of the descriptions in *London Street Games:* ". . . you go up to a boy smaller than yourself and take him by the throat and say *Pin, Button, or Marble.* And that's all you have to do. Because then he must turn out his pockets and thank God if he doesn't get a thrashing into the bargain. It isn't exactly what you'd call even chances, but it's quite all right, especially if you happen to be the big boy; because the big boy generally wins at this game."[23] We see in this passage what may be a reflection of Douglas' allegiance to the principle of the survival of the fittest, a popular concept in nineteenth-century science and one which impressed him as particularly valid.

However, many of these instances of cold-bloodedness may be consciously iconoclastic. Douglas obviously found a good deal of sly amusement in shocking the public. Smug and unrealistic morality was the enemy against which he struck in all his books and in much of his conversation and behavior as well. The *épater le bourgeois* motif can be found in English literature at least as early as Byron and was especially popular in London during Douglas' formative years, the last decades of the nineteenth century. In *Looking Back* he reports with obvious relish his various violations of accepted ethical standards. For instance, his practice of borrowing money with little hope or serious intention of returning it: "far from having a horror of such conduct, [I] regarded these temporary contributions as my due, and each succeeding cheque (there were not nearly enough of them, nor were they nearly big enough) as a tribute to my persuasive powers . . . (78)."

It is also possible that much of Douglas' unethical behavior— his dexterity in fleecing the rich, his willingness to be "kept," his ungenerous "looking out for himself" policy—is in some part the result of the milieu in which he found himself as a young man fresh from school. Young and handsome aristocrats of limited means were expected, indeed trained, to prosper in a parasitical kind of relationship to society in which taste rather than morality was the basis. Even the diplomatic service in which Douglas trained and served was at that time a kind of corps of professional gentlemen—the very word *diplomacy* still connotes suaveness rather than honesty.

In the autobiographical sections of *Together* appear a number of details which may well have been included for their "shock" value but which nevertheless indicate that there was little sentimentality in Douglas, even as a child: the childhood custom of decapitating the dolls sent to his sister as gifts and the prank of rolling a stone through a peasant's hay hut. The strange interest in the mentally ill which marked the children of the Douglas family may also be disturbing to the sensibilities of some readers. Norman and his sister liked nothing better than to visit asylums in the neighborhood and to amuse themselves by watching the mentally ill: "There is a fascination about real idiots. They have all the glamour of a monkey-house, with an additional note of human pathos (13)." It is not so much the behavior of the children that is shocking as the tone in which it is recounted by the adult. And the peculiar interest in insanity remained strong. On the walking tour of his native Vorarlberg which he took with his friend Mr. R. in the early 1920's, one of the promised sights was the "dorftrottles" (village idiots "of the genuine alpine breed"). But, alas, these proved disappointing— too intelligent, able to do such things as knit and chop wood. "These things call themselves idiots," he complained. "Even idiots, it seems, have degenerated nowadays (38)."

Several critics have suspected that a rigorous, Calvinistic background may have been indirectly responsible for Douglas' hatred of Puritantical values and ultimately of anything that resembled them or that received their sanction. His friend John Davenport suggested that "The ghost of a Scottish moralist may have lingered behind the garden god."[24] And V. S. Pritchett, in his memorial article in the *New Statesman and Nation,* said: "His laughter . . . has the short, tolerant scorn, the touch of brutality, sometimes the mad, fantastic ring of the ex-puritan; there is a note of amused vengeance in it. I do not know anything about the early life of Norman Douglas; yet one cannot but suspect that at some early age, the Scottish devil must have been made irresistibly attractive to him and that *South Wind* is the calvinist's as well as the pleasure seeker's hedonist's [sic] revenge (307)."

No one, it seems, including those of Douglas' friends who have written about him, knows much more about his early life than he chose to tell in his own books. But, on the basis of what he related concerning his early schooling, Pritchett's theory makes sense. Yet Douglas would no doubt have set aside discussion of his "touch of brutality" in much the same way that he defended the harsh actions of Emperor Tiberius: "Brutality and common sense are not rarely different names for the same thing. There are men who call surgeons brutal, because they amputate limbs."[25]

John Davenport has written of Douglas: "Tempered in the abstract, his love of mankind individually was passionate. . . ."[26] And this summarizes the contradictory nature of Douglas' attitude toward his fellow men. Despite his scorn for the "herd" as such and his indifference to social problems, he had a vein of kindness and consideration for individuals—especially for those in need or in trouble. Several of the reminiscences by friends and acquaintances printed in Nancy Cunard's *Grand Man* testify to his willingness to help others, not only with money, but with his services. He once heard that Ouida, a writer whom he admired but had never met, was in financial difficulties. He sent her fifty pounds immediately. Even D. H. Lawrence, who was not tolerant of Douglas' moral vagaries, had to admit that Douglas ". . . has never left me in the lurch."[27] In Douglas' books, too, one finds indications of this concern for the downtrodden: his defense of Ouida and of Maurice Magnus, his plan to drain the Pontine swamps for the control of malaria, his twelve-page attack on the conditions of French reformatories, his complaints about the sacrificing of lambs in Athens at Easter.

His love of children and their love of him are referred to by his friends. He liked to talk with children and to give them food or money. Nancy Cunard has recorded the determination with which he tried to adopt a refugee child from the Spanish Civil War. This action was his way of reacting toward the war in which he refused to take sides as other intellectuals were doing. Perhaps children recognized under the rascally exterior a certain paradoxical innocence. As one reviewer said, here was "not a wicked old man" but a "naughty old boy."[28]

IV *The Pleasure Seeker*

The virtue which Douglas endeavored to practice and to

cultivate in his reader was "that tough, cheerful egotism, which, sanely regarded, is but sanity itself."[29] The "end" of such behavior could only be pleasure. He wrote, "The business of life is to enjoy oneself; everything else is mockery."[30] He disclaimed any interest in the habits, tastes, and beliefs of others, holding that they should be free to pursue their own pleasure as he insisted that he should be free: "Others are free to . . . enjoy oysters and champagne, or nursing the sick, or learning Chinese, or whatever their own uncontaminated fancy may suggest."[31]

The egotism which is a marked characteristic of his personality was also a part of his conscious philosophy. A parable contained in *Siren Land* says: "When they asked the Leontine philosopher how he managed to live a hundred years with such glowing health and jollity, the sage was wont to shake his hoary locks and roar out: 'because I never went a step out of my way to please anybody but myself (206).'" This statement is, of course, whimsical and intended to amuse, but it also represents a point of view that was attractive to Douglas. He has frequently been labeled a hedonist and an Epicurean, and doubtless this aspect of his life and writings appealed to the aesthetes who admired him during the 1920's. And yet he was, according to friends, never the "bohemian" sensualist that these people thought him to be. Douglas himself preferred to be considered an Epicurean rather than a hedonist.[32] And certainly the pleasure which he sought was ordinarily intellectual in nature. "Knowledge is power, they say. Knowledge is not only power; it is good fun."[33] The pleasure with which he devoted himself to various kinds of research has already been discussed, and it is obvious that sequestered scholarly life—consider Eames of *South Wind*—held a great appeal for him. The felicities of the life of the scholarly recluse are described in *Siren Land:* ". . . around the bibliographer's table there lies a passionless calm, unruffled by politics or sex-problems; we all become tender-hearted toward the innocuous enthusiast who writes for the delectation of one odd lunatic-scholar in every hundred years (55)."

An important part of this ideal is the tranquility. Douglas' desire, especially in old age, to escape from the perplexities of society into a life of the mind—into Epicurus' garden—is reminiscent of Lucretius' picture of the wise observer, peaceful and detached in a quiet citadel, contemplating the battle of life raging on the plain below. This sort of life brought Mr. Keith of *South Wind* back to Nepenthe each spring and autumn, and it is, one hopes, the sort of life that Douglas enjoyed during those last years at Kenneth Macpherson's villa on Capri. For nothing was to him so prized as leisure, which had produced "everything which distinguishes man from animals. . . ."[34]

But in all the talk of leisure and solitude, there is an element missing. The idyllic "Theocritan" existence, like that of the recluse scholar, had its appeal; and yet it was too passive a thing to satisfy a Norman Douglas—except perhaps the octogenarian Norman Douglas who was tired from fleeing tourists and wars. He described the ideal bibliographer as an "innocuous enthusiast," but Douglas himself was never quite that. His pleasure-seeking was marked, until late in his life, by a certain strenuous grasping of experience—a willingness to pick up and travel to whatever region beckoned, or to throw himself upon a new project with the intensity of the omnivorous researcher. In reading Douglas' nature descriptions, especially those of scenes caught at particular times and under particular lights, or of places visited at certain seasons when some special plant was in blossom, one is reminded of Pater's eloquent plea in the conclusion of *The Renaissance* for life as experience:

Every moment some form grows perfect in hand or face; some tone on the hills or sea is choicer than the rest; some mood or passion or insight or intellectual excitement is irresistibly real and attractive for us,—for that moment only. Not the fruit of experience, but experience itself is the end. A counted number of pulses only is given to us of a variegated, dramatic life. How may we see in them all that is to be seen in them by the finest senses? How shall we pass most swiftly from point to point, and be present always at the focus where the greatest number of vital forces unite in their purest energy?

This passage, famous as the credo of aestheticism and hedonism during the 1890's, may well have been known to the young man-about-town Norman Douglas. But whether he read it or simply imbibed it from the intellectual atmosphere of the times does not matter. The strenuous hedonism which counterbalances the need for calm repose in Douglas owes something to the tradition to which Pater belongs. Eames, the scholar of Nepenthe, has the desired solitude and pleasant intellectual pursuits, and yet his life is not complete. Though treated for the most part sympathetically he is also lightly satirized as a fool who missed the good things of the other sort—wine, sex, and conversation.

Nancy Cunard agrees with the Epicurean emphasis, but Davenport, who also knew Douglas well, qualifies: "... she too devotedly allows his claim to be not hedonist but epicurean, a claim made on the strength of his enjoyment of things of the mind as well as of—well, oysters and champagne. But his reaction from Puritanism was too violent for epicurean balance."[35] And Richard Aldington, who in *Pinorman*, makes a great deal of Douglas' unrestrained and unorthodox sex life, will not hear of the Epicurean claim: "He was no modest follower of Epicurus, practising frugality as pleasure. I should say he went far beyond Aristippus in praising purely sensual pleasure without the restraint of any moral law, the very existence of which Norman denied (119)." Moral judgments apart, it is hard to avoid feeling that Douglas wasted a great deal of intellectual energy on the undisciplined and purposeless kind of existence which he considered the art of living.[36]

A recurrent note in Douglas' hedonism is his interest in food. No memoir, whether it be a brief column of reminiscences or a full-length profile such as that of Nancy Cunard, is without its depiction of the "grand man" in the restaurant, badgering the waiters, disappearing into the kitchen to thunder at the chef, and weighing the wine because no southern Italian had the least respect for anyone who could be cheated. Although he was no doubt as familiar with Italian cookery as any other foreigner and had a knowledge of Italian dialects which served him well, he was apparently not so much the true connoisseur as he was a man who knew what he liked and was determined to get it. There is a good deal of pose involved—the role of the connoisseur pleased him as did that of the tryant—and his meticulous taste was to a good extent a matter of whim and prejudice. The most amusing among many renditions of Douglas *au restaurant* is that by D. H. Lawrence, whose ability to catch the tone of people's conversation has been praised by critics who knew the models.

"—you just run down and absolutely prevent them from boiling that bird in the old soup water . . . if you need force, fetch me."
    "*Cos' é? Zuppa? Grazie. No, niente per me. No! No! Quest' acqua sporca non bevo io.* I don't drink this dirty water. I—What—What's that in it—a piece of dish clout? Oh, Holy Dio, I can't eat another thing this evening—"[37]

But Douglas did apparently take his eating seriously and often philosophized on the subject. He equated good eating with civilization, professing to distrust anyone who was undiscerning in his choice of food: " 'I don't care what I eat!' " What a confession to make! Is it not the same as saying I don't care whether I am dirty or clean? When others tell me this, I regard it as a pose, or a poor joke . . . . A man owes something to those traditions of our race which have helped to raise us above the level of the brute. Good taste in viands has been painfully acquired; it is a sacred trust. Beware of gross feeders. . . . Will they not act, on occasion, even as they feed?"[38]

So central a value was physical well-being that it became involved in Douglas' ethical principles. One should not be surprised to find such emphases in a morality supposedly based on the order of nature, where there is no place for the unhealthy. He believed that nothing is beneficial except what is physiologically desirable, and hence that any sound morality should derive its sanctions from the laws which govern the body. He attributed much of the "crabbiness" and "pessimism" with which the modern world is plagued to dyspepsia and constipation. His preoccupation with the latter problem was nearly obsessive. (One lengthy treatment is to be found in *South Wind* when Mr. Keith discourses at great length on the purgative properties of Turkey Rhubarb.) In more than one instance he related cultural phenomena to nutrition: "The Jews, so long as they starved in Palestine, were the most acrimonious bigots on earth. Now that they live and feed sensibly, they have learnt to see things in their true perspective—they have become rationalists. Their less fortunate fellow Semites, the Arabs, have continued to starve and swear by the Koran—empty in body and mind."[39]

In a discussion of Douglas' thought and values, the subject of his sexual attitudes demands some treatment. Here again we find somewhat unorthodox views, and again probably a mixture of sincerity and pose, conviction and iconoclasm. Although there are those who believe that Douglas' sexual proclivities formed a significant factor in his career, there is also the danger of overemphasizing the matter.

The violent moral reaction that the young Douglas underwent after his "escape" from the Puritanical regime at Uppingham has already been mentioned. The Karlsruhe period was marked by a freedom from restraint in various respects and a reveling in pleasure previously beyond reach. In *Looking Back* he recounted some of the liaisons of that period with a lack of reticence that some reviewers found disturbing. There were Ethel, "a complaisant little English girl"; Auguste, "fair and none too slender"; and Miriam, "whom I now also squeezed into my Harem (40-41)." One receives the impression that the young man was engaged in a determined flouting of conventional morality, and the boastful tone with which the older man reminisces indicates that the attitude remained.

In the years following Karlsruhe there were more "affairs," all of them ending with Douglas' departure from the vicinity, culminating in the Russian affair that caused his resignation from the Foreign Office. He admitted that he often "found it difficult to remain faithful to a single person, where women are concerned."[40]

According to several reports it was after the failure of Douglas' short-lived marriage that his sexual direction changed, or perhaps one should say widened. Henceforth his rebellion against accepted moral institutions became overt and pronounced. In *Old Calabria* (1916) he expressed his respect for the "third sex." Concerning some newspaper articles on Sappho, he wrote: "... I do perceive a certain Writing upon the Wall, setting forth, in clearest language, that $1 + 1 = 3$, a legend which it behoves them not to expunge, but to expound. For it refuses to be expunged; and we do not need a German lady to tell us how much the 'synthetic' sex, the hornless but not brainless sex, has done for the life of the spirit while those other two were reclaiming the waste places of the earth, and procreating, and fighting—as befits their horned anatomy (119-120)." The basis of his arguments on the subject seems to be that the homosexual is a natural type and has much right to existence as any other.

In *Late Harvest* he included some suggestions on the matter which he had contributed to a correspondence in a London weekly: "Here we have a constant and well-marked variety or 'sport' of our species—a variety which has existed from time immemorial among all races and men in every walk of life—a variety which has given to mankind, *caeteris paribus,* as much of beauty or of use as any other section of the community—a variety which, in typical specimens, is as persistent as the blue-winged teal, though not so rare (8)."

His principal concern, as might be expected, was that homosexuals should be allowed their right to seek pleasure in any way they chose, and that they should not be persecuted by narrow legal codes—pleas with which people far less eccentric than Douglas might well agree. And the blame for the injustice is placed, again as one would expect, on Christianity:

The heterosexual and the blissfully contented monosexual may take care of themselves; in prescribing for the homosexual a little sanity would not be out of place. And the first step toward sanity is to take over the more reasonable provisions of the Napoleonic code. If English divorce laws are a disreputable tangle, our enactments on this head are a sinister joke, the source of multiple and unmerited suffering. . . . What calls for treatment is not so much homosexuality as the diseased attitude adopted toward it in non-Latin countries. This attitude is the outcome of Judaea-Christian teaching, as interpreted by Puritanism. (5)

It is useless to deny that the extravagances to which Douglas' hedonism led him formed a distasteful aspect of his career. His unorthodox sexual activities, although they may not have constituted a considerable factor in his writing, did affect his life. Aldington mentions " many scrapes with outraged parents or the police which arose from his peculiar habits." In *Pinorman* he describes Douglas' sex life with considerable frankness: "He was quite literally *Paiderastes*, a lover of boys, and it is falsifying his whole existence to ignore it. In the late nineteenth and twentieth centuries he behaved in Western Europe as if he were living in Eastern Mediterranean countries at some period between the age of Plato and that of Hadrian (83-84)." Nor will Aldington allow Douglas' habits to be considered, as such aberrations are considered by many, as a kind of mental illness: ". . . I must record my conviction that in Norman's case these deviations were not the result of psycho-physical misfortunes but simply due to what old-fashioned people called 'vice'. He was looking for new sensations, and an experiment became a habit (116)."

Douglas apparently did not have the effeminate qualities associated in the popular mind with the homosexual; his writings attest to this. Nancy Cunard, a woman with whom he seems to have had a long and close relationship—although, according to her own statement, not a sexual one—has emphasized his masculine qualities. And another friend, John Davenport, agrees with her emphasis: "She fully realizes his essential masculinity, which has been too often obscured by some of those who share certain of his sexual proclivities, and for whom he reserved opprobrious terms in several languages."[41]

Douglas' ambivalence in the matter of sex is further attested to by Graham Greene, in reference to the "dozen or so living tokens" that Douglas left "here and there," and to the "old gypsy family from northern Italy who traveled all the way to Capri to spend an afternoon with Douglas and proudly exhibit another grandchild (ix)." And Frank Swinnerton sums up the comprehensiveness of Douglas' hedonism by saying that he loved "life, women, boys, food, drink, and knowledge."[42]

V *The Individualist*

A great many of Douglas' attitudes might be gathered under the term "individualism." His thought is virtually predicated on his belief in the right of any individual to live as he sees fit and to seek his well-being and his pleasure in whatever fashion he chooses. A corollary of this principle is his dislike of the "wishy-washy" tendency to depend on others, or to live according to conventions—to follow what he like to call the "herd" instinct. Accordingly, he was intolerant of "the masses" and of "social" legislation designed for their benefit; on the other hand, he was ready to praise anyone who was strongly individualistic or unconventional. Among the eccentrics and "Ishmaels" whom he admired were Crawford Tait Ramage, the strange British traveler who was one of the first writers of modern times to visit Calabria; Edgar Allan Poe, the "anti-vulgarian" who abandoned the "ethical moment"; Isabelle Eberhard, the adventurous Russian girl who lived among the Bedouins as a man; Charles Waterton, another travel-writer and a "prince of eccentrics"; Major Frederick Potter and Mr. Augustus Browne, who lived together at Olevano for many years without exchanging a word; and Maurice Magnus, the unconventional American journalist. The sorts of men whom Douglas admired were those "who can evolve notions independently of other folk, men who can think without thinking what they are expected to think, men who tend to diverge from the common rut and are able to contemplate with fresh eyes what is going on around them."[43]

Although ready enough to come to the support of anyone who was asserting or practicing his individuality or his individual rights, Douglas was opposed to "social" action of most kinds. His attitude in such matters might be described as a lack of what is sometimes called "social consciousness." In *Good-bye to Western Culture,* his most violent attack on the mores of English society, he wrote: "No individual cares tuppence what his neighbour does, provided he be not hurt thereby. Mass-conscience is a newspaper-manufactured article—all make-believe and playing to the gallery (210)." This echoes his statement in the earlier *Alone:* "Consider well your neighbour, what an imbecile he is. Then ask yourself whether it be worth while paying any attention to what he thinks of you (136)."

Good-bye to Western Culture is, in the main, a blast against over-legislation and modern man's effort to achieve social stability through the regulation of individual behavior. Douglas saw all such effort—legal controls and social legislation—as leading to standardization—to following of the herd: "I imagine it would puzzle those old feudals—our oriental preoccupation with other folk, our craving to lean up against each other for mutual support and betterment. Flabbiness, they might have called it. We call it 'solidarity'. . . . We invent such words to shadow forth a desire more or less vague, more or less reasonable; and forthwith flatter ourselves that we have succeeded in creating a thing. Solidarity! Mankind is a jellyfish. How comes a jellyfish to want a backbone?"[44]

Naturally any kind of collectivism or state control was anathema to Douglas. An amusing manifestation of this antipathy is his hatred of ants and bees. He considered these creatures far too orderly, proper, industrious, and communistic; and he found a number of occasions to deprecate them. In *Together* he related that as a boy he had fostered and fed insects called "ant lions." "But, oh, to be an authentic anteater on a Gargantuan scale—omnipresent, insatiable of appetite—and engulf that entire tribe of automata!" He once left a specimen skull on an anthill to be cleaned, and returned to find it gone. ". . . the methodical socialists had mislaid it. . . ." He secured a rake and leveled the hill. (124)

The bees come in for a drubbing in *Birds and Beasts of the Greek Anthology:*

. . . men have held in veneration this contankerous and fussy insect which, by dint of specializing in communistic habits, has lost every shred of individuality. (182)

....

[The bee] loafs for half the year, and is orderly only because it lacks such independence of character and imagination as even a louse possesses. (186)

This personal war against the socialistic insects is interesting not only as an example of a particular element of Douglas' humor and of the diversified and unusual nature of his subject matter but also as a demonstration of how deeply ingrained was his sense of the value of individualism.

Although Douglas' beliefs were, to a great extent, deeply felt prejudices which pervaded his thought and writings, there was in him a sort of tolerance—though this may be using the word somewhat loosely. He frequently professed that he was not interested in converting others to his ideas: "Let each think as he pleases. I have better uses for my leisure than to try to bring others round to any convictions of mine, such as they are; far better uses. Enough for me to have watched the virus at work. . . ."[45] He seldom proposed remedies, although he constantly condemned existing institutions. The reformer he deplored as a type of "meddler." In the early pages of *Good-bye to Western Culture* he established his position:

The reader will find no suggestion of remedies in these pages. I am not the stuff of which reformers are made; rather than indulge in that variety of meddlesomeness I would sweep a crossing. Nine-tenths of the reformers of humanity have been mischief-makers or humbugs. I have no desire to be added to the list. A man who reforms himself has contributed his full share towards the reformation of his neighbour.

Let Europe and Asia do what they please: good luck to them! I observe, and I pass on. (5)

Although he does not completely fulfill the conditions of his agreement (many remedies—ranging from the Napoleonic Code to Turkey Rhubarb—are proposed in the pages of this book), a certain note struck here is to be found throughout. *Good-bye to Western Culture*, like all of Douglas' writings, is not aimed at those who, so to speak, need it. It has rather the tone of a conversation between men of sanity, good taste, and self-sufficiency who are amusing themselves with a discussion of the weak, contemptible herd and its absurd activities. Although critics have often used the word *toleration* to describe this "hands off" policy which Douglas favors, it seems hardly appropriate to call such a hurler of invective *tolerant*. In any event, the point to be understood is that in Douglas one is dealing not with the zeal of reform but with the zeal of disapproval. A catharsis of spleen was, for Douglas, its own reward.

Apparently ethical and political views such as those which have been described here need not be thought of as invariably destructive. Muriel Draper, who knew Douglas and sympathized with his point of view, finds a constructive aspect to his thought. She refers to the lines from *Good-bye to Western Culture* which have just been quoted: "His acquired cynicism fights with his natural idealism, and when he says that 'a man who reforms himself has contributed his full share toward the reformation of his neighbor,' it is an indication that herein lies, for him, the possible cure of much that is vulgar, somnambulistic, ugly, and stupid in our flurried and purposeless lives."[46] Of course individual action toward individual goals was the only action Douglas approved. But insofar as Mrs. Draper's statement implies that Douglas proposed this or anything else as a cure for the state of things, she has gone too far: she has let the reformer in by the back door, and Douglas would have been the first to eject him again. His lack of interest in the Millennium is made clear in a passage from "Cold Comfort." He has just pointed out that he finds nothing wrong with the world itself; he is satisfied with the position of the equator; the attitudes of the North Pole and the Galapagos Islands strike him as "irreproachable." But as to humanity,

. . . let it muddle along between pragmatism and paradise till the next Buddah-Messiah holds out a bait more appetizing than the last; and so on, till the day of judgment—the day, to wit, on which the moon will be converted to ripe green cheese. Let it wallow in unreason and moral biliousness, if so disposed. People who cultivate their ego at the expense of its environment deserve all they can get. . . . I can only suggest, as a means of cleansing certain Augean stables of sentimentalism, the old-fashioned remedy of a little honest work and an occasional dose of Turkey Rhubarb. (412-13)[47]

If Douglas believed that improving oneself was a way of improving the universe, it was not because he believed or desired that others would follow suit; rather it was because he believed that one's universe should be a self-contained sphere independent of the help or interference of others. Thus, learning to enjoy life, one's own life, and to take society with a grain of salt, would improve one's universe.

Douglas might also be called anti-progressive, for he disapproved of a great deal of what is usually considered material or technological progress. Dawkins has pointed out that Douglas' attitude toward machines is reminiscent of that of Samuel Butler (32). Railways struck him as unsightly and uncomfortable, and the tramcar became a kind of symbol of the ugliness, noise, and confusion of modern life. He was disturbed by the "repulsive" telephone wires which had disfigured his native village: "... the women of the place, instead of feeding chickens or mending the children's clothes, spend their lives in gossiping with each other at long distances, and God alone knows the nonsense they find to chatter about. . . . Now why do people want all this ridiculous electricity rushing up and down the country? Solidarity. Brotherhood of men. . . ."[48] In *Late Harvest* he mentions motion pictures, calling them a negative and pernicious force which fosters mental laziness.[49]

The kind of social, political, and material progress that has produced efficiency, convenience, and order in modern society he liked to call the "Prussian" kind. He saw it as "subversive" of civilization, as "fatal to the finer tissues." Thus *Good-bye to Western Culture* contains vehement attacks on such practices and institutions as officialdom, passports, visas, *cartes d'identité*, curfews, taxes, and various kinds of "red tape." The United States, a sort of symbol of progress, receives some of Douglas' sharpest invective:

The variegated riff-raff now weltering in that witches' cauldron— . . . . These men have cut themselves off from their several homely memories, and look with rancorous envy upon the orderly and time-honored institutions; they are inflamed with all the ferocious pushfulness of the Prussian and his determination to *get there* at whatever cost to others; they have the same boastfulness . . . and relentless self-assertion; the same lack of candour in public life; the same cringing love of the boss who rules them with rod of iron . . . .[50]

Metropolitan living, a significant characteristic of the modern world, is an abomination to the side of Douglas which loves nature, solitude, and simplicity: "... has any good ever come out of that foul-clustering town-proletariat, beloved of humanitarians? Nothing—never; they are only waiting for a leader, some 'inspired idiot,' to rend to pieces our poor civilization. Whereas out of the very dregs of country-folk has arisen, by the operation of that dark law which regulates the meteoric appearance of 'sports,' a Lincoln, a Winkelmann, to guide men's footsteps in the path (35)!"

Douglas lived long enough to see the increasing prevalence of the very things that he most detested: growing city populations, increased governmental controls, bigger and better gadgets, larger swarms of tourists overrunning the quiet places that he loved. In one of his last statements on the subject, in *Late Harvest*, he summed up his old complaints: "Goodbye to the past. With those revolting termites as their ideal, a mob of visionaries is driving us straight into the jaws of that obscene monster the community. Family life—doomed; personal freedom tottering to its grave; ourselves regimented to such a degree that leisure has become a privilege of domestic animals. A cheerful prospect (71)."

To the strenuous and unsentimental nature of Norman Douglas, strife—wholesome struggle such as that which is to be observed everywhere in nature—was an essential and healthy element in life. And any well-practiced deception, any show of superiority, was to him—as it was to the ancient Greeks—worthy of admiration. He reported, in *Alone* and elsewhere with some show of pride his unprincipled borrowing from rich tourists. In *Looking Back* he recorded his cheating of a tailor, who could more easily lose the money than he. Dawkins describes his attitude as belief "in the inevitability, and, so far as such a man can use the word at all, in the rightness of the struggle for life in its fiercest forms . . . (12)."

The inequality of men was to Douglas an incontestable fact, and he was therefore opposed to the pampering of the mediocre through legislation, education, or any other means: "wet-nursing the unfit—dirty work . . . ."[51] One reviewer of *Good-bye to Western Culture* called Douglas' attitude that of an "aristocrat for whom democracy and vulgarity are identical."[52] And certainly this book, more than any other, shows his unqualified contempt for the so-called "masses": ". . . when they have learnt to consider themselves as good as anybody else because some fool has drilled them up to the standard of a grocer's assistant, then it will be time (as the Persians say) to put one's trust in God (32)." He approved of the caste system of India and felt that it "rests on firmer foundations than anything which the Western world has hitherto devised (164)." Caste feeling was behind all forms of refinement and was "man's best prophylactic against the mass-feeling which would make a cypher of him (163)."

He further regretted that the Western world has no warrior caste to save the lives of its artists, teachers, scholars, and inventors (167).

Another object of Douglas' disapproval was modern educational practice—another force tending toward the destruction of individuality. He considered government a conspiracy against the superior man, and compulsory education one of its principal weapons: "...it is the business of schooling . . . to crush down the race till we are as alike as two peas." A great many pages of *Good-bye to Western Culture* are devoted to this subject. In fact, after over-legislation, over-education constitutes the principal theme of the book. Douglas' accusations are that compulsory education creates a type instead of character; instills uniformity, the enemy of civilization; inculcates nationalism, another enemy of civilization; and destroys originality of outlook, curiosity, initiative, and directness of vision. "Education is a State-controlled manufactory of echoes (25-26)."

Douglas' positive suggestions in this matter are vague, in keeping with his professed lack of interest in reform. But he obviously would have preferred a system of education which allowed the student greater freedom to develop his own personality and interests:

. . . one of the secrets of happiness is curiosity. Life is full of untapped sources of pleasure, and education, instead of breeding dis-content as it does, should train our curiosity to discover and exploit those sources. Does it? Often enough curiosity is not roused but repressed; not repressed but strangled to death. A child of eight is many-sided. By eighteen most of his auspicious angles have been polished away; he is standardised; transformed perhaps into the perfect citizen. Your perfect citizen may be a fine fellow; he is not the perfect man.[53]

His attitude toward universal education reflects the bias called here "aristocratic," although it is, in the main, an aristocracy of the intellect and the will. In *Good-bye to Western Culture* he regrets the passing of the simple, honest illiterate and the growth of a pseudo-educated class, a "brood of cads."

The western notion seems to be this: some dogs can learn tricks, therefore all dogs must learn them. Are we ever going to realize that we have our unteachables too, and that to keep them in school is wasting not ony *our* money but *their* time? Presumably not. The school-age is continually being raised. Soon we shall be doing sums when we might be getting married. . . . The consequence is that England is full of well-groomed adolescents of twenty-five, with no more poise or self-reliance than a Newfoundland puppy. (22-23)

Like most of the rantings in *Good-bye to Western Culture,* the strictures concerning modern education have their grains of truth. Although few would approve the unrestrained and un-qualified nature of the attack, few would deny some tendency on the part of educators, in America, at least, to lower stan-dards and to teach to the least-common-denominator, produc-ing quantity rather than quality.

VI *The Nietzschean*

Douglas' aristocratic point of view and much of his individual-ism show a close affinity to the thought of the German philoso-pher Friedrich Nietzsche. There are sharply distinguishing fea-tures, but the central attitudes are similar; both men predicat-ed their ethics on the assumption that nature's evolution is di-rected toward the creating of individual genius rather than toward universal betterment of the species. One passage from Nietzsche's *Beyond Good and Evil,* a description of the nature and aims of the "free spirit,' should sufficiently demonstrate the affinity between the thought of Nietzsche and that of Douglas, as it has been described:

What they [the levelers] would fain attain with all their strength, is the universal green-meadow happiness of the herd, together with security, safety, comfort, and alleviation of life for everyone; their two most frequently chanted songs and doctrines are called "Equality of Rights, and "Sympathy with all sufferers"—and suffering itself is looked upon by them as something that must be *done away with.* We opposite ones, however, who have opened our eye and con-science to the question how and where the plant man has hitherto grown most vigorously, believe that this has always taken place under the opposite conditions. . . . We believe that severity, violence, slavery, danger in the street and in the heart, secrecy, stoicism, tempter's art and diviltry of every kind,—that everything wicked, terrible, tyrannical, predatory, and serpentine in man, serves as well for the elevation of the human species as its opposite. . . . Having been at home, or at least guest, in many realms of the spirit; having escaped again and again from the gloomy, agreeable nooks in which preferences and prejudices, youth, origin, the ac-cident of men and books, or even the weariness of travel seemed to confine us; full of malice against the seductions of dependancy which lie concealed in honors, money, position, or exaltation of the senses; grateful even for distress and the vicissitudes of illness, because they always free us from some rule, and its 'prejudice,' grateful to the God, devil, sheep, and worm in us; inquisitive to a fault, investigators to the point of cruelty, with unhesitating finger for the intangible, with teeth and stomachs for the most indigestible, ready for every adventure, owing to an excess of "free will"; . . . hidden ones under the mantles of light, appropriators, although we resemble heirs and spendthrifts, arrangers and collectors from morning till night, misers of our wealth and our full-crammed drawers, economical in learning and forgetting, inventive in scheming; sometimes proud of tables of categories, sometimes pedants, sometimes night-owls of work even in full day; yea, if necessary, even scarecrows—and it is necessary nowadays, that is to say, inasmuch as we are the born, sworn, jealous friends of solitude, of our own profoundest mid-day and midnight solitude:—such kind of men are we, we free spirits![54]

Although there are points here with which Douglas might disagree, it should be obvious that he fits well the pattern of the Nietzschean "free spirit."

The similarities in the thought of the two can be multiplied. Both saw life as a struggle in which the fittest survive, and hence both equated strength with virtue and weakness with evil. Both preferred pride to humility, intelligence to altruism, and power to justice. Both considered democracy opposed to natural law and therefore disapproved of Utilitarianism, Socialism, and what ordinarily goes under the name of progress, as well as of pity, sentimentality, and idealisms. Both affirmed, on the other hand, energy and vitality; and each tended to value the physical, the instinctive, and the natural, thus finding a place for the simple man, though not as a leader.

Good-bye to Western Culture is dedicated to Douglas' friend Oscar Levy, the translator of Nietzsche; and several writers who are often regarded as Nietzschean—H.L. Mencken and Clive Bell—are quoted or alluded to with respect. Douglas summarizes the contributions of the German philosopher with a tone of approbation that he did not accord to many: "Seriously concerned with the spiritual welfare of mankind, he took their little eccentricities to heart and cursed them roundly, and rightly. His explosions have made a clearing in our jungle of unreason; one of those bare, sporadic patches where the sun can penetrate to earth, and where a gentleman can take his pleasure (161)."

But Douglas is not seriously "concerned with the spiritual welfare of mankind"; moreover, he is not a poet, which Nietzsche was, but a scientist, which Nietzsche was not. The German was not able to go all the way with Darwin and his followers. He was aware of the biological discoveries of his day, and the "survival of the fittest" theory lies behind much of his thought. But he was not able to accept its full implications. Douglas wrote of Nietzsche that the true import of the advancements which had been made by the English scientists "seems to have escaped him altogether (159)." In *Alone* (1921) he related that he had recognized this weakness in Nietzsche some time before, presumably as a young man:

Nietzsche was also then to the fore, and it pleases me to recollect that even in those days I detected his blind spot; his horror of those English materialists and biologists. . . . To his way of thinking the human mind is so highly organized, so different from that of beasts, that not all the proofs of ethnology and physiology would ever induce him to accept the ape-ancestry of man. This monkey-business is too irksome and humiliating to be true; he waves it aside, with a sneer at the disgusting arguments of those Englishmen. (126)

In *Good-bye to Western Culture* Douglas granted Nietzsche higher praise than he accorded to any other philosopher, calling him ". . . so austere, so superior to all of them in ruthless integrity . . . with his passion for communing with nature . . . reverence for the 'terrible beauty of solitude.' (159)" But, in the last analysis, Nietzsche remained for Douglas too much the idealist, too little the naturalist and scientist: ". . . a smattering of palaeontology, and a glance at Sirius now and then, would have helped to steady Nietzsche's views in regard to creatures whose capacity for assimilating knowledge is so limited, and who, whatever their capacity, would be polished off the face of the earth by a few additional degrees of heat or cold (161-162)."

VII *The "Dandy"*

In considering the sources and correlatives of Douglas' ideas, one must keep in mind the fact that he was a young man in the London of the 1890's. These were formative years for him, and it is not surprising that he reflects the ethical and literary attitudes that were fashionable. The fact is that one need go no further than the philosophy of the nineteenth-century "dandy" to find the general outlines of Douglas' thought. The love of eccentricity; the emphasis upon the sensual; the cynical and paradoxical response to accepted values—all were the fashion of the time among a certain group, the group which would have appealed to a young, intellectul aristocrat in revolt against puritanical restrictions. Of course Douglas did not have, or had lost by the time his career in literature began, many of the tenets of the aestheticism of the 1890's (some of them— the preference for art over nature—were not compatible with his older values); but he also retained some of the central attitudes all his life.

It is always difficult to pin down the ethics or the politics of the "dandies," not only because these men were not much interested in society, but also because the "dandy," as Barbey d'Aurevilly pointed out in his essay on the subject, does not necessarily express his own beliefs, but rather seeks to create an effect, like that of Brummel or Byron.[55] In Wilde's *Picture of Dorian Gray*, people are always saying of Lord Henry that he doesn't really mean what he says. His answer is that Englishmen are less interested in the truth of an idea than in the sincerity of the purveyor. Some of this questionable intent is also present in Douglas, and it is similarly difficult in his case to deduce a consistent ethical system from his writings. Oscar Wilde, however, thought more systematically on these matters than some, and it is not difficult to cull aphorisms from his work which might as easily have been written by Douglas. The following are from *The Critic as Artist:*

. . . the development of the race depends upon the development of the individual.

————

That humanitarian sympathy wars against Nature, by securing the survival of the failure, may make the man of science loathe its facile virtues.

————

Offensive busybodies have destroyed the simple and spontaneous virtue that there is in man.

————

. . . who [is] the true man of culture, if not he who by fine scholarship and fastidious rejection has made instinct selfconscious and intelligent?

————

Aldington, who sees Douglas as heavily indebted to Wilde, both stylistically and philosophically, quotes the following remarks of Lord Henry in *The Picture of Dorian Gray* as representing the hedonism which Douglas learned from Wilde: "Don't squander the gold of your days listening to the tedious, trying to improve the hopeless failure, or giving away your life to the ignorant, the common and the vulgar. These are the sickly aims, the false ideals of our age. Live! Live the wonderful life that is in you! Let nothing be lost upon you. Be always searching for new sensations. Be afraid of nothing. A new hedonism—that is what our century wants."[56] Although one reluctantly equates the philosophy of a fictional character with that of the author, the fact remains that Lord Henry is an epitome of the "aesthete," created by one who was an expert on the subject. And the views expressed—reminiscent as they are of that manifesto of the aesthetic movement, Pater's famous plea for experience-for-its-own sake in the conclusion of his *Renaissance Studies*—are views that Douglas frequently expressed and indeed tried to realize in his life.

Whatever the direct influence of Wilde, or of the "aesthetic" movement generally, it is clear that Douglas represents part of the general revolt against Victorian values. It is also clear that he belongs to the earlier wave of that revolt—the wave that began in the 1870's and 1880's and culminated in the "decadence" of the 1890's—rather than to the twentieth-century movement that included figures such as Lawrence, Huxley, and Joyce. *South Wind*, which echoes the old while it inspires the new, might be said to form a kind of link between these phases.

VIII *The Anti-Liberal*

The reaction of the left wing of the literary world to *Good-bye to Western Culture* appeared in Edmund Wilson's review in the *New Republic*, since reprinted in *Shores of Light*. Wilson attacked Douglas for the "escapist" philosophy which allowed him to censure Western society from an isolated and passive vantage point on Capri. "Norman Douglas, who writes so clearly, does not think any more clearly than any other dilettante of Epicurean tastes who desires to figure as a champion of all the moral and aesthetic values without being willing to deal with the problem of how these values are created or lost."[57] Wilson finds inconsistencies in Douglas' tendency to approve meddlesomeness and lawmaking when it concerns something in which he happens to be interested. He recalls Douglas' denouncement of French prison conditions although the victims were the very sort of riffraff whom Douglas says we are "breeding as carefully as if they were Pekingese spaniels." "Very well"; says Wilson, "should he not, as a Nietzschean, be willing to let them die?"

Of course there are contradictions in *Good-bye to Western Culture*, as there are elsewhere in Douglas' writings—he was not and did not pretend to be a systematic thinker. He once quoted Renan: "*Malheur à qui ne se contredit pas une fois par jour!*"[58] But Wilson ignores several factors. When Douglas says that some person or some group "should be underground," few readers will take him entirely literally. This sort of exaggeration is a characteristic of his method, and is neither without precedent nor without a certain value—although it may be mainly a propaganda value. What is involved is actully that certain practices of hyperbole common to conversational discourse are carried over to writing. As a stylistic trait, this brutal exaggeration is not attractive to the sensitive; and, at best, it is not subtle. But, nevertheless, it seems unfair to censure Douglas for not being consistent to attitudes which are essentially ironic. And there are other flaws in the charge of inconsistent Nietzscheanism. What Douglas condemned were the herd followers—the cranks, the prudes, and all those who were inferior according to his own individualistic criteria. This condemnation does not necessarily include the inmates of the French reformatories. Also, since Douglas would undoubtedly have denied being a follower of Nietzsche, or of anybody else, why should he be given the obligation of consistency to Nietzsche's principles? And lastly, it could well be argued that letting these members of the inferior group die is no more consistent with the principles of Nietzsche than with those of Douglas.

Wilson's observations concerning Douglas' tone constitute a more telling criticism. He quotes such words and phrases as "shoddiness," "ingrained vulgarity," and "fetid masses"; and he suggests that this diction is designed to establish an understanding that author and reader share a certain refined aristocracy, that they are superior to the ordinary man in intellect, taste, and general worth. Wilson correctly points out that this is exactly the persuasive technique employed in "slick" advertising. Of course any piece of writing establishes some sort of hypothetical understanding between author and reader, and such understandings frequently call upon both to assume roles that are in some way artificial; but it is seldom that a piece of writing attempts to create such a meretricious contract—a league of supermen—as does *Good-bye to Western Culture*. Wilson concludes his review with the comment that, although he respects the independence of Douglas' career and his refusal to be intimidated by conventions, "the kind of social criticism represented by *Good-bye to Western Culture* . . . seems . . . essentially trivial (491)." After all the qualifications are made, this judgment is not, in the main, unfair.

It appears that Douglas should have been sympathetic to some of the reforms of the Fascist regimes, as well as to much of their philosophy. The Fascists were certainly unsentimental—except where sentiment formed part of their propaganda programs—and intolerant of "soft" idealism. But their programs crushed individual rights and demanded conformity to party lines, and these were things that Douglas could never approve. During the Spanish Civil War, Nancy Cunard compiled a book called *Authors Take Sides* and asked Douglas for a contribution. His answer was characteristic:

"I cannot excite myself over nations and causes and creeds—my contempt for humanity in general is too great. Individuals are the only things that interest me. If Spaniards like to cut each other's throats and get Germans and Russians to help them—why not let them? It's not my affair. If they eat each other up to the last man, like Kilkenny cats, let them! Nobody is going to compel me to 'take sides.' To hell with sides. If Fascists annoy me, I hop it. If Communists annoy me, I hop it. Everything that ends in 'ism' is just b————, so far as I am concerned."[59]

But he added that he was "perfectly ready to take charge of [a] Spanish child—orphan or otherwise."

Douglas had no love for the Fascist officials of his adopted country. Although they were sufficiently amoral in the pursuit of their goals, they also had the newfound nationalism and puritanism which Thomas Mann described so vividly in *Mario and the Magician* and elsewhere. And, although they made the trains run on time, they also prosecuted dilettante Englishmen who published obscene limericks. In retrospect, in *Late Harvest,* Douglas describes the effects of the Fascist period upon Italy: "Hardly a village in the land has escaped some scratch of the Facist claw in the unnecessary suppression of old things and the unnecessary erection of new. The result? Our wives and mistresses are enabled to appear more often than formerly in new hats and new motor cars. For the rest, these people are merely carrying on the tradition of the House of Savoy (56)."

Douglas has been accused of anti-Semitism, and indeed he frequently places the blame for what is to him the destructive tradition of Christianity upon the Jews. Ordinarily, however, he attacks the ideas and not the race. In *Alone* he wrote: "Far be it from me to disparage the race of Israel. I have gained the conviction—firm-mixed, now, as the Polar Star—that the Hebrew is as good a man as the Christian (12)." An American writer, Louis Golding, wrote an imaginary dialogue for the *Menorah Journal* using Douglas as a mouthpiece for anti-Semitism.[60] Douglas mentioned this article briefly in *Experiments*, wondering why Golding had not used someone more qualified, "Hilaire Belloc, for instance." He added: "He might with some plausibility have introduced me as anti-Christian. . . . But I shall not wrangle over the religious aspects of the matter; they are not worth wrangling about, since Christians are only an anaemic variety of Jews (255)."

IX *The Primitivist*

There is in Douglas' thought a strain of what generally goes under the term "primitivism": a dislike of the complexities and sophistications of civilization, and a liking for the simple, the natural, the childlike, and even, occasionally, the savage. In a passage in "Aspects of Russia," he wishes that he could wipe out many of the traditions which have made up Western civilization:

Only think: no Old Masters, no Cinque-Cento, no Calvinistic cant with its spawn of pruriency and hypocrisy, no metaphysics, no incubus of classical tradition! Never to have addled your (national) brain with the Thing in Itself and probabiliorism and Gandarene Pigs: never to have made yourself ill about sins non-existent; never to have babbled of Plato and Jacapo Bellini; never to have enjoyed a single one of the thumb-screwing interludes that lie between the flamboyant cretinism of the Greek Church and the gracious serenity of Anatole France. (249)

Thus it is that he seldom discussed the art or the writing of his contemporaries; in fact the usually put a stop to such discussions when he encountered them with his scornful "Isn't that rather

Cinque-Cento, my dear?" He preferred the company and conversation of children and old people, plying them with sweets and snuff, respectively. In *London Street Games* and elsewhere he lamented the fact that children are not as longer fresh, unspoiled, unprejudiced, and imaginative as they used to be. Education, city living, commercial toys, and cricket are responsible for this degeneration. He also lamented the loss of the simple dignity of the illiterate peasant. He complained that conscription and emigration were destroying the old dignified peasantry of southern Italy who "combine the manners of Louis Quatorze with the profiles of Augustus or Plato, and who still recall, in many of their traits, the pristine life of Odyssean days."[61]

The appeal that children had for Douglas is based on their individuality, curiosity, and freedom from conventional ideas:

A man who has tried to remain a mere citizen of the world and refused to squeeze himself into the narrow methods and aspirations of any epoch or country, will discover that children correspond unconsciously to his multifarious interests. They are not standardised. They are more generous in their appreciations, more sensitive to pure ideas, more impersonal. Their curiosity is disinterested. The stock may be rudimentary, but the outlook is spacious; it is the passionless outlook of the sage. . . . How refreshing to converse with folks who have no bile to vent, no axe to grind, no prejudices to air; who are pagans to the core; who, uninitiated into the false values of externals, never fail to size you up from a more spiritual point of view than do their elders; who are not oozing politics and sexuality, nor afflicted with some stupid ailment or other which prevents them doing this and that. To be in contact with physical health—it would alone suffice to render their society a dear delight, quite apart from the fact that if you are wise and humble you may tiptoe yourself, by inches, into fairyland.[62]

Of course those who, like Richard Aldington, imply that Douglas' interest in children grew from his particular "vice" would probably choose to read between the lines of a passage such as this. But, whatever the truth, there is here, in the world of childhood, a picture of the ideal life of the era of the satyrs in *In the Beginning,* an era of open minds and closeness to nature. And this is the kind of world which Douglas would have preferred.

Occasionally, beneath Douglas' erudition and refined taste there is perceivable an even more profound sort of primitivism, an attraction to the elemental and savage. In *Fountains in the Sand* there is a description of a beast-dance performed by ". . . two fine negroes . . ., depicting the amorous rages of panthers or some other cat-like feral . . . purely sadistic." . . . Extremes meet. Performances such as these are beyond good and evil. They are for the wholly savage or the wholly civilized. We complain considerably just now of the swamping of class distinctions in our lands, but a man of culture has a prerogative to which the biliously moral middle classes can never aspire: to be an Arab, when it suits him (70-71)."

A passage in *South Wind* reflects something like the kind of primitivism one finds in the later Lawrence. The shy and confused young Englishman, Denis, has been told by the worldly Keith that he must "externalize" himself and that the best way to do this is to visit the cave of Mercury in the full of the moon: "Familiarize yourself with elemental things. The whole earth reeks of humanity and its works . . . tell people to go to Hell, Denis . . . (66-67)." The cave of Mercury had once been consecrated to "some mysterious, primaeval, fecund Mother of Earth (141)"; and later, under the Romans, to Priapean rites. In the transforming atmosphere of the cave, Denis remembers his conversation with Keith:

Earth-worship: the cult of those generative forces which weld together in one mighty instinct the highest and lowliest of terrestrial creatures. . . . The inalienable right of man and beast to enact that which shall confound death, and replenish the land with youth, and joy, and teeming life. The right which priestly castes of every age have striven to repress, which triumphs over every obstacle and sanctifies, by its fruits, the wildest impulses of man. The right to love!

Musing thus, he began to understand why men of old, who looked things squarely in the face, should have deified this friendly, all-compelling passion. He reverenced the fierce necessity which drives the living world to its fairest and sole enduring effort. Be fruitful and multiply. He recognized for the first time that he was not a longely [sic] figure on earth, but absorbed into a solemn and eternal movement; bound close to the throbbing heart of the Universe. There was grandeur, there was repose, in being able to regard himself as an integral part of nature, destined to create and leave his mark. He felt that he was growing into harmony with permanent things—finding himself. He realized now what Keith had meant. (141-42)

This attitude toward nature, call it what one will, sums up

a number of Douglas' values—sensuality, simplicity, and so on. In the last pages of *Old Calabria* there appears a plea for this primitive relationship with nature, a plea which deserves quotation for its creation of atmosphere and its felicitous expression. It is part of a description of Cape Rizutto, across the bay from Cotrone on the sole of the Italian boot:

This corner of Magna Graecia is a severely parsimonious manifestation of nature. Rocks and waters! But these rocks and waters are actualities; the stuff whereof man is made. A landscape so luminous, so resolutely scornful of accessories, hints at brave and simple forms of expression; it brings us to the ground, where we belong; it medicines to the disease of introspection and stimulates a capacity which we are in danger of unlearning amid our morbid hyperborean gloom—the capacity for honest contempt; contempt for that scarecrow of a theory which would have us neglect what is earthly, tangible. What is life well-lived but a blithe discarding of primordial husks, of those comfortable intangibilities that lurk about us, waiting for our weaker moments?

The sage, that perfect savage, will be the last to withdraw himself from the influence of these radiant realities. He will strive to knit closer the bond, to devise a more durable and affectionate relationship between himself and them. Let him open his eyes. For a reasonable adjustment lies at his feet. From these brown stones that seam the tranquil Ionian, from this gracious solitude, he can carve out, and bear away into the cheerful din of cities, the rudiments of something clean and veracious and wholly terrestrial—some tonic philosophy that shall foster sunny mischiefs and farewell regret. (338)

X *Homo Mediterraneus*

Douglas' preference for the Mediterranean lands in which he spent most of his adult life and about which he wrote his best books was part of his philosophy. Many of the attitudes he displays or approves are characteristic of the Southern peoples, and the lands themselves seemed always able to stimulate him with their beauty and their legendary associations: "Adventure and discovery are lurking on every side. These painted clouds with their floating banners and citadels, yonder mysterious headlands that creep into the landscape at this hour, those islets emerging, like flakes of bronze, out of the sunset-glow—all the wonder of the Odyssey is there!"[63]

He finds in southern Italy a proper balance between man and nature. Whereas in the northern countries the sun withholds its full power and man must struggle with the elements, and in the equatorial lands it becomes an overpowering demon that strangles man with vegetation, on the shores of the Mediterranean it ministers to man, and his works are made to stand in just relation to nature. This is the very climate of moderation.

A large part of the charm which the Mediterranean area held for Douglas lay in its historical associations. This element is revealed in a passage in *Siren Land*: "Here, too, an ancient world, our ancient world, lies spread out in rare charm of colour and outline, and every footstep is fraught with memories. . . . No person of culture, however prosaic, will easily detach himself from such scenes and thoughts—is it not the prerogative of civilised man to pause and ponder before the relics of his own past? (250)"

The best spokesman for this "Mediterraneanism" is Count Caloveglia of *South Wind*, who believes that the Mediterranean basin will someday become again the center of Western civilization. His values are, in the main, those of his creator. He finds a "kernel of hard reason . . . enclosed within the soft imagination of the *homo Mediterraneus*." The northerner, on the other hand, has a hardness on the surface but is apt to be "in a state of fluid irresponsibility" inside (86). The southerners listen to the prompting of nature, believing them to be reasonable and right; and even the priests, despite professions to the contrary, share this belief and live according to it. By nature anti-ascetic, these people have yet retained the ancient Hellenic ideal of temperance "which avoids troubling the equilibrium between man and his environment."[64] They base their ethic upon aesthetic considerations: "They never call it wrong. Their mode of condemnation is to say that it is not pretty. The ethical moment, you observe, is replaced by an aesthetic one."[65] Mr. Keith, another spokesman for the author, stresses the childlike simplicity of the southerner, a characteristic which drew Douglas to the Italians, at least to those who had not been to America: "There was an element of the child in every Southerner; . . . refusing to believe what is improbable, [they] reserve their credulity for what is utterly impossible . . . (385)."

Count Caloveglia's most extensive exposition of his Mediterraneanism is based on the relationship between climate and culture. This is a matter which Douglas took seriously and which is very near to the theme of *South Wind*. Civilization is a product of leisure, and only in a climate where nature allows man this leisure can there be a life of reason and of creativity.

We have only a certain amount of energy at our disposal. It is not seemly to consume every ounce of it in a contest with brute nature. Man is made for better things. Whatever fails to elevate the mind is not truly profitable. Tell me, sir, how shall the mind be elevated if the body be exhausted with material preoccupations. Consider the complex conditions under which a Northern family is obliged to live. Think of the labour expended upon that unceasing duel with the elements—the extra clothing and footwear and mufflers and mantles, the carpets, the rugs, the abundant and costly food required to keep the body in sound working condition, the plumbing, the gas, the woodwork, the paintings and repaintings, the tons of fuel, the lighting in winter, the contrivances against frost and rain, the never-ending repairs to houses, the daily polishings and dustings, and scrubbings and those thousand other impediments to the life of the spirit! Half of them are nonexistent in these latitudes; half the vitality expended upon them could therefore be directed to other ends. At close of day, your Northerner is pleased with himself. He has survived; he has even prospered. His family is adequately housed and clothed. He feels "presentable," as he calls it, in the eyes of those who share his illusions. He fancies he has attained the aim and object of existence. He is too dazed with the struggle to perceive how incongruous his efforts have been. What has he done? He has sacrificed himself on the altar of a false ideal. He has not touched the fringe of a reasonable life. He has performed certain social and political duties—he knows nothing of duties toward himself. I am speaking of men from whom better things might have been expected. As for the majority, the crowd, the herd—they do not exist, neither here nor anywhere else. They leave a purely physiological mark upon posterity; they propagate the species and protect their offsprings. So do foxes. It is not enough for us. Living in our lands, men would have leisure to cultivate nobler aspects of their nature. They would be accessible to purer aspirations, worthier delights. They would enjoy the happiness of sages. What other happiness deserves the name? In the Mediterranean, Mr. Heard, lies the hope of humanity. (84-85)

Douglas' belief in the importance of pleasant climatic conditions to the well-being of man—aristocratic man, at least—even draws him at times toward sun worship. In *Siren Land* his digressive pen falls upon the subject of Mithraism, and it occurs to him that here is, or was, a religion perhaps better fitted than any other to appeal to the intelligent and the civilized.

The following passage is actually an eloquent plea for naturalism, but it seems apropos to a discussion of Douglas' deep affinity for the lands of "sunny mischief": "The wise man of all ages will not hesitate whom to adore when he beholds the Great Fire by whose operation all things derive their first breath of life and the faculty of continued living; when he remembers that the ruby is kindred not in colour only, but in substance, with the arterial life which flows through his veins—a kinship of blood binding the cosmos to himself, whose body contains the common properties of the earth, whose humours, they say, are swayed by her satellite, whose very thoughts are but expressions of solar virtues. (191)"

XI *The Hellenist*

Not the least of Douglas' feeling for the Mediterranean area lies in the fact that it was the land and the sea of the Greeks and was hence for him haunted with memories of the Homeric epics and of the days when reason ruled the world. It is no accident that he preferred southern Italy to the northern parts of the country, even though he spent many years in Florence. In those provinces which he called *Old Calabria*—in Magna Graecia—lay the reminders of the Greek civilization, and these he found provocative of Classical musings and thus useful to his travel writing.

Professor Dawkins, himself a Classicist, has called Douglas "...the man of all others in the present world of letters who stands nearest to the ancient Greek point of view."[66] Certainly there is hardly a facet of Douglas' thought which does not have its precedent in the attitudes of the Greeks. We should note immediately, however, that his affinity lay not so much with the values of the Periclean Age as with those of earlier centuries. By the fifth century B.C. the subjectivism which Douglas deplored had made inroads. Democracy—even Athenian democracy—was anathema to him; Plato was the villain of Western thought; even Socrates was too uninterested in natural science and too respectful of his mystical "daimon." The civilization which appealed to Douglas was that which existed in Ionia in the sixth and seventh centuries before Christ, a culture in which there was sufficient wealth for leisure and in which the arts of life were sufficiently developed to provide men with delicate and refined pleasure. The primitive religions were no longer taken seriously by the intelligentsia, and philosophers had begun to ask scientific rather than religious questions. It was a period with an intellectual atmosphere of naturalism, aristocracy, and refinement; and it was also the great age of the Greek lyric, the only poetry, with the exception of the *Iliad* and the *Odyssey*—also probably Ionian—that interested Douglas. W. K. C. Guthrie in his excellent study of Greek religion describes those times, demonstrating that the poets whom Douglas admired and the natural philosophers who were the fathers of the philosophical tradition to which Douglas belonged were products of the same culture:

At first sight there is little in common between the poetry of Mimnermos and the thought of men like Thales, Anaximander, and Anaximines, the founders of European natural philosophy. Yet both are typical products of the same general state of society, presupposing alike intellectual freedom, a high material standard of life, and abundant leisure. The spirit of their age and class was materialistic. Their interests lay in this world, they had not much faith in another, and seeing no reason to suppose that the gods had man's interests at heart, they felt at liberty to leave them alone. Poet and philosopher shared this outlook, though the one looked inward to the microcosm, mourned his ephemeral nature and took refuge in the consolations of the love and wine, whereas for the other an interest in this world took the form of a consuming curiosity about the macrocosm.[67]

Douglas seems to have combined both reactions described here, the hedonistic and the scientific. In fact, all of the attitudes which Guthrie mentions as characteristic of this Hellenic culture are ones that Douglas espoused.

That Douglas shared the Greeks' regard for the human body and their consequent antipathy for the concepts of inherent sin and life beyond the grave is made clear in several passages in *Siren Land:*

The idea that we entered into the world tainted from birth, that feeling of duty unfulfilled which is rooted in the doctrine of sin and has hindered millions from enjoying life in a rational and plenary manner—all this was alien to their mode of thought. (193)

To those Greeks, the human frame was a subtle instrument to be kept lovingly in tune with the loud-voiced melodies of earth and sky and sea; these were their realities; as for a life beyond, let the gods see to it—a shadowy, half-hearted business, at best. (165)

The Greek doctrine of the Golden Mean was one to which Douglas frequently professed his allegiance. Temperance is described in *South Wind* as "the exercise of our faculties and organs in such a manner as to combine the maximum of pleasure with the minimum of pain." And our bodies will tell us "exactly how far we can proceed with impunity (322)." This is a striving for pleasure, sensual or intellectual, with no restraint except nature's own. But it is necessary to keep the balance, to mantain nature's equilibrium: "All excess is unlovely." Count Caloveglia, that epitome of the Classic point of view, "knew the story of Polycrates, the too-fortunate man. He knew what lies in wait for the presumptuous mortal who oversteps the boundary of what is fair and good. Nemesis! (402)"

Even the implicit selfishness—the hard, extroverted egotism which is so apparent in Douglas' life and writings—has a precedent in the attitudes of the Greeks. They were a selfish people, a race of bargainers and traders whose hero was Odysseus "of the many devices." Dawkins demonstrates this side of the Greek character by reference to their language: "The ancient word for *good, agathós,* has now in common usage a slightly contemptuous shade of meaning; we might translate it by *mild, easy-going,* or even *simple.* The word for to laugh, *geló* now means not only *to laugh,* but *to cheat,* to *deceive;* especially that form of deceit which consists of inducing a man to believe what is not true. The man who is so simple, so *agathós* that he can easily be deceived, is an object of derision (13)." Douglas reported this same tendency—to call those who are easily gulled "good people"—among modern Italians;[68] and, if we are to believe some of the things that have been written about him, Douglas himself was adept at these sophistical tricks which the Greeks admired.

But despite these important affinities, Douglas had few illusions concerning the ancient world. He knew that it was not "a schoolmaster's pale Platonic dream."[69] In *Siren Land* he referred to the Greek "crowd" as an "intemperate set of bigots and ruffians (12)," and in *One Day,* written in Greece, he said: "... one remembers what certain enthusiasts would have us forget: that the old Greeks, though humaner than ourselves in some respects, were in others as ferocious a pack of fanatics as ever breathed."[70] His dislikes among things Greek were as strong as his likes: the Philistine Spartans; the "oriental dreamer" Plato; Pythagoras, "strongly tainted with Orientalism"[71]; the Orphic mysteries, "stuffed with Eastern lore";[72] stoicism, "—a dumb protest against the environment."[73] He particularly disliked the mystery cults and the tendency they represented:

[What drove men toward them?] . . . the anti-Hellenic impulse to escape from actualities; it was fear of a fact: that death is the end of all things. They craved for comfort. . . . So they underwent that rite which, like other such buffooneries, gave them a sense of superiority over their unenlightened, because uninitiated, fellow-creatures; they went in as gentlemen, and came out as prigs. And why the proceedings in that dark hole were never disclosed is intelligible on another hypothesis: that the mysteries themselves were some sublime farce which these good people were ashamed of themselves for having witnessed, and therefore ashamed to reveal. Hence that conspiracy of silence (ask any intelligent Mason).[74]

As much as Douglas was attracted by the values which he chose to consider characteristically Greek, he was repulsed by those which he considered characteristically Roman. He found the Romans too businesslike, too practical, and too unartistic. A passage in *Good-bye to Western Culture* places the blame for almost everything upon the Romans: "The shoddiness of our ideals . . . social and political is a heritage from those unimaginative Roundheads, with their ingrained vulgarity, their imperialism, their pernicious doctrine of the *raison d'état*, and the welcome they gave, as vulgarians naturally would give, to imported pinchbeck like Christianity (238-39)."

XII *Pagan Melancholy*

Not infrequently the "tough cheerful egotism" of Douglas' outlook is penetrated by a note of melancholy. Several critics have mentioned the presence of "elegaic cadences" in his prose, and his friends have reported the depression which frequently appeared in his personal life. Nancy Cunard relates that "there were occasions when he seemed to worry more than would appear logical in conjunction with such good spirits and sound foundations (13)." She found two opposed facets in Douglas' personality—"two faces . . .: the lusty, spontaneous, jovial, assertive one, with its wonderful gifts of inventiveness, laughter and irony *in excelsis;* and that other, the unexpected dreaminess, a mist over the fen at evening (5)." This description is obviously as kind as it is overwritten. The fact is, apparently, that Douglas became in later years a chronic "crank" whose conversation and letters were filled with complaints about food, conditions, laws, and the world in general. All this was no doubt to some extent a role—the fussy, old Scottish gentleman—which Douglas enjoyed playing. But, despite the whimsicality, exaggeration, and pose, there was a degree of sincerity. His criticisms were based on a consistent point of view which he held with some conviction.

So long as Douglas' dissent took the form of irony, it was acceptable and amusing. H. M. Tomlinson mentions this melancholy and biting tone in a reminiscence of Douglas' conversation: "I remember now that to hear him talk, at a London street-corner, blithely but cryptically melancholy, his words as sharp as his nose, of whatever irked him at the moment, his very eyebrows querulous, and then for him to go, with a last smile of lurking mockery, kept one on the spot for a moment, pondering."[75] But the quality which was engaging in the younger man became nagging and annoying as age brought him nearer to the death which was, for him, the end of all. Everything which he valued was part of physical life and the physical world, and not only was all this drawing inexorably toward its close, but all society seemed leagued to destroy the good things with which the hedonist would fill his brief span. Tomlinson said: "He is a sad and lonely man, confined to his Chott country, all that is left to him, because that sterile salt depression alone is exempt from potato planters, military parades, and improvements by politicians (47)."

For the true hedonist and sensualist, old age is no happy prospect. *Paneros,* in some ways the testament of an aging voluptuary, contains these lines, filled with regret for the passing of youth and with disdain for the prolongation of sterile age: "Why prolong life save to prolong pleasure? What pleasures are comparable to those of youth? And what ecstasy, of all of them, is more fervid than that of young lovers locked in voluptuous embracement, beside which every other joy of earth sinks to the consequence of a trifle . . .?"[76] And yet death can never be welcomed because, for the naturalist, it must necessarily be considered the end of personal existence. It is "a torment, a terror, a wintry thing, which comes to hug us to its body and drag us underground, away from friends and sunshine, into that uncomfortable night of nothing; there to rot like a carrion dog (2)." One thinks of the terms in which the aged Douglas was accustomed to answer questions concerning his health: "Putrefying, my dear, putrefying."

Again, one recognizes a pagan note in Douglas' melancholy, a tragic note to be found especially in the literature of people whose religion includes no conception of an afterlife. Among the early Greeks it formed a particularly poignant element in the attitudes of a people who displayed an intense delight in life combined with an acute awareness of its brevity. In the *Iliad* we read: "As is the life of the leaves, so is that of men. The wind scatters the leaves to the ground: the vigorous forest puts forth others, and they grow in the spring season. Soon one generation of men comes and another ceases."

Douglas commented on this Greek melancholy in *Siren Land*: "And if Greek life was heaving with a soft undercurrent of melancholy, it was the melancholy not of psychic constipation but rather of wistfulness; it was what Pater called a 'pagan melancholy.' They did not brood; a sane mind broods over nothing; it insists upon being distracted. The death of a comrade needs must convulse our organism, but, if sound, it resents the intrusion and seeks to regain its equipoise (193)." And in *One Day* he described the attitude toward death characteristic of the poets of the Greek anthology: "For the most part they view the inevitable end in a spirit of calm contemplation. May you be happy down there, the survivors seem to say, if indeed any joy comes to the dead. Such is their outlook—cleansing and purging; nor can one peruse the saddest of epitaphs without realizing how much blither the world then was, how remote from our conception of a *vale of tears* (44)."

Thus while the naturalist in Douglas dictated a "spirit of calm contemplation," the hedonist deplored the loss of sensual pleasures. The solace of Epicurean resignation proved empty, and Douglas did not meet approaching death too gracefully. Aldington says that he "desperately wanted to go on living" and records an incident in the railroad station in Florence in 1937. "Norman takes me aside and urgently reminds me that I have promised to let him know at once if I find in the scientific periodicals I read any means of prolonging life."[77] One is tempted to equate Douglas' position with that of that other Scottish rationalist, Mr. Keith:

. . . that infamous apparition . . . he most ardently desired to forget. His laughter died down. Wanly he looked at his mirthful pagans, the embodiment of joy. Yes; these were his distraction, his playmates, his elixir of life, his antidote against the only disease, the only sin, crime, vice which he recognized on earth—a vice nonetheless, because it happened to be the inevitable—the vice of old age. And all the time that pallid swarm came crowding on: messengers from the inexorable spectre. He felt them creeping about with ghostly tread, blighting the radiance of his life, tainting the very air he breathed. Hateful intruders! They wailed among his lilies. The garden was full of their horrid footsteps.

In their presence Mr. Keith began to experience an uncomfortable sensation, a kind of chill—as though something evil had stepped between himself and the brave light of the sun. (298-99)

XIII *The Literary Critic*

There remain to be considered Douglas' critical attitudes, and these are not of great significance. Although he wrote many book reviews during the period of his work for the *English Review,* he cannot be considered a literary critic of any importance. Throughout most of his life he was almost entirely uninterested in modern literature. He wrote in *Late Harvest* of his period as a critic: "I managed during that period to hit out now and then and say what I thought, while becoming more and more—how shall I say?—more and more venal as the months rolled by . . . . Dirty work. And not over-paid (45-46)."

Although his reviews were sometimes shrewd and biting in their exposure of cheap emotionalism and melodrama in the third-rate novels that were produced during World War I, he was obviously not at home in the work and was very likely to digress into some "hobby-horse" topic suggested by the book under consideration. His extroversion and his violent dislike of messy emotion and of anything that struck him as mystical seem to have left him with a blind spot in the matter of poetry; he was apparently lacking in the requisite sensitivity. In *Fountains in the Sand* he said: "Take away from modern poetry what appeals to primitive man—the jingle and pathetic fallacy—and the residue, if any, would be better expressed in prose (61)." This judgment seems less absurd if one recalls that it was made in 1912, the year Edward Marsh published the first volume of *Georgian Poetry.* W. Y. Tindall has written of the poets of that period that "Being up-to-date meant accepting the frames of Wordsworth and Tennyson and the rhetoric of Keats, purged of richness and strength, however, in order to achieve the condition of Housman."[78] One would hardly expect poetry of this sort to appeal to a hater of the pathetic fallacy, of sentimentalism, and of English scenery ("like living in a salad"). It should also be noted that Douglas was among the first critics to recognize

Robert Frost, whose concreteness and understatement pleased him.[79]

The essay on Edgar Allan Poe (1909) Douglas called his first appearance before a literary audience. In it he praised Poe, a writer in whom he had been interested for some years, for his abandonment of the didactic element: "[Poe's] influence upon literature was a civilizing and purifying agency. Poe is a great anti-vulgarian. As such, he has discarded the ethical moment, and in doing so, he has followed the footsteps of the masters of all ages. Why is it that didacticism in poetry was so offensive to him? Because it constitutes an intrusion of ethics into art, an intrusion which arouses, even in ordinary minds, a sense of incongruity and impropriety."[80]

This point of view is consistent with Douglas' anti-puritan feelings and with his dislike of meddlesome morality. But it is a critical position which was already dated and which, like many of his other views, belongs to the late nineteenth century rather than to the twentieth. Ford Madox Ford, in "A Haughty Generation," an article printed in the *Yale Review* of July 1922, noted the fact that Douglas' literary tastes seem to have been arrested somewhere near the turn of the century: "In a sense Mr. Douglas is a writer of an older generation—of a generation infinitely old, critically. To come upon passages of appraisement in 'Alone' is to be bewildered by feeling that one's young, young youth has returned. You have Ouida and Mathilde Blind—Mathilde Blind of all people!—exalted at the expense of James. . . . There is hardly anyone old enough to remember *that* literary point of view (XI:711)." But Douglas not only believed that his generation was intellectually and artistically superior to those which followed it; he even pretended to believe that the body temperature of modern young men was several degrees lower than that of his contemporaries.[81]

Douglas' criticism consists, in the main, of the application of his particular values and ideas to the work in question. Although he seems to have recognized a certain inadequacy in such criticism, he questioned the validity of other types. Life was his business; and life, he assumed, was the business of other writers. He therefore believed himself justified in bringing his experience to bear upon their books in an effort to evaluate their ideas and their reasoning. Beyond this, all else was individual taste. In *Late Harvest* he discussed the function and the requisites of the reviewer:

To judge a man's writing on its literary merits is one part of the critic's business and one part only, seeing that a book is both a mental product and a social one. A knowledge of the British Museum Library will never suffice to make a respectable reviewer. He must have a knowledge of life, of men and their ways, a fair dose of personal worldly experience—the requisite outfit, in fact. This is what they sometimes lack, and it accounts for a certain thinness, a certain anaemic quality, in their appraisals. . . . Is it justifiable to approach all writers from one and the same angle, with an unchanging set of predetermined opinions? Should a reviewer be what he sometimes is, a mentor with a fixed point of view? Certainly he should, where mere questions of intellectual discipline, of good or bad writing, of crooked or straight thinking, are involved. . . . Beyond this province, the canons are variable and complex, and he is the critic who discovers and applies the right one. (45)

Douglas avoided the issues involved in the realm of "variable and complex" canons. He judged books according to his own "unchanging set of pre-determined opinions" to such a degree that his critical outlook can only be described as narrow. His judgments of the classics of literature were often startlingly unorthodox; yet they reflected the integrity with which he held to his views, as well as the confirmed independence of his thought. The *Divine Comedy* was a "monument of bigotry . . . [its] detestable sentiments . . . are enough to prejudice any feeling mind against the faith which it proclaims." Douglas condemns the book because he personally cannot bear the idea of "eternal imprisonment."[82]

He praised Milton's style as a "felicitous alloy of Mediterranean grace and Saxon mettle," but he was convinced that *Paradise Lost* was plagiarized from the *Adamo Caduto*, a tragedy by a seventeenth-century Italian, Serafino della Salandro. Far from disapproving of Milton's Latinism and Italianism, as he found some contemporaries doing, Douglas suggested that "our language has become enriched by steady gleams of pomp and splendour due, in large part, to the peculiar lustre of Milton's comely importations."[83]

He reports having passed through a Shelley period in his youth, but his mature view could not accept Shelley's idealism: "He lacked the master-key. An evangelist of a kind, he was streaked, for all his paganism, with the craze of world-improvement. One day he escaped from his chains into those mountains and there beheld a certain Witch—only to be called back to mortality by a domestic and critic-bitten lady. He tried to translate the Symposium. He never tried to live it. . . ."[84]

A writer whom Douglas was always ready to praise was Ouida, whose works he felt should be read for "their tone, their temper; for that pervasive good breeding, that shining honesty, that capacity of scorn."[85] D. M. Low has made a convincing case for Ouida's influence upon Douglas in such matters as her religious skepticism, her individualism, and her lack of illusions about progress, the perfectibility of man, and the magical power of education.[86] From that literary point of view that—in Ford's words, "hardly anyone is old enough to remember"—Ouida's criticism is preferable to that of Henry James. In *Late Harvest*, Douglas wrote: ". . . I will commit myself to the statement that the critical utterances of James already, at this short distance of time, read curiously stale and senile, when compared with Ouida's. And why? Because . . . Ouida's have the "milk of humanity" in them. Nobody can say that of anything Henry James ever wrote (38)."

D. H. Lawrence, with whom Douglas carried on a feud over the Magnus affair, received the censure of the older man for his tendency to put real people thinly disguised into his novels. Douglas claimed to hold "the old fashioned view that all . . . social curiosity is vulgar and therefore to be avoided."[87] He described Lawrence as a sexual adolescent who had "never recovered from the shock of puberty,"[88] a view which, despite its oversimplification, has something to be said for it. He was willing to admit, however, that Lawrence "could write good descriptions and his travel books are excellent." And he called *Sons and Lovers* "one of the really good novels of our time."[89]

Douglas' views on the drama seem to be those spoken by one of the characters in *South Wind*. They point up the characteristic which hindered his appreciation of imaginative literature— the egocentric point of view which made it difficult for him to identify himself with the plights of others. "When I watch *Hamlet* or *Othello*, I say to myself: This stuff is nicely riveted together. But, in the first place, the story is not true. And secondly, it is no affair of mine. Why cry about it? (395)"

Among the kindest remarks concerning Douglas' critical views are those of Sherard Vines in his book *Movements in Modern English Poetry and Prose:*

Though he is a topographer and novelist in the first instance, he has produced a small amount of literary criticism that cannot be passed

over in silence, and anyone who has read his article on Doughty's *Arabia Deserta*, and on Charles Waterton will no doubt
agree. Like his junior, Mr. Huxley, he has the art of throwing aphorisms on the (comparatively) universal while ostensibly engaged
with the particular; in the essay on *Arabia Deserta* may be found a
plea for recognition of the value of the dream or fantasy element in
art, a dig at utilitarianism and a significant comparison of the Anglo-
Saxon with the French literary spirit in topography. He goes "bald-
headed" for the paralysing effect of the Academy; and such an attack launched by such a man at a time when rigidity and formality
are in danger of excessive admiration should be salutary in its effect.[90]

Although Douglas' remarks on travel writing, among the most
cogent of his criticism, are to considered later, it seems in order
to touch upon the *Arabia Deserta* essay here. It represents, as
Vines points out, Douglas' clearest statement of his aestheticism
as well as of the "dreamlike" contemplation of natural beauty
for its own sake with which he filled his own writing and
which he valued in the writings of others. The sense and the
force of his argument are demonstrated in the following passage:

Is there no prosperity other than material? It is surely time to
have done with this utilitarian nonsense; to reverse the proposition
and argue, if need be, in favour of the value of *mere illusions*. An
argument of sufficient force when one realizes, for instance, that much
of what is best in our literary tradition—that heritage of beauty to
which a man will cling when he has learnt to forsake and deride all
his other natal gods—has its roots in dreams, in nature-worship, the
communion between man and wild things; and could never have
come into being but for that subtle harmony "which the profane cannot hear."[91]

Douglas' opposition to didacticism in literature is grounded
in his preference for the concrete: "The minutest hint of a moral
lesson is a generalization: generalizations cannot awaken emotions like single images, and therefore morality should not in-
trude where the awakening of emotion is the primary object."[92]
This is, for the most part, a sound maxim, and it served Douglas well. But he was little more able than the next man, to avoid
generalization; and such preachings as the reader encounters in
Good-bye to Western Culture and elsewhere in Douglas' work
seem clearly to contradict his principles.

Belief in the importance of objectivity and concreteness underlies Douglas' preference for the Greek lyric poets. The brief, spare poems of these ancient writers are among the few poems which he praised. Here was the atmosphere in which he was at home, the tone to which he aspired—unsentimental, unmystical, clear in line and form, and concrete. The only poems he published were an Anacreontic that appeared in *Unprofessional Tales*, a slight but not unpleasant piece, and some imitations of Greek epitaphs which accurately reproduce the tone of the Greek lyric. His discussion in *One Day* of the poets of the Greek Anthology may well be the most valuable criticism he produced:

Here we have these eternal wants of mankind—the cry for food and drink and love. . . . the best of these poets . . . felt like children and spoke like men. They were sensitive in the right spot. To talk of the crystalline contour of the verses, their wit, tenderness, and directness of vision—it is true enough. You will go on to discover that they have the *inevitable* ring; that this truth, whatever it be, has now been uttered once and forever. (38)

They looked outward and saw themselves surrounded by a host of tangible things, fellow-creatures and beasts and mountains and woodlands and waters; they regulated their behavior in accordance with these mundane necessities and so attained terrestrial values. Whence, in the older epigrams, that sense of direct contemplation of nature, that eye for detail, that touch of earth—bitter or sweet. Slowly it fades away. Even before the commencement of the Christian era concrete imagery tends to be replaced by abstractions. The process was never arrested. They, the Christians, could not allow these things of earth, dear to pagans, to be of much account. They looked inwards, guiding their conduct no longer in relation to tangible objects but to an intangible postulate; and so attained ghostly values. Ghostly is the impression they leave. A kind of spiritual dimness had begun to creep over the world. (40-41)

Douglas' literary standards are thus clearly consonant with his values in other matters: he preferred writers who presented nature with clarity, objectivity, and concreteness—and without moralistic designs upon the reader.

III Methods

L YTTON STRACHEY once wrote Norman Douglas, concerning *Alone:* "Your books are so full; there is so much of so many things in them—so much experience, so much learning, so much art, so much humour, so much philosophy, and so much proof that there is so much more, so very much more underneath, that is unexpressed."[1] This is the effect of Douglas' books upon his devotees. The fullness and variety, and the richness of personality and scope of learning that he brought to his books, make them more than the "hints to tourists" and cliché "word-painting" that so many travel books are.

Douglas' methods—and much of what is said about them here applies not only to the travel books but also to the fiction, which is to be treated later—were consistent and somewhat individual. Around a thread of personal narrative he wove a fabric of observation that embraced the whole nature of the region he was writing about: its topography and geology, its plants and animals, its history and literature and institutions, its villages and cafés, and something of the spirit of its people. And shining through at all points, though seldom unpleasantly obtruded, is the distinctive personality of the author—frequently eccentric to the point of annoyance, but always perceptive of natural beauty and informed by the philosophy that experience is its own reward.

Although the travel books are usually presented in the form of a journey, with various towns and places as well as the events experienced in them treated in the order of their appearance in the itinerary, the organization is ordinarily quite loose. The essays on places or topics which constitute chapters are joined only tenuously, and the books derive their unity from the fact that the material has been suggested by the same region and from the personality and point of view of the author. The reader is traveling in a leisurely way with Norman Douglas through some particular region, usually off the beaten track, and sharing Douglas' random walking, talking, and dining. And, more important, he is listening to Douglas' views on philosophy, religion, art, and the art of living.

When the treasures of town or village are turned up—some cave used for worship during the Middle Ages, the ruins of a villa where Horace once stayed, a collection of rare coins in the local museum, or just some unusual vantage point which allows an especially attractive view of the landscape at sunset—the reader finds that his guide and companion is able to discourse on almost anything with the authority of wide learning and with the perception of an artist. The history of the region, its legends and literature, references to it by ancient writers—all are tapped as sources of the urbane and free-flowing discourse. Although seldom treated with anything resembling completeness, these subjects are discussed interestingly and casually.

The reader feels assured that the author has nothing of what Keats called "a palpable design" upon him. He finds himself also learning things—in what seems almost an accidental fashion—about the topography of the region, the geographical composition of its cliffs, the make-up and condition of its forests, and the names and appearance of the flowers which grow on its hillsides and in its sequestered valleys. Nor is the populace excluded from this view, for the inhabitants of a region, along with their customs and beliefs, also form part of the essence, the peculiar "genius" which Douglas believed every region has and which he strove to express.[2]

The tone of Douglas' books is that of a conversation between casual friends who are cultured and wise in the ways of the world, versed in many things, interested in almost everything, and neither very pious nor very easily shocked. If people of another sort appear by mistake in his audience, they will be likely, at best, to flounder because of lack of background, or, at worst, to be scandalized by some flash of refined but biting cynicism. Douglas knows this and perhaps intentionally designs a few traps for such people. He never writes down to them, never includes textbook history to "fill them in," and never attenuates his point of view to save their sensibilities, even though it is very likely that he could have widened his audience and achieved more popular success by recourse to some to these expedients.

Some insight into Douglas' tastes and literary practices is to be found in a passage in *Looking Back* in which he tells of a tutor named Frau Schenkh, who taught him Italian during the Karlsruhe days and who introduced him to the work of Gregorovius:

Frau Schenkh was so conscientious and capable a teacher that soon enough, and probably by way of arousing my interest in Italy, she was making me translate into Italian the delightful chapters in Gregorovius which deal with Porto D'Anzio and Nettuno, the Pontine Marshes and the Cape of Circe. I liked Gregorovius even then, and in later years learned to appreciate more fully his humanism, his alloy of learning and descriptive power; I am inclined to detect his influence in some of my own things; that veneer of erudition. . . . No doubt his fondness for scholarly research sometimes looks like pedantry, but, glancing into him again, I do not find him oppressive after the manner of many of his countrymen, and he certainly knows how to squeeze delicate effects out of the language.[3]

In describing the methods of Gregorovius, Douglas was describing, as he well knew, his own methods. The approach, with its combination of scholarly, scientific, and humanistic interests—its "veneer of erudition"—was his own. His requirements for successful travel writing were those he described in *Alone*—curiosity, learning, and time.[4] And these are the ingredients of his own best books. It is, of course, a more complex and rarer combination of interests and energies which enabled him to produce books of unusual originality and enduring interest on such over-described and tourist-infested regions as Capri and Naples. Aldington lists these ingredients: as ". . . sea excursions and long wanderings afoot, local friendships, scholarly collections, prolonged studies among documents in the libraries of Naples and Cava, enthusiasms for geology, natural history, botany, afforestation, old customs, out-of-the-way history, departed manners."[5] There is something here for everyone, and thanks to clear and pleasing presentation, even readers whose interests are considerably more limited seldom find themselves bored for long.

Some threats to reader interest are present, however, in Douglas' travel books. The discursive organization, with its lack of a real narrative core, may deter the reader who is accustomed to having his descriptions of regions presented in a more orderly and systematic fashion, or with some sort of romanticized plot line. Moreover, the closeness of detail with which Douglas occasionally attacks some favorite topic may prove annoying, especially if the digression involves a subject in which the reader

is not especially interested or a point of view with which he
cannot muster much sympathy. And of course Douglas' attitudes
are such that they are bound to disturb occasionally. Thus
Cornelius Weygandt writes of *Siren Land* and *Old Calabria:*
"There is something sinister in them . . . and always a pottering
over petty details,—very differing impediments, the one repellent, the other boring."[6]

I *Observation and Personality*

But Douglas was not writing systematic descriptions: he had
given that up when he found that it did not pay. He was simply
giving the reader an opportunity to share with him a particular
atmosphere—an atmosphere which owed as much to Douglas'
personality and interests, including his eccentricities, as to the
region involved. This approach produced a peculiar sort of experience which some readers seemed to enjoy and were willing
to pay for; the rest could go their way. In *Siren Land* he ex-
cused an abrupt change of subject with the following explanation: "Were I writing a guide-book or historical account of this
region, I would endeavour to give a systematic description of
these legendary islets, supplemented with measurements and
hints for travellers. But I am doing nothing of the kind; I am
only dreaming through the summer months to the music of
the cicadas, and dreams are irresponsible things that flit about
aimlessly, dwelling with absurd gravity upon unconsidered
trifles and never quoting statistics (41-42)."

Douglas' remarks about a philosophy of travel literature which
occur in his essay on Doughty's *Arabia Deserta* constitute valuable literary criticism and throw more light on his own work than
anything else one might say. The essence of his view was that
travel books should result from a combination of observation
and personality. When a proper rapport is established between
author and reader, the same things are of interest and significance to both, and only then can the reader accept the author
with natural ease as his guide. Although he favored this balance
between the objective and the personal, Douglas recognized
that the great travel writers have been such mainly because
they had appealing and individualized personalities and were
able to express these, without obtruding them, in contact with
the material being described. Of course he deplored the subjective and introspective, and yet he emphasized the need, in
travel writing, for the presence of a mind with an individual

point of view behind the ostensible surface of external description and narration: "... an impersonal travel book is a horror." He describes the ideal writer of travel books as "the inspired or at least enthusiastic amateur" and adds:

One would not take it amiss, furthermore, were he obsessed by some hobby or grievance, by idiosyncrasies and prejudices not common to the rest of us. And it goes without saying that he must be gloriously indifferent to the opinions of his fellow creatures. Can professionals ever fulfill these conditions? No! They should therefore never attempt to write travel-books.
They have lost their innocence. (3)

Thus the reader of the travel book should be always in contact with a personality as well as with a region, and that personality should be worthwhile one—which to Douglas means a strong and independent one—so that the reader indirectly learns to understand himself as well as the region involved. The passage in the essay on *Arabia Deserta* in which Douglas develops these ideas is worth extensive quotation:

Here is not only information; here is character, a human document. The image of the poet-traveller is no blur. Doughty has etched his lonely figure against this desolation of sand and Lavacrag, and we are glad to see how the thing has been accomplished; it does one good to be in contact with a companion full of natural resources and listen to his tale; one leaves him with regret, as one bids farewell to some friend of robust and well-stored mind, perceiving that, all unconsciously, his words have been of use in revealing us to ourselves. They have helped us to rectify and clarify our own perspective. (Can anything be called a book unless it forces the reader by one method or another, by contrast or sympathy, to discover himself?) So *Arabia Deserta* is the antithesis of the purely pictorial . . . inasmuch as therein we enjoy that feeling of intimacy for which every sensitive person must crave, while wandering with his author through strange places. It seems to me that the reader of a good travel-book is entitled not only to an exterior voyage, to descriptions of scenery and so forth, but to an interior, a sentimental or temperamental voyage, which takes place side by side with that outer one, and that the ideal book of this kind offers us, indeed, a triple opportunity of exploration—abroad, into the author's brain and into our own. The writer should therefore possess a brain worth exploring; some philosophy of life—not necessarily, though by preference, of his own forging—and the courage to proclaim it and put it to the test; he must be naïf and profound, both child and sage. Who is either the one or the other in these days, when the whole trend of existence makes for the superficial and commonplace, when a man writes with one eye on his publisher and the other on his public?

This may account for the insipid taste of many travel-books printed just now; lack of personality on the part of their authors. It is not enough to depict, in however glowing hues, the landscape and customs of distant regions, to smother us in folklore and statistics and history, and be-sprinkle the pages with imaginary conversations or foreign idioms by way of generating "local colour." It is not enough. We want to take our share in that interior voyage and watch how these alien sights and sounds affect the writer. If he lacks that compulsion of the spirit which is called character, or lets his mind linger on contingencies hostile to frank utterance, he will be unable to supply that want and leave us dissatisfied. . . .

[The earlier travellers] were "gentlemen scholars" who saw things from their own individual angle. Their leisurely aristocratic flavour, their wholesome discussions about this or that, their waywardness and all that mercurial touch of a bygone generation—where is it now? (8-10)

Douglas apparently strove to achieve the "leisurely aristocratic flavour" of Doughty, whom he knew personally, and of the older travel writers who manifested their personalities and individualities in their books. He gave much of himself, his opinions, and his tastes in his books, and a good deal of autobiography as well. Yet, on the other hand, he did not approve of the sort of travel writing which amounts to a relating of subjective visions prompted by the place visited. For him the best of the travelers were those who, like Doughty, presented their subjects and themselves honestly and, in a sense, objectively, thus establishing the delicate balance. He recognized the increased subjectivity of modern literary values—the "soul-baring" approach of some modern writers, and the "prying" tendency of some readers—and saw the dangers involved:

Readers are becoming more and more connoisseurs of sensations; they commune with an author not only for what he writes, but for what he is; they endeavor to spy into the windows of his soul and to overhear him chronicling his most casual needs and impressions. They want to learn how things affect him. It is a feature of today—the personal trend. A self-consistent writer—one who rings true—can therefore secure more attention by the personal method than by the other one. For we are all creatures of impulse liable to unguarded moments, and there is a contagion in wisely premeditated *asides* on the part of such a man; from sharing his opinions we are insensibly led to adopt his views. But the chronicling of moods depends on whose moods they are. Whoever is not constitutionally honest, had better remain impersonal.[7]

Although Douglas doubtless believed that he had the required "constitutional honesty" and although he certainly injected his personality into his writings, he nevertheless exercised a very definite restraint which protected him from readers who would spy into the windows of writers' souls. Despite the autobiographical help he offers to the student of his character and thought, he seldom actually withdraws the mask from his innermost concerns, and one is hence never quite able to see clearly the deepest workings of his mind. H. M. Tomlinson writes: "He has no tricks but only the idiosyncrasies of an original man, good-natured and humorous, of whom you will learn nothing but what he chooses to disclose. He has the sudden reticences of a gentleman who has appeared to be open and intimate. He has said enough. If you seek for more than he has given he changes the subject so delicately that you forget your sudden disquiet in a new interest (73)." The evaluations which appeared at the time of Douglas' death noted this strangely impersonal aspect of the writings of a man whose very personality was one of his greatest appeals. The *Times Literary Supplement* said, "...he never thrusts his personality into the foreground."[8] And V. S. Pritchett, writing in the *New Statesman and Nation*, said, "Douglas is an excellent writer of works of travel: he has the necessary independence of mind, his loneliness, the face that gives nothing way (307)."

Dawkins has contrasted Douglas' extroverted approach with the more personal-subjective approach of such writers as Kinglake and, more recently, Sacheverell Sitwell: "All through, his books are the exact opposite of the books of those people who use their theme mainly as a means of embodying their own esthetic appreciations and feelings, they themselves being the real subject of the book. What sets Douglas in motion is the external world and nothing else; he lets himself appear, it is true, but only indirectly (75)." Dawkins finds that Douglas' books invite the reader to the scene described; whereas those of the introverted writers, especially the best of them, tend to frighten the reader away from the region, since the reader realizes that he is dealing with a kind of fantasy and fears that encountering the reality will break the spell his author has created.

... when it is Douglas who is writing and I find myself delighted or interested, I feel the strongest desire to go and see it all for myself, and everywhere I savour most the descriptions of things or places with which I am already fairly familiar. Douglas is a guide to the show, and he makes me see far more than I should ever be able to see for myself with only my own eyes. But the reader of such a creation as *The Gothick North* can be content to sit quietly at home, unaffected by the fall in the pound. Incidentally too the man whose eyes gaze always outward finds the whole external world so interesting that he never has the least difficulty in finding a subject: they press in upon him. (77)

The travel writer of the inward glance, who writes out of himself rather than out of the region, may produce artistic products of a sort; but his writing has a certain artificiality, almost a falseness, which the scientist in Douglas could never have abided. Douglas would have considered that such a writer had lost touch with his subject and that his observations had been inaccurate. He deplored the passing of what he called "the artist's eye—the eye for detail":

Such is that curious trait of many of our bards to pass from the particular to the general, instead of *vice versa*: surely this blunts the edge of the reader's appetency? Again, if art is but the expression or the revelation of the artist's personality, and if, in eight cases out of ten, that personality be neither strong nor interesting—why go within? Why not become a little objective for a change? This brooding preoccupation with self is aesthetically unjustifiable. We cannot all be Childe Harold, and he was bad enough.[9]

He complained similarly of modern poets, in whom he found a "tendency . . . to deal with fixed types rather than trust to the loving and precise observation which is the hall-mark of true poetry." One of the few poets whom Douglas praised was, as we have noted, Robert Frost, who had the required individual touch, but who was nevertheless perceptive and honest in his treatment of nature. He wrote of Frost: "Nowhere on earth, they say, is more derivative nonsense printed under the name of poetry than in America; Mr. Frost is an American. All the more credit to him for giving us a picture of things seen with the eye. There is a wild, racy flavour in his poems; they sound that *inevitable* response to nature which is the hall-mark of true lyric feeling."[10]

Despite Douglas' many prejudices and unqualified attitudes, there is a certain honesty and integrity in his writing. He kept his eye on his subject and treated it with a scientific kind of exactness. This particular approach may not appeal to all read-ers, but to some it is one of the principal appeals of his work. Pritchett writes:

. . . his intellect was scientific—like Butler's—and the beauties of his writing are contrived from an exactitude of eye and from the ironies of research. The landscape of *South Wind* is a superb collec-tion of well-placed geological and botanical observations, of notes on climate; one remembers the crinkled sun, the changing tempera-tures of the island, those draughts of cold air coming from the buried caverns, their suggestion of physical cataclysm and terror, and their usefulness to the natural philosophers of engineering on the island. (307)

Douglas was, as an artist must be, true to his response. His ability to catch the atmosphere of places was a result of this intellectual honesty. He received a series of significant impres-sions and was left with a special sense of the beauty, ugliness, or whatever of the place he had seen. He was able to convey this essence to his readers successfully only because he was willing to hide nothing, or at least to select details in such a way that nothing was concealed that had contributed significantly to the conclusion. This attitude breeds confidence in the reader and fosters the partnership of sympathy and interests which Douglas thought important.

The honesty of Douglas' methods, which has reminded some critics of the attitude of the ancient travelers, does not allow him to hide his disgust with inferiority or inhospitality when he finds it. He was ready to condemn anything from the lack of an adequate reforestation program to bad wine or unclean beds. And despite his admiration for the Mediterranean peoples, he was not ordinarily guilty of the sort of uncritical tolerance which is a product of sentimental humanitarianism and altruism. He judged by his own values, which were aesthetic and, with-in certain limits, pragmatic; he never compromised himself for the sake of subject or reader. In *Late Harvest* he wrote regard-ing certain criticisms of his treatment of the saints: "They would have liked me to take a more spiritualistic point of view in re-gard to those events, in other words, to allegorize facts instead of letting them speak for themselves. The spiritual interpreta-tion of unpalatable facts is not to my taste, signifying, as it does, that an intelligent observation of them has been thrown out of gear. The delightful word 'spiritual' is not to be trusted; on occasion it allows 'muddle-headed' to step into its shoes (49)."

Just as he was free from false altruism and religious bias, Douglas was free also from other forms of sentimentality. His genuine love of the beautiful, the curious, and the antique is qualified by his constant awareness of the falseness and affectation which so often corrupt modern attitudes toward them. Occasionally, when his atmosphere has hints of artificiality, a cleansing irony saves the day and one sees that the effect throughout has been conscious and intentional. His cynicism tempers his veneration, and the most serious moods are likely to end in an ironic smile. This device is an important one in *South Wind* and the other satires, but it appears in the travel books as well. The following interlude appears in *Siren Land*:

I remember a long-drawn, golden evening among the Cyclades. A spell had fallen over all things; the movement of Nature seemed to be momentarily arrested; there was not a sound below; overhead, the sunbeams vibrated with tuneful melodies. Janko, the fisherman, had dropped his oars, and our boat, the only moving object in that preternatural stillness, was drawn by an invisible hand toward the ruddy pool in the west. Athwart our path lay a craggy islet, black and menacing against the background of crimson conflagration. Soon it came in upon us in swarthy confusion of rock and cloven ravine, a few gleams of emerald in its sheltered recesses. Here if anywhere, methought, Sirens might still dwell unmolested. The curly-pated rascal steered with cunning hand towards a Lilliputian islet; like a true Greek he appreciated curiosity in every form. He resolutely refused to set foot on shore. I began my explorations alone, concluding that he had visited the place before.

It was no Siren islet. It was an islet of fleas. I picked them off my clothes in tens, in hundreds, in handfuls. Never was mortal nearer jumping out of his skin.(9)

Douglas wrote most of his travel books several years after material was collected—that is, after the tour which the book related. He preferred a method based on a sort of "emotion recollected in tranquillity." The passage of time mellowed his memories and created a nostalgia which motivated his writing. He described this process in *Alone:*

. . . a haze of oblivion is formed by lapse of time and space; a kindly haze, which obliterates the thousand fretting annoyances wherewith the traveller's path in every country is bestrewn. He forgets them; forgets that weltering ocean of unpleasantness and remembers only its sporadic islets—those moments of calm delight or fiercer joy which he would fain hold fast for ever. . . . He comes for the sake of its mirage, that sunny phantom which will rise up later out of some November fog in another land. Italy is a delightful place to remember, to think and talk about. (199-200)

The emotions evoked by particular recollections and the moods which his memory had spun from them determined Douglas' choice of details and perhaps also produced his surprisingly unified atmospheres. Places which other travelers found uncomfortable or lacking in objects of interest were for Douglas touchstones of pleasant memories. He never lost his nostalgic loyalty to places where he had been happy. And these memories, dwelt upon years later and often in another country, evoked moods which he was able to translate infectiously into prose. Though time and distance might blur details, it was the mood that mattered, the mood to which he was true. "How strange," he wrote, "is that process of mental association, and how a mood, the most volatile of things on earth, will often persist and grow into a suggestion and become attached to some locality, twining itself inextricably among houses and fields and pathways!"[11]

Douglas noted carefully the associations which particular scenes aroused—he was an admirer of Proust—investigating them persistently and making of them some of the finest passages in his books. For instance, Tunisia, which was so unlike his native country or his adopted country, often reminded him nevertheless of familiar scenes, and such memories helped him to bring landscapes to life and to draw upon the entire body of his experience, whatever his immediate subject. The headwaters of the Seldja—with some assistance from hashish—produced this excursion into memories:

I sat alone, screened from the midday heat, drowsy and content. It was a pleasant resting-place, under that leafy arbour, through which only a few rays of light could filter, weaving arabesque designs that moved and melted on the floor as the wind stirred the foliage overhead. And a pleasant occupation, listening to those amiable amphibians in the mere below—they carried my thought back to other frog concerts, dimly remembered, in some other lands—and gazing through the green network of branches upon that sun-scorched garden, where now a silvery thread of water began to attract my attention as it stole, coyly, among the flower-beds.

The day is yet young, methought; it is too hot to think of marching home at this hour. Now is the time, rather, for a pipe of *kif*—

Four pipes, reverentially inhaled . . . it was almost too much, for a mere dilettante.

But the mystery of the frogs, the when and where of it, was solved. Slowly and benignly the memories travelled back, building themselves into a vision so clearcut and elaborate withal, that I might have been holding it, as one holds some engraving or miniature, in my hand. It was in the Rhine-woods, of course; long years ago, in summertime. But the frog-music here was not amiable at all; never have I heard such angry batrachian vociferations. They came in a discontented and menacing chorus from ten thousand leathery throats, and almost drowned our converse as we crept along through the twilight of trees that shot up from the swampy earth.

These Rhine-woods are like pathless tropical jungles; everything is so green and luxuriant; and morning grew to midday while we threaded our way through tangles of interlacing boughs and undergrowth. Yet we knew, all the time, that something else was in store for us, some joy, some surprise. And lo! there was an opening in the forest, and we suddenly found ourselves standing up on the summit of a high bank at whose foot there rolled a sunlit and impetuous torrent. Too staid for the formation of ripples, too swift for calm content, the river seemed to boil up from below in a kind of frolicsome rage. A blissful sight.

"*Er spinnt*," my companion was saying.

In what obscure chamber of the brain had those words slumbered, closely folded, for thirty years? It was indeed an authentic weaving of arabesque designs upon the even texture of the living liquid mass; multitudinous rings and ovals and lozenges were cast up from the green depths as from a mighty over-bubbling cauldron; some fiercely engulfed again, others torn hither than thither into new and pleasing shapes, fresh ones for ever emerging; only a few contrived to linger unchanged, floating in sunny splendour down the face of the waters. A blissful sight! The dark and mazy woodlands, now, were left far behind—the croaking of the frogs sounded strangely distant. We gazed in ecstasy upon that shining flood. . . .[12]

A passage from *Alone* goes some way toward explaining the method Douglas used, in the writing of that book at least, and demonstrates that a certain idealization of actuality is involved in his reminiscences:

. . . generally, delving down into memory, a man can bring up at least one clear-cut fragment, something still fervid and flashing, a remembered voice or a glimpse of landscape which helps to unveil the main features of a scenario already relegated to the lumber-room. And this detail will unravel the next; the scattered elements jostle each other into place, as in the final disentangling of some complicated fugue.

Such things will do for a skeleton. Imagination will kindly provide flesh and blood, life, movement. . . . One supresses much; why not add a little? Truth blends well with untruth, and phantasy has been so sternly banned of late from travellers' tales that I am growing tender-hearted towards the poor old dame; quite chivalrous, in fact—especially on those rather frequent occasions when I find myself unable to dispense with her services. (257-58)

Time glazes the memories of incidents, smooths the rough edges, deepens the hues, and intensifies the experience; and it seems that Douglas was not reluctant to exploit its properties. Nor does this statement necessarily contradict what has been said about his honesty and objectivity. His honesty, as we have said, was an honesty to his response: he recreated exactly what he had felt, a method which had a place for the subjective consideration as well as for the objective. Although time may cheat the memory, does it not also synthesize, bring perspective and insight? If the winnowings of memory led Douglas to the essence of his experience, were not some of the most important conditions of art realized thereby?

II *The "Veneer of Erudition"*

One feature that characterizes Douglas' writing—fiction as well as travel writing—is the constant use he made of his wide knowledge in several fields. Other writers may have had a comparable mastery of one or another of these areas, but few have had such a grasp of all of them—and even fewer have so openly and almost systematically exploited such a wealthy storeroom of abstruse information.

Douglas kept himself well informed generally during a good part of his adult life—let us say through the *English Review* period. He had kept up with contemporary letters and with scholarly developments in all the fields in which he was interested. But in his later years he found himself unable to maintain such an active program of reading and research, and apparently concluded that it was not worth the trouble. Henceforth he seems to have read very little, virtually nothing of his contemporaries, and to have fallen behind in many respects. His tastes and reading experience never actually went much beyond the Edwardian period; and the significant modern developments in psychology, philosophy, sociology, anthropology—all areas which had once interested him—slipped by unnoticed. Such names as Freud, Jung, Malinowski, Benedict, Meade, Fraser, Harrison, Dewey, Croce—the leaders of twentieth-century thought in some of Douglas' chosen fields—are unmentioned in his books. But all this did not prevent him from continuing to utter his nineteenth-century views with the greatest conviction. He simply rationalized, as only the egotist can, that what he did not know was not worth knowing.

On the other hand, in such areas as ancient, medieval, and Renaissance writings, antiquarian lore, and mythology, as well as in the elements of botany, zoology, and geology, his vast erudition, acquired early, remained available to him. Books and flowers do not often change; nor does the body of Greek lyrics, the description of Pausanius, or the history of Tacitus or Suetonius. Here Douglas was master, and few could challenge him. Particularly in the history and literature of Italy was his knowledge prodigious. Aldington writes: "His mastery of out-of-the-way Italian and Italian-Latin literature is enormous, far beyond anything dreamed of by Burkhardt and Addington Symonds. Walter Pater is a mere amateur in comparison. There is not a professor in the world with Douglas' knowledge of the history and thought and archeology of South Italy."[13]

Douglas incorporated his knowledge and researches into his writings wherever possible, making of his erudition not so much an embellishment as a part of the very fabric which he wove. In his travel books he discussed matters of geology, biology, history, literature, and religion, not as interesting sidelights but as essential aspects of the region. This is not to say that these subjects were treated systematically, for nothing could be further from the truth. He did not write textbooks. But all these areas were included in the province through which he allowed his pen to roam. His erudition was usually embodied in references, allusions, or digressions. He assumed an audience interested in such material and never considered the possibility of a reader whose interests were in the more ostensible and superficial features of the area—the tourist attractions; in fact, he took for granted considerable knowledge on the part of the reader. An example of allusion to Italian history, from *Old Calabria*, shows the sort of historical background which he assumed:

Then my thoughts wandered to the Hohenstaufen and the conspiracy whereby their fate was avenged. The romantic figures of Manfred and Conradin; their relentless enemy Charles; Costanza,

her brow crowned with a poetic nimbus (that melted towards the
end into an aureole of bigotry); Frangipani, huge in villainy; the
princess Beatrix, tottering from the dungeon where she had been
confined for almost twenty years; her deliverer Roger de Lauria,
without whose resourcefulness and audacity it might have gone
ill with Aragon; Popes and Palaeologus—brilliant colour effects;
the King of England and St. Louis of France; in the background,
dimly discernible, the colossal shades of Frederick and Innocent,
locked in deadly embrace; and the whole congress of figures enlivened and interpenetrated as by some electric fluid—the personality of John of Procida. That the element of farce might not be
lacking, Fate contrived that exquisite royal duel at Bordeaux
where the two mighty potentates, calling each other by a variety of
unkingly epithets, enacted a prodigiously fine piece of foolery for
the delectation of Europe. (7-8)

Few readers would be able to reconstruct this story in any
detail. But to anyone who has read in medieval history, these allusions bring the pageant back to life. As to the reader who has
no associations at all with these names and events, Douglas does
not care enough about him to supply the kind of background
information he would need in order to make sense of the passage.

Douglas' knowledge of languages and his interest in etymology
enabled him to extract stories from place names and thus to en-
rich the pages of his travel books. And the greater the reader's
knowledge of these matters, and of ancient and medieval literature, the greater the pleasure of anticipation and recognition
derived from Douglas' references and discoveries. For instance,
in *Siren Land*, mentioning the ridge which limits the Sorrentine
Peninsula, he digresses on the history of the name and in so
doing enriches the reader's knowledge of the district in several
dimensions:

The ridge or backbone which divides the gulfs of Salerno and
Naples is called "Le Tore"—an obscure and venerable word which is
common all over this region and takes us back to Mount Taurus
in Cilicia and to the Celtic and Sinaitic Tor. Perhaps the poet Statius
was referring to these Tore when he spoke of the "green Taurubulae"
of Sorrento or Capri, but unfortunately nobody can tell us exactly
what he meant, as in the whole of ancient literature the word occurs only in this one passage. A modern scholar derives the "Tore"
from the Greek $\Tau\alpha$ $\ddot{o}\rho\eta$, the mountains; which, if not correct, is at
least simple. There is a village called Torco on the southern slope
of the ridge just below Sant' Agata, whose name has been drawn

by some from the Latin *Torqueo*, because the road "turns" there (which it does not; it just ends), and by others from the Greek *theorica* because, they say, a religious procession of youths and maidens used to wend thither in olden days. Though the church of Torco is one of the oldest in the district, there are no classic remains whatever in the neighbourhood, and I rather disbelieve this tempting theoricaderivation, although it is adopted in his *Magic and Astrology* by Maury who copied it, I suspect, from the old Sorrentine writer, Onofrio Gariulli. It seems more natural to connect the word Torco with this backbone or Tor. (26)

The question as to when this sort of thing is carried too far is largely a matter of personal taste.

Douglas' knowledge of natural history also contributed to the texture of his descriptive passages. His naming of specific flowers and rocks adds considerable exactness to the descriptions, at least for those who are familiar with these names, or are willing to look them up. His use of such technical knowledge is not quite for its own sake, for he ordinarily has recourse to it only when it involves significant features of the landscapes, or when some special interest is attached to it. His early scientific interests were subordinated or integrated into the larger pictures of regions and locales which form the purpose of his more mature books. The early cataloging, listing, and systematic describing of biological and geological data gave way to the more leisurely and wider-ranging approach of *Old Calabria* and *Siren Land*, where the purpose is in the main aesthetic rather than scientific and where the technical details are supplied only when they form some part of the whole picture. Such details are seldom overemphasized or allowed to grow out of just proportion. Here is a description of the Siren Islets which comes precariously near to being too technical and also contains something of the sort of snobbery of which Douglas is sometimes guilty; and yet it is hard to deny that the passage throws light on a significant feature of the region:

And so they are at this present moment; uncultivated, treeless and, in summer, aflame with heat; struck by the sun's first beams, they glister through the livelong day and remain fiercely glowing, like incandescent rubies, long after the coast-line is drowned in the shades of evening. Yet there are wandering breezes and a harmonious wavelapping suggestive of coolness. They lie in a rough circle, and anyone but a geologist familiar with the inevitable "quaquaversal dip" would take them to be the relics of a submerged crater, an illusion

which is strengthened by the outward slope and half-moon shape
of the greater islet, and by the riven pinnacles of stone gnawed
by the waves into bizarre shapes and painted, wherever the spray
can reach them, to a murky brown. And this is exactly what one
old traveller called them—a mistake for which he was sternly
rebuked by Breislack. So Dumas talks of the "granitic ramparts"
of Capri, and a Swiss, writing only three years ago, praises its
"parois verticales de porphyre et basalte." A deplorable lack of
general intelligence, seeing that the principal charm of all Italian
scenery, its graceful outlines and much of its delicate aerial tints,
is exclusively due to a peculiar natural formation. Limestone, and
no other rock, is able to produce them. (40-41)

The balance between man and nature which Douglas claimed to have found in the Mediterranean lands is present in his
description of them. Topographical and "scientific" details are
balanced with matters of "humanistic" interest. The descriptions
of scenery and atmosphere are more effective for appearing only
occasionally, being dispersed among narrative passages—reminiscences, anecdotes, and history—personal opinions, and abstract argument. The reader is not troubled by the almost constant description that he finds in the work of some travel writers.

In his fiction also Douglas depended heavily upon his peculiar sort of erudition. In *South Wind*, for instance, much of the
atmospheric effect and humor stem from the knowledge of the
antiquities of Capri which the author had acquired while writing the Capri monographs. The lives of St. Dodekanus and St.
Eulalia are of course derived from the "more than fifty" saints'
lives which Douglas said he had read. The life of the abstemious
St. Eulalia especially owes a good deal to that of Sister Serafina,
who really lived on Capri and in "Siren Land." The description
of the fabulous fountain of Nepenthe follows Iasolina's account
of the mineral baths of Ischia. Mr. Eames' beloved historian of
the island, Monsignor Perelli, resembles Fabio Giordano, whom
Douglas had studied, as well as probably hundreds of other such
commentators. And in this novel, as in the travel books, there are
to be found the almost scientifically precise descriptions of
rock formations, cliffs, caves, and other geological features. Douglas wrote in *Late Harvest* regarding the early monographs on
the Summer Islands: "I utilised the geological features of this
group, over-coloured for literary purposes, to describe the cliff-

scenery of Nepenthe in *South Wind,* whereas the pumice stone industry of that imaginary place, as well as its decayed bathing-establishment of St. Elias, were inspired by what I saw elsewhere, on Lipari. The minerals mentioned in *South Wind* are such as occur on Ponza—nearly all of them (31-32)."

The extent to which Douglas drew upon his reading for the purposes of his fiction is demonstrated by the listing of sources in the preface to *They Went:*

> The unicorns occur in Vertumanus and other old travellers; Armorican radishes are mentioned by Pliny the Elder; . . . Athanaeus describes the Celts—their huge mustaches and banqueting habits, together with other social features less commendable; the sturdy pigs and trumpets for summoning them are to be found (with much else!) in Dottin, the bent swords in Déchelette, that "old-fashioned buckler, embossed with coral"—you may inspect it at the British Museum; details of manners and costume and speech have been taken from Joubainville, Pictet, Jullian, La Monneraie, Goffic—I really cannot remember all their names; every item, for instance, in that list of beast-gods is authentic though I defy you to discover my authority for Boulianus. (It is, *entre nous,* the chronicler Albert of Morlaix.)[14]

Needless to say, scientific, historical, and literary knowledge do not make a man able to produce good travel books or good novels; other considerations are more important, the foremost among them being the ability to write, and Douglas' ability to put technical and scientific material into a palatable and usually interesting form testifies to his power of expression. Whatever his subject, he was almost never dull or pedantic. As H. M. Tomlinson states, "He can render examples of plutonic rocks as buoyant as a conversation on Nepenthe between ladies who are merry because they have lost their husbands and illusions. . . . With Norman Douglas, erudition is as airy as the bright balls a conjurer weaves fascinatingly aloft (12)."

Another essential quality of Norman Douglas as a writer of travel books is his sense of history. He was an amateur antiquarian, a reader of old histories, and a collector of old books and prints. In addition, he had, during his younger years at least, a lively interest in archeology. The past was always alive for him, and his books are testimony to this. He always knew the localities that had been referred to by the Classical writers, and when, and by whom, and in what connection. He had an eye for the topographical characteristics which indicated that a villa or a theater or a temple had once existed on the site. And he was always acutely and nostalgically conscious of the changes that time had wrought not only in man's works but in man himself. Certainly one of the characteristic qualities of *Old Calabria* is the running historical commentary it contains; and *Siren Land* has as a sort of unifying theme the conception of the Sirens, their evolution from Homer to the present, and the changes in culture which that evolution reflects.

With the historian's awareness of the importance of perspective, Douglas preferred the long view of civilizations and cultures, and the insight which such a point of view brings. Count Caloveglia of *South Wind*, by temperament and tastes an ancient Greek, had no wish to have lived in Classical times: "Great things can only be seen at a proper distance. Pheidias [to his contemporaries] may have been little more than an amateur, struggling with brute material in the infancy of his trade or calling. No, my friend! I am glad not to be coeval with Pericles. I am glad to recognize Hellenic achievements at their true worth. I am glad to profit by that wedge of time which has enabled me to reverence things fair and eternal (121).

It has already been mentioned that much of Douglas' interest in the Mediterranean area lay in the historical associations which it held for one so well versed in antiquities as he. A land without cultural "roots" would almost certainly have provided a less rich subject for his pen, and this background probably accounts, in part at least, for his lack of interest in visiting the Americas. His books on Austria and Tunisia, regions in which he was still able to trace a few Roman footsteps, are not quite so popular nor so highly regarded as his books on southern Italy; and one of the reasons is probably that, although they have compensating qualities, they lack the historical dimension.

It must be admitted, however, that Douglas' historical sense was seriously flawed. He did not avoid the hoary error of seeing the past as inevitably better than the present. Although he protested otherwise, it is obvious that his continual deprecation of things modern is usually ill-considered and that, although he is aware of the failings of the cultures of other periods, he is inclined to minimize these. His understanding of the past was better than his understanding of the present. And, while he was able to see the historical sources of traditions and ideas, he was not always able to understand or even to interest himself in the nature of their historical development. Hence Christianity and the Platonic tradition became *bêtes noires* in which Douglas could see no constructive value or historical purpose. As in other matters, his egocentrism often caused him to concentrate his attention on those historical periods or conditions which interested him and to ignore those to which his temperament made him unsympathetic. Nevertheless, we owe to his particular tastes and proclivities such treatments of historical subject matter as his study of the free-living Tiberius; his delightful excursions into hagiography, Siren legends, and so on; and the attitudes which give to his books their peculiar flavor—an individualized adaptation of certain Classical traditions and viewpoints.

III *The Humor of Caricature*

An all-important requisite of the satirist, and part of the equipment of the travel writer as well, is humor. Douglas had the commodity in no small measure, but it is frequently found, especially in the satires, accompanied by a certain sinister note—a harshness and lack of warmth—which some readers find repellent. In the travel books and in the miscellaneous writings, the humor is to be found in occasional amusing descriptions and anecdotes. It is always unannounced; frequently it is so well disguised that it may go undetected. Douglas' many violent prejudices, returned to again and again in his books and proclaimed with a great show of serious and righteous indignation, are almost certainly intended to cause a smile. In this category one would include such idiosyncrasies as his abomination of beech trees and margarine; his fondness for the insane; his belief in the universal efficacy of Turkey Rhubarb; and his solemnly professed belief that all rabbits served in Italian restaurants were cats. Richard Aldington is not quite able to accept this sort of humor, which he calls "a verve which sometimes ran away with him . . . that vein of *simplicissimus* caricature and whimsicality. . . ."[15] The kind of exaggeration that Douglas used in *Siren Land* when he spent pages in describing a horde of small boys pursuing and ultimately tearing to shreds a chicken which the restaurant owner had instructed them to catch for the author's dinner seems to be too much for Aldington. He complains of Douglas that " . . . both in talk and writing he indulged that gift of his for amusing caricature to the point where the exaggeration becomes preposterous. . . ."[16]

Douglas' humor can appear in a brief description, such as this one of an English bed (another of his prejudices):

You clamber into such a receptacle and straightway roll downhill, down into its center, into a kind of riverbed where you remain fixed fast, while that monstrous feather abomination called a pillow, yielding to pressure, rises up on either side of your head and engulfs eyes and nose and everything else in its folds. No escape! You are strangled, smothered; you might as well have gone to bed with an octopus. In this horrid contrivance you lie for eight long hours, clapped down like a corpse in its coffin. Every single bed in rural England ought to be burnt. Not one of them is fit for a Christian to sleep in. . . .[17]

Or in an anecdote such as the one in *Old Calabria* about a certain Italian priest whose workmen were lazy: " 'Ha, loafers, rogues, villains, vermin and sons of *bastardi cornuti!* If God had not given me these garments and thereby closed my lips to all evil-speaking (seizing his cassock and displaying half a yard of purple stocking)—wouldn't I just tell you, spawn of adulterous assassins, what I think of you!' (60)"

A reviewer of *Alone* wrote: "As a humorist Norman Douglas has few equals. While he can seldom be called precisely subtle, there is a certain quality in his humor at which we can smile, smile in the knowledge of superiority over the average individual."[18] And it is this sense of amused superiority that is probably the reader's response to Douglas' handling of the saints' lives. Some of his best humor is managed at the expense of the saints. He was an avid reader of hagiography, and its main appeal must have been that it amused him. He repeated these stories in his books, selecting the most bizarre details and making a pretense of complete scholarly objectivity. There is seldom any direct indication that the author is anything but completely credulous, but the tacit understanding is always there that both author and reader are so far beyond believing these fantastic tales that it would be absurd to mention the fact; one merely smiles. His only stricture—the humorist compromising with the scientist— is that "such relations of imperfectly ascertained and therefore questionable wonders . . . tend to shake our faith in the evidence of well-authenticated ones."[19]

Douglas made a great point of noting the similarities among saints' lives. In "Southern Saintliness," reprinted in *Old Calabria,* he made of his observations a sort of theory of influences; but it is actually part of the fun. The humor lies in the selection of detail and in the straightfaced presentation with its pseudo-scholarly tone and rather obvious irony:

But a little acquaintance with the subject will soon show you that, so far as the range of their particular Christianity allowed of it, there is a praiseworthy and even astonishing diversity among them. Nearly all of them could fly, more or less: nearly all of them could cure diseases and cause the clouds to rain; nearly all of them were illiterate; and every one of them died in the odour of sanctity—with roseate complexion, sweetly smelling corpse, and flexible limbs. Yet each one had his particular gift, his strong point. Joseph of Copertino specialized in flying, others were conspicuous for their heroism in sitting in hot baths, devouring ordure, tormenting themselves with pins, and so forth. (263-64)

The special gift of St. Giangiuseppi della Croce (born 1654) was prediction, especially foretelling the deaths of children, "which he almost always accompanied with jocular words (*scherzi*) on his lips."

He would enter a house and genially remark; "O, what an odour of Paradise"; sooner or later one or more of the children of the family would perish. To a boy to twelve he said, "Be good, Natale, for the angels are coming to take you." These playful words seem to have weighed considerably on the boy's mind and, sure enough, after a few years he died. . . . To a little girl who was crying in the street he said: "I don't want to hear you any more. Go and sing in Paradise." And meeting her a short time after, he said, "What, are you still here?" In a few days she was dead. (265)

The venerable Fra Egidio of Taranto could bring animals and people back from the dead. This he accomplished with half an hour of prayer and perspiring, repeating, "Not dead, but only asleep."

Thus a cow belonging to Fra Egidio's monastery was once stolen by an impious butcher, and cut up into the usual joints with a view to a clandestine sale of the meat. The saint discovered the beast's remains, ordered that they should be laid together on the floor in the shape of a living cow, with the entrails, head, and so forth in their natural positions; then, having made the sign of the cross with his cord upon the slaughtered beast, and rousing up all his faith, he said: "In the name of God and of Saint Pasquale, arise, Catherine!" (Catherine was the cow's name.) At these words the animal lowed, shook itself, and stood up on its feet alive, whole and strong, even as it had been before it was killed. (272)

The most amusing of all is the life of Joseph of Copertino, the flying monk. He was a simple and humble creature, and the chapter which Douglas devoted to him in *Old Calabria* is especially amiable in tone. There is not the slightest direct indication of disbelief as Douglas quotes the choicest details from the official life: ". . . his most remarkable flights took place at Fossembrone, where once 'detaching himself in swiftest manner from the altar with a cry like thunder, he went, like lightning, gyrating hither and thither about the chapel, and with such an impetus that he made all the cells of the dormitory tremble . . . (73).'" On another occasion he was asked to perform for the Spanish ambassador, and, after some hesitation, agreed to descend from his room: ". . . hardly had he entered the church and raised his eyes to a statue . . . situated above the altar, when he threw himself into a flight in order to embrace its feet at a distance of twelve paces, passing over the heads of all the congregation; then, after remaining there for some time, he flew back over them with his usual cry, and immediately returned to his cell (73)." Joseph, who died in 1663 at the age of sixty-one, ". . . had been suffering and infirm for some little time previous to that event, but managed to take a short flight on the very day preceding his demise (77)."

The same sort of straightfaced but not invariably subtle humor is to be found in some of Douglas' book reviews. For instance, in a review of *The Angel Warriors at Mons,* which tells of supernatural warriors turning the tide of the battle for the British forces, Douglas pretended to admonish those who might disbelieve: "If an angel appeared to Abraham under the oak, there is obviously no reason why an angel should not appear unto Lance-Corporal Richard Snooks, of the 69th Punjab Pushers, somewhere in France." With mock patriotism he pretended to find fault with the censorship office for having allowed this information to be disclosed: "we cannot help thinking that the general public ought to be maintained in the fond illusion that our brave Tommies held their own, unaided by the obsolete weapons of these exotics."[20]

A good deal of humor can be found hidden away in the indexes of Douglas' books. In the index of *Together,* for instance, are the following entries:

Brunnemacher (father), mountaineer, presumably hirsute, 25; (son) mountaineer, indubitably hirsute, 23

Cider, getting tipsy on, 237

Grandmother, paternal, devours roly poly *pour encourager les autres,* 104

Poets, should avoid towns, 84; generally born naked, 168; talk nonsense about pomegranates, 206

Squirrel, with malformed teeth, 10; death of a tame, 28

IV *The Parsimony of Limitation*

There remains to be considered here a general characteristic—perhaps it is better called a limitation—of Douglas' talent which has already been touched upon indirectly. He was not a highly creative writer. The ideas, characters, settings, and other materials that went into his books seldom sprang fullblown from his imagination. They were rather drawn from his reading, as we have seen, or from his personal experience. Of course, it could be argued that this is true of any writer, that no one can do other than write from his own experience; but in Douglas' case there was less of the synthesizing and transforming power that marks the truly creative artist. His attempts at fiction were few; he seems to have preferred the kind of studies which enabled him to present factual material embellished with cursory commentary, or travel writing in which he was reproducing incidents and feelings which he had actually experienced and not created.

Even in his novels, Douglas preferred to recreate situations that were familiar to his experience or had been encountered in his reading, places which he had seen, and characters taken from life or literature. We have seen in the preface to *They Went* his list of details borrowed from earlier writers and have noted the extent to which *South Wind* was indebted to his studies. Nepenthe is topographically a combination of Ischia, Ponza, and Capri; and the characters, as we shall see, also have their counterparts. In fact, Francis Brett Young, a resident of Capri, says *South Wind* is simply "transcribed from life."[21] Even minor details and incidents are often based on something Douglas remembered seeing or something he had read in a newspaper. For example, in *Looking Back* he mentioned having seen, during his stay in Russia, children bathing naked in the Tshornaia Rietshka near St. Petersburg (64); and this detail found its way into *South Wind* in a scene showing the members of the Russian sect bathing naked in the sea near Madame Steynlin's villa.

His ability to devise a fictitious situation and sustain it as a plot line was not strong. *South Wind* is considered weak in the matter of plot, and the plots of the other fiction—*Nerinda, They Went,* and *In the Beginning*—are all to some degree derived from Classical writings, a venerable practice but one which the modern novelist does not usually follow. The fact is that Douglas was not a novelist by temperament or proclivity; his talents lay rather in the direction of topographical description and the familiar essay. His travel books are actually series of essays held together by little more than their common source in the history and localities of a single region, plus the unity derived from a single, strong point of view. The novels tend to follow a similar pattern of construction.

Writing of any kind came rather hard for Douglas. He worked with almost painful care, insisting upon accuracy (once holding up a book for three months in order to verify a passage from eighteenth-century German incunabula)[22] and revising repeatedly. He once wrote, "After a short interval I am generally dissatisfied with everything I have written and curse my folly for allowing it to go to press."[23] He did not consider literature to be his reason for existence, but took it as a means of living because it seemed his only lucrative talent. He was under no illusions as to his creative power, and frequently he refused requests to write stories, articles, and travel books, probably because he simply did not feel able at the time. The same factors are no doubt involved in the unusual frugality with which he used and reused his materials, and stored up ideas, both his own and those of others for future use. D. H. Lawrence once remarked, "Douglas keeps everything," and this penchant is readily observable in the most cursory study of his bibliography. The early *Herpetology of the Grand Duchy of Baden,* of little or no literary value, was reprinted in *Three of Them.* The weak short stories of *Unprofessional Tales* and also some of the indifferent reviews from the *English Review* were collected in *Experiments.* The Capri materials, although they had to be privately printed and brought Douglas little return, were by no means wasted. Aldington writes: "I question whether anything in them of the slightest literary interest has been wasted by not being used elsewhere.[24]

To demonstrate Douglas' parsimonious methods, especially in the use of his early researches, we need only consider the contents of his important books and note the previous appearance of the material. Chapter I of *Siren Land,* called "Sirens and their Ancestry," had first appeared as "Sirens" in the *English Review* of May, 1909. Chapter II, "Uplands of Sorrento," had appeared under the same title in December, 1909. Chapter III, "The Siren Islets"; Chapter IV, "Tiberius"; and Chapter V, "The Philosophy of the Blue Grotto," had all appeared in slightly different form in the Capri monographs. Chapters IX and XI, "The Life of Sister Serafina" and "On Leisure," had both occurred in "Islands of Typhoeus" (*English Review,* February, 1909), and Chapter XII, "Caves of Siren Land," under the same title in the *English Review* of February, 1911. *Old Calabria* is similarly made up for the most part of articles that had appeared in the *English Review,* the *North American Review,* and the *Cornhill Magazine;* a large part of *Alone* was first printed in the *Anglo-Italian Review* and *Living Age.* Even the early official *Report on the Pumice Stone Industry of the Lipari Islands* was not forgotten. In *South Wind* Mr. Keith, strolling along with Bishop Heard, suddenly remarks:

"I observe you are interested in those people. A singular illusion, is it not?"

He referred to a group of men and boys who, stripped to the waist, were bearing aloft immense masses of some argent-coloured rock.

"It is pumice-stone—one of the old industries of the place. They excavate it on the hill-side yonder. Volcanic stuff. . . . Light as foam. But who can believe it? The bearers move within a few feet of us and yet it resembles the most ponderous limestone or granite. Then you ask yourself: How is it possible? If their burden were what it seems to be, they would be crushed to earth instead of striding proudly along. Admirable figures! As you say, the spectacle takes one back into mythological times. Would you not call it a procession of Titans, children of the Gods, storing up mountain-blocks for some earth-convulsing battle?" (81-82)

Thus a strong impression which Douglas had once received and included in his official report turns up ten years later in a novel.

Douglas avoided the need for genuine imaginative creation whenever he could, and the strange nature of several of his books reflects this effort. *London Street Games,* for instance, must certainly be the only thing of its kind. It might even be conjectured that, after collecting the material at the cost of a great deal of time and effort, Douglas found himself unwilling or unable to shape it into a formal or informal treatise and hence decided to reproduce practically verbatim and almost without commentary the descriptions of the games which the children had given him. But this is only conjecture; Douglas himself offered a different explanation of his methods and purposes:

> Those of them who could write described the games in their own fashion on scraps of paper . . .: I made them control each other's descriptions, and these holographs, which I still possess, from a bundle weighing 900 grammes. I have copied for every separate class of game, one or more of these playing-rules in the original language, without the alteration of a single letter; and no two of them are by the same child.
>
> I wished to produce not a set informative treatise—this had already been done, however inadequately—but a social document. And it should have an impromptu flavour: that struck me as the most appropriate treatment for a subject such as this one. My point, my only point, was the astounding inventiveness of those poor children. . . . The book therefore, to obtain its full psychological effect and full momentum, should be read aloud without a break, from beginning to end. It should be rehearsed as what it is, a "breathless catalogue." Hence the apparent disorder in my recital, which was deliberately contrived to convey that impression of breathlessness.[25]

The singular little book which resulted is, astonishingly enough, capable of being read. But its formlessness makes it undeniably monotonous.

Another example of this "cataloging" sort of book is *Birds and Beasts of the Greek Anthology,* in which Douglas simply collected references to animals from the Greek lyrics (the actual collecting was probably done by his friend Brooks, the real-life Eames of Capri, who also did many of the translations).[26] Douglas added a few leisurely comments to each—references to legends regarding the particular animal, remarks concerning its present distribution, and so on. Although it is an erudite and frequently witty performance, *Birds and Beasts* is not an act of sustained artistic creation.

When Douglas came to do a full-scale volume of reminiscences, *Looking Back,* he again had recourse to an unusual method, and again it was one which reflected his liking for collecting and cataloging. As we have already noted, he presumably went over the large collection of calling cards which had been gathered over the years in an old vase, took them up at random, and recorded in an entirely discursive fashion the memories which they evoked. A great deal of autobiography is presented in this haphazard fashion, as well as many interesting vignettes of various friends and acquaintances, some famous, some obscure. But there is no clear organization—not even an attempt to retain the chronology of the cards or the memories.

Most reviewers found the system refreshing and the result spontaneous and conversational. Some complained about the confusion of dates and periods into which the reader is unavoidably led. Richard Aldington thinks that the method was less "casual and haphazard" than it looked, for Douglas managed to say "something about almost every year from 1878 to 1928." Aldington even suspects that the calling cards may never have actually existed. He adds: "The plan certainly had advantages. By seeming to write always of people he had known he was able to write at length about himself and yet avoid the appearance of egotism and vanity which is such a snare in autobiography."[27] One wonders whether this might not have been another avoidance of the necessity of constructing a narrative, even an autobiographical one; one wonders whether Douglas did not doubt his imaginative ability to realize even his own life in the form of an artistic structure. The products of Douglas' last decade—*Late Harvest, Almanac, Footnote on Capri,* and *Venus in the Kitchen*—are all collections, or selections from or comments on earlier work.

Douglas had things to say himself on the matter of the creative imagination. In his article on Poe, he considered a charge similar to the one that has been made against him: "Poe was prodigious in intellectual versatility—in variety of material, singularly poor. But this organic poverty must not be confounded with artificial simplicity, with the deliberate repetition of set words and images whereby the haunting charm of his verse and tales is often contrived (113)." Presumably in calling Poe "singularly poor" in "variety of material" Douglas was referring to the sameness of atmosphere, mood, subject, and setting in Poe's poems and stories. What he meant by "prodigious in intellectual versatility" is not so clear. Douglas himself is, of course, often praised for versatility, and he, too, showed something less than a fertility in respect to variety of material—at least he found it necessary to recast old material to an unusual extent. The "deliberate repetition of set words and images," also characteristic of Douglas' style, will be discussed later. It is a method which was no doubt adopted by preference by both Douglas and Poe, and which has a great deal to be said for it. And yet it, too, is a method which avoids the necessity of supplying the richer variety that one expects of more inventive writers.

But one should not allow such strictures to obscure the more important fact that Douglas, like Poe, was able to accomplish a great deal within the limits of his powers. In the introduction to *They Went* Douglas wrote: "Can our imagination ever create? Or must it not rather content itself with forming new combinations; with readjusting material that already lies at hand, if we care to pick it up? (xi)" And who can argue? For the question of literary quality is at bottom less a matter of material than a matter of handling—of the manner of the "readjustment" and the nature of the "raw combinations" that the writer forms. Douglas complains that modern writers are too concerned with the choice of subject: "... this is beginning at the wrong end. ... The tritest and most wayward theme responds to originality of treatment, and Browning alone might have taught them that gold can be extracted out of dust-heaps."[28] There may be a note of rationalization here, but there is a note of truth as well. Obviously Douglas' forte was in "treatment" rather than in invention, and his value lies not so much in *what* he wrote about as in *how* he wrote about it—to whatever degree such a separation is valid. But he worked too much with the "dust-heaps," and the expenditure of effort and skill required to extract gold from them was apparently tedious and not always successful.

CHAPTER 4

The Novels

D OUGLAS' three novels—*South Wind, They Went,* and *In the Beginning*—are usually considered satirical. Satire is difficult of definition. Its tone is one of disapprobation; its tools are irony, wit, humor, and exaggeration. And it is theoretically didactic, since its implied purpose is the renovation of society. Douglas' novels are witty and humorous, employing the kind of exaggerated characterization associated with satire and striking at human foibles and self-delusion. Certainly Douglas would have been scandalized by the suggestion that he intended to reform society. And such a suggestion needs qualification. But it is clear that he held values which he believed to be better than those of most of his fellow men and that the approach of his novels—indeed, of everything he wrote—was designed, consciously or otherwise, to influence the intelligent reader to his way of thinking. Like all satirists, he saw clearly that men fall short of the moral and social standards to which they profess allegiance; and, like all satirists, he scorned the hypocrisy with which men pretend to lofty ideals while they live lives based on selfishness and egotism.

Of course Douglas hated the selfishness and egotism less than he hated the hypocrisy. As we have seen, he believed that the individual should be self-sustaining and that pleasure was a justifiable end. He advocated an approach to life in which few values were absolute and in which actions were deemed good or bad in relation to their ends; whatever did not conduce to a leisurely, undisturbed existence and to a controlled exploitation of the senses was humbug. What he deplored most was that intelligent men should fail to recognize these facts and hence sacrifice the natural pleasures to a set of absurd and outmoded ethical values to which the great majority of people paid only lip service. Disapproving attitudes, expressed in a tone and manner that would probably be called satiric, had appeared incidentally in the travel books, but they first received full treatment in satiric fiction in *South Wind.*

I South Wind: *a Bishop Mediterraneanized*

The material of *South Wind* (1917) was a remarkably felicitous selection, and Douglas was never again to find a subject
so perfectly suited to his talent and temperament. Its themes
were ideas that Douglas had long cherished—the relativity of
morals, the futility of false ideals, the importance of climate as
a factor in social and cultural conditions. Its setting enabled him
to exploit his practiced ability to describe Mediterranean scenery.
And its plot was such that atmospheric factors, which Douglas
always handled adeptly, played a more important role than narrative or dramatic action, which did not come so easily for him.

Joseph Conrad had written Douglas in 1908: ". . . think seriously of writing a novel. . . . Place it in southern Italy if that will
help. . . . Don't make it a novel of Italian peasant life—not
yet! . . . Place European personalities in Italian frame. European
here means an international crowd. Try and make it a novel
of analysis on the basis of some strong situation."[1] Some years
later, when Douglas undertook *South Wind*, he followed Conrad's advice almost entirely. He wrote a novel of analysis with a
setting that fit Conrad's suggestion, although perhaps the situation was not so strong as his friend might have desired. The
scene was a fictitious island named Nepenthe, a Mediterranean
island with an Italianate populace and near a mainland on
which there was a volcano. It was peopled with a cosmopolitan
crowd, mostly English. Its model was plainly Capri.

On Nepenthe, Douglas created his own kind of Utopia—a
device familiar to the satiric tradition—where people lived, for
the most part, a casual, leisurely existence, doing the things they
wanted to do and attaching importance only to things that Douglas thought important. Many of the characters represented
aspects of Douglas' own personality—one was a hedonist, one
a Classicist, one a recluse-scholar, one a geologist. It was as if
the author's own personality had been passed through a spec-
trum and separated into its various components.

Perhaps the most important character in *South Wind* is the
atmosphere of Nepenthe, which seems to have a life of its own.
By deft handling of the geological features of the island, exaggerated from those of Ponza which he had described in *Summer
Islands,* and by clever allusions to the sirocco which blew inces-
santly, Douglas created a strange and infectious mood, at once
attractive and sinister, salubrious and debilitating. But whatever

the ambiguous properties of the climate and the south wind, the salient feature of Nepenthe's atmosphere was its power to induce clear-sightedness. As Mr. Keith explained:

This coast-line alone—the sheer effrontery of its mineral charm— might affect some natures to such an extent as to dislocate their stability. Northern minds seem to become fluid here, impressionable, unstable, unbalanced—what you please. There is something in the brightness of this spot which decomposes their old particles and arranges them into fresh and unexpected patterns. That is what people mean when they say they "discover themselves" here. You discover a mechanism, you know, when you take it to pieces. (200-01)

Into this atmosphere comes Mr. Heard, English Bishop of Bampopo in Africa, who is stopping over on Nepenthe to visit his cousin and to escort her back to England, since her second husband, Mr. Meadows, cannot leave his post in India. A reasonable and intelligent man, Mr. Heard cannot become overly perturbed about the waywardness and the ethical eccentricities of the African natives. But he still labors under some "serious delusions": he idealizes women, and he clings to the beliefs of his church.

Don Francesco, a genial but lascivious priest met on the boat, introduces the Bishop to the American Mrs. Steynlin, called the Duchess of San Martino, a leader of Nepenthean society who is about to become a Catholic through the influence of Don Francesco, and to her guest Denis Phipps, a pleasantly naïve and impressionable English student. Bishop Heard subsequently meets other unusual Nepentheans, such as Mr. Keith, a wealthy hedonist with a penchant for exotic cookery; Count Caloveglia, a Classicist and antiquarian who professes Hellenic values; Eames, an amiable and innocuous bibliographer of the island's literature; Edward Marten, an indigent Jewish minerologist; Freddy Parker, supposedly the Commissioner of Finance from Nicaragua but actually the devious proprietor, along with his "barn-like" step sister, of the local drinking club; the Commissioner's friend, the red-headed, Mephistophelian magistrate, Malipizzo; and the alcoholic Englishwoman, Miss Wilberforce, who undresses in public.

The first days of the Bishop's fortnight visit to Nepenthe are filled only with leisurely conversation in which the distinctive qualities and interests of the various inhabitants are revealed.

He attends the colorful festival of the local saint, St. Dodekanus, and calls on his cousin, who is strangely displeased to see him. Then he discovers that "things are beginning to happen." There are ominous reports that one of the island's springs has dried up and that unusual births have occurred; Freddy Parker's stepsister dies of a mosquito bite and that suspicious personage learns that his patron in the Nicaraguan government has also died and that his empty but esteemed title of Commissioner of Finance may be revoked. Finally, the volcano begins to erupt, raining ashes on the island. Miraculously, further catastrophe is averted by a procession in honor of St. Dodekanus proposed by Commissioner Parker, who is not even a Catholic.

The mysterious dangers past, the life of Nepenthe becomes again a series of friendly gatherings and rambling conversations. Bishop Heard hears about Van Koppen, the American millionaire who yearly visits Nepenthe on his yacht, which is always the scene of disreputable parties. He learns of Denis Phipps' inability to find a purpose in life, and of the plan to build a clinic for Miss Wilberforce, a project disapproved by Mr. Keith, who believes everyone should be permitted to do as he pleases. He watches Count Caloveglia, dignified pronouncer of virtuous principles, sell a fake antique statue to the millionaire Van Koppen, who knows that it is a fake but admires the Count's ability to dupe the experts. And finally, while sitting among the cliffs with Denis, Mr. Heard sees his cousin, Mrs. Meadows, walk out of her house with a man he recognizes as one Mr. Muhlen he met on the ship and has since learned is actually a blackmailer named Retlow. And he sees his cousin push this man off the cliff. Remembering how unpleasant Retlow had been and remembering that Mrs. Meadows' first husband had been named Retlow, the Bishop concludes that his cousin has been the victim of an obnoxious blackmailer and that her act was justified.

Unfortunately, a native boy is accused of the murder when a gold piece that had belonged to Retlow is found in his possession. The evil Malipizzo hopes, by convicting the native, to discredit the Church, since the boy's cousin is the village priest. But a lawyer named Morena, famous as a member of the Black Hand, is called in by the priest to defend the boy and is successful through his sentimental eloquence. And under these conditions, despite the ostensible immorality of the events, the

Bishop does not feel it necessary to divulge his knowledge of the matter.

Denis, having also been worked upon by the atmosphere of the place, is "beginning to know his own mind," and asserts himself to stop the windy harangues of Mr. Keith, thus performing "the first virile achievement of his young life (413)."

Heard's stay on Nepenthe produces the necessary change. The provocative conversation of the articulate Mr. Keith, who insidiously propounds his rationalistic hedonism, has its effect. And Bishop Heard watches various situations which mellow his point of view. But most important of all, the magical atmosphere of the place permeates him, and the south wind sweeps the cobwebs from his mind. The transformation is complete when he is able to face the act of murder, performed by one whom he considers an epitome of the English womanly ideal, and not only overlooks it as a trivial matter but justifies it as a moral necesssity.

In *Late Harvest* Douglas described the purposes of *South Wind* as follows: "*South Wind* was the result of my craving to escape from the wearisome actualities of life. To picture yourself living in a society of such instability, of such 'jovial immoderation' and 'frolicsome perversity' that even a respectable bishop can be persuaded to approve of murder—this was my aim(52)." The "wearisome actuality"—the stodgy, complacent social mores and the impractical ethical code upon which they were supposed to be based—is the true target of the satire. Thus Douglas sets up a society which flouts stability and respectability—a society which is his kind of utopia. Bishop Heard, "respectable but rather drab . . . whose tastes and needs are fashioned to reflect those of the average drab reader," is introduced into this society, and it is demonstrated that such a person cannot resist its influence. The Bishop—the observer and interpreter of the events—sees, as the reader is expected to, that a reasonable person should live a reasonable existence in a carefree pursuit of civilized pleasures with no pretense of subscribing to outmoded and false conceptions. The reader is being asked, implicitly, "Could you resist?"

H. M. Tomlinson, discussing *South Wind*, concludes that the only practical suggestion which the book makes is:

that the more likeable of us should migrate to the sunny south, to be thawed out—loosened from the frost of the north, and Christianity and other inhibiting elements. The suggestion approaches the diabolical, for we know it cannot be only a matter of climate; he himself notes elsewhere the mortification of the flesh, which to him is the sin against the light, may be witnessed as frequently under the warmer skies of the south as where northern blasts chill us into a miserable apprehension of our sins. (65-66)

And, of course, the theme should not be interpreted as the insistence that only a Mediterranean sun can make possible the kind of rebellion against Christian morality which *South Wind* sympathetically depicts. That the southern climate is no complete panacea is part of the irony, and it is a "diabolical" irony because it includes the unstated but always plausible possibility that nothing is really of much help. The atmosphere is artificial; Nepenthe is as unreal as Erewhon. But that it is more like Italy than like any place else is not surprising, since Douglas assuredly believed that the sunny south was the best hope of civilized men; other men—most men—had no hope.

While Douglas may have been under no illusions as to the possibility of universal amelioration, his Mediterraneanism was deep seated. It was to be expected, as Conrad saw, that this attitude would form part of Douglas' first serious effort at fiction. As we have already noted, Douglas believed that climate and region influenced the human outlook. In *Siren Land* he had written: "The landscape . . . and not only the hour and the man, plays a part when gods are to be created (36)." And now in *South Wind*: "But certainly the sun which colours our complexion and orders our daily habits, influences at the same time our character and outlook. The almost hysterical changes of light and darkness, summer and winter, which have impressed themselves upon the literature of the North, are unknown here (325)." He had likewise spoken in *Siren Land* of the cathartic properties of the southern Italian regions:

Here, on these odorous Siren heights, far removed from duty's sacred call—for duty has become the Moloch of modern life—it may not be amiss to build a summer hut wherein to undergo a brief *katharsis*, of purgation and readjustment. For we do get sadly out of perspective with our environment in the fevered North, out of touch with elemental and permanent things. . . .
. . . many of us would do well to *mediterraneanise* ourselves for a season, to quicken those ethic roots from which has sprung so much of what is best in our natures. To dream in Siren Land, pursuing the

moods and memories as they shift in labyrinthine mazes, like shadows on a woodland path in June; to stroll among the hills and fill the mind with new images upon which to browse at leisure, casting off outworn weeds of thought with the painless ease of a serpent and unperplexing, incidentally, some of those "questions of the day" of which the daily papers nevertheless know nothing—this is an antidote for many ills. There is repose in Siren land; there is none of that delirious massing-together in which certain mortals, unable to stand alone, can lean up against one another and so gain, for a moment, a precarious condition of equipoise. (37-38)

This is the atmosphere Douglas attempted to recreate in *South Wind*—the repose, the solitude, the naïve light, the nearness to elemental things. By following the process of the mediterraneanizing of Bishop Heard, we can learn something of how Douglas managed his problem.

To begin with, Bishop Heard is not a hopeless case; if he were, Douglas would not be interested in him. Having spent considerable time in Africa, the Bishop is somewhat mellowed. The natives there had something of the same "spirit of unconquerable playfulness in grave concerns" that he now notes in the Nepentheans. His favorites were the Bulanga: "And the Bulanga. . . . Really the Bulanga were the worst of the lot. Not fit to be talked about. And yet, somehow or other, one could not help liking them. . . . (36)" Bishop Heard is a reasonable man; and he is ripe for Nepenthe. When he has been on the island only a few days he is already reflecting on the new, open-minded attitude of which he has become aware:

Happiness—an honourable, justifiable happiness—how was it to be attained? Not otherwise, he used to think than through the two-fold agency of Christianity and civilization. That was his old College attitude. Imperceptibly his outlook had shifted since then. Something had been stirring within him; new points of view had floated into his ken. He was no longer so sure about things. The structure of his mind had lost that old stability; its elements seemed to be held in solution, ready to form new combinations. China had taught him that men can be happy and virtuous while lacking, and even scorning, the first of these twin blessings. Then had come Africa, where his notions had been further dislocated by those natives who derided both the one and the other—such fine healthy animals, all the same! A candid soul, he allowed his natural shrewdness and logic to play freely with memories of his earlier experiences among the London poor. Those experiences now became fraught with a new meaning. The solemn doctrines he had preached in those days:

were they really a panacea for all the ills of the flesh? He thought upon the gaunt bodies, starved souls, and white faces—the dirt, the squalor of it! Was that Christianity, civilization? (85-86)

Before long the Bishop feels himself on the verge of something:

Whatever it was he seemed to be no longer his own master, as in former days. Fate had caused his feet to stray towards something new—something alarming. He was poised, as it were on the brink of a gulf. Or rather, it was as if that old mind of his, like a boat sailing hitherto briskly before the wind, had suddenly encountered a bank of calm, of utter and ominous calm; it was a thing spellbound; a toy of circumstances beyond human control. The canvas hung in the stagnant air. From which quarter would the quickening breeze arrive? Whither would it bear him? (185)

The influence of new and unusual friends, of a new sense of leisure, and of the omnipresent south wind makes of his mind a pliable and impressionable thing, giving his own good sense a chance to operate. Old conceptions are beginning to vanish, the rigid sense of duty to dissolve, and an insidious doubt to enter:

He tried to get himself into perspective. "I must straighten myself out," he thought. Assuredly it was a restful place, this Nepenthe, abounding in kindly people; his affection for it grew with every day. Rest without; but where was that old rest within, that sense of plain tasks plainly to be performed, of tangible duty? Whither had it gone? Alien influences were at work upon him. Something new had insinuated itself into his blood, some demon of doubt and disquiet which threatened his old-established conceptions. Whence came it? The effect of changed environment—new friends, new food, new habits? The unaccustomed leisure which gave him, for the first time, a chance of thinking about non-professional matters? The South Wind acting on his still weakened health? All these together? Or had he reached an epoch in his development, the termination of one of those definite life-periods when all men worthy of the name pass through some cleansing process of spiritual desquamation, and slip their outworn weeds of thought and feeling. (184-85)

Soon afterwards we find him entertaining a new realization of the importance of the individual and of the inevitability of individual weakness. He thinks to himself that perhaps the American millionaire Van Koppen, who reportedly keeps a number of young ladies on his yacht, cannot help being what he is; perhaps this very coarseness in Van Koppen has helped him to become a renowned philanthropist. And most startling of all, perhaps even ladies have such coarse impulses:

Certain human attributes were mutually exclusive—avarice and generosity, for instance; others no doubt mysteriously but inextricably intertwined. A man was an in-dividual [sic]; he could not be divided or taken to pieces; he could not be expected to possess virtues incompatible with the rest of his mental equipment, however desirable such virtues might be. Who knows? Van Koppen's doubtful acts might be an unavoidable expression of his personality, an integral part of that nature under whose ferocious stimulus he had climbed to his present enviable position. And Mr. Heard was both shocked and amused to reflect that but for the co-operation of certain coarse organic impulses to which these Nepenthe legends testified, the millionaire might never have been able to acquire the proud title of "Saviour of his Country." [Van Koppen's fortune was the result of his monopoly of certain ingeniously contrived rubber goods.]

"That's queer," he mused. "It never struck me before. Shows how careful one must be. Dear me! Perhaps the ladies have inevitable organic impulses of a corresponding kind. Decidedly queer. H'm. Ha. Now I wonder. . . . And perhaps, if the truth were known, these young persons are having quite a good time of it—" (190-91)

Various other incidents and impressions have their effect on Bishop Heard. There are the Russians, the simplehearted sect of "Little White Cows," and their demagogic leader who show him what incredible "chimaeras" the "hyperborean mists" of northern Europe can engender. And there is the murder trial, with its comic opera confusion, which shows him how undependable is the justice of organized society. Everything prepares him for the climactic situation in which he witnesses the murder and, far from being outraged, he is able to take the matter in stride and to attribute it to the "immutable instincts of mankind." "One dirty blackmailer more or less; what on earth did it matter to anybody? . . . A contemptible little episode! He decided to relegate it into the category of unimportant events (404-05)."

His conclusive view is that Nepenthe has done him good:

There was something bright and diabolical in the tone of the place, something kaleidoscopic,—a frolicsome perversity. Purifying, at the same time. It swept away the cobwebs. It gave you a measure, a standard, whereby to compute earthly affairs. Another landmark passed; another milestone on the road to enlightenment. That period of doubt was over. His values had righted themselves. He had carved out new and sound ones; a workable, up-to-date theory of life. He was in fine trim. His liver—he forgot that he ever had one. Nepenthe had done him good all round. And he knew exactly what he wanted. A return to the Church, for example, was out of the question. His sympathies had outgrown the ideals of that establishment; a wave of pantheistic benevolence had drowned its smug little teachings. The Church of England! What was it still good for? A stepping stone, possibly towards something more respectable and humane; a warning to all concerned of the folly of idolizing dead men and their delusions. The Church? Ghosts! (399)

A criticism to which *South Wind* is probably open is the weakness of its story line. One reviewer said, "There is no story, or none that matters."[2] And Richard Aldington is quite severe on this matter:

. . . there was a theme for an extravaganza or short story of novelette length if properly constructed, but the author doesn't know his trade. True, he has created here and there an ambience and "atmosphere" of genial and irresponsible paganism, for which I praise him. But about one third of his chapters are irrelevant to his theme and therefore from an artistic point of view useless excrescences, however excellent they may be in themselves as essays. The author's real problem was admittedly a difficult one, and, in view of its preposterous nature, the Bishop's conversion from Christianity to low-class South Italian immoralism could only take place in an extravaganza. The Bishop ought to have been shown by a series of skilfully contrived and interwoven incidents and experiences, gradually condoning one by one breaches of Anglican morals until he arrives at murder. . . .[3]

Douglas, annoyed by the reviewers' charges concerning the weakness of the plot of *South Wind,* undertook to answer them in *Alone* with a rather lengthy discussion of the novel:

I see no reason why a book should have a plot. In regard to this one, it would be nearer the truth to say it is nothing but plot from beginning to end. How to make a murder palatable to a bishop: that is the plot. How? You must unconventionalise him and instil into his mind the seeds of doubt and revolt. You must shatter his old notions of what is right. It is the only way to achieve this result, and I would defy the critic to point to a single incident or character or conversation in the book which does not further the object in view. The good bishop soon finds himself among new influences;

his sensations, his intellect, are assailed from within and without. Figures such as those in Chapters 11, 19, and 35 [these are respectively the story of Bashakuloff and the Little White Cows, that of the Good Duke Alfred, and that of Commendatore Giustino Morena]; the endless dialogues in the boat; the even more tedious happenings in the local law-court; the very externals—relaxing wind and fantastic landscape and volcanic phenomena—the joval immoderation of everything and everybody; they foster a sense of violence and insecurity; they all tend to make the soil receptive to new ideas.

If that was your plot, the reviewer might say, you have hidden it rather successfully. I have certainly done my best to hide it. For although the personalities of the villain and his legal spouse crop up periodically, with ominous insistence, from the first chapter onwards, they are always swallowed up again. The reason is given in the penultimate chapter, where the critic might have found a *résumé* of my intentions and the key to this plot—to wit, a murder under those particular circumstances is not only justifiable and commendable but—insignificant. Quite insignificant! Not worth troubling about. Hundreds of decent and honest folk are being destroyed every day; nobody cares tuppence; "one dirty blackmailer more or less— what does it matter to anybody?" There are so many more interesting things on earth. That is why the bishop—*i.e.* the reader— here discovers the crime to be a "contemptible little episode," and decides to "relegate it into the category of unimportant events." *He was glad that the whole affair had remained in the background, so to speak, of his local experiences. It seemed appropriate. . . .* That is the heart, the core, of the plot. And that is why all those other happenings find themselves pushed into the foreground. (168-69)

There is little that can be said to contradict this explanation— or to support it. Douglas' assertion that *everything* contributes in some way to the central problem is rather strong, but it could probably be defended. Final recourse must be to the response of the individual reader; and, while the effect of the book is not particularly one of economy, most readers probably find it, in the main, unified. Nevertheless, the structure of the novel is not so strong as that of many less important novels. Almost the entire first half is devoted to exposition, establishment of characters, and development of atmosphere. With the threatened eruption of the volcano, accompanied by various fantastic portents, a tension is created which subsequently snaps. Dramatic things then begin to happen: the Little White Cows riot; Mrs. Meadows murders her first husband; Freddy Parker dies; and finally the Count sells his fake statue. The resolution of the plot takes place within the mind of the Bishop, and the denouement appropriately involves everyone's getting quietly and whimsically tipsy.[4]

II *The Gallery of Eccentrics*

Douglas was more interested in the souls of places than in the souls of individuals. He preferred to observe life generally rather than to study psychology and individual behavior. As a result, his characters do not have the kind of depth and verisimilitude that we have come to expect in the modern novel, where the naturalistic tradition is strong and where subtle psychology is demanded. One cannot chart their unconscious minds or follow the various hereditary factors and traumatic incidents which make them what they are. In this sense, they might be considered superficial and lacking in realism. V. S. Pritchett writes:

Douglas is an observer of human nature who depends upon his first impression for his effect; he is not a novelist in the sense that he proceeds any deeper into his people. He certainly is not "in" them and has little sympathy. He is a brilliant satirical talker, the egotist who is the unrelaxing circus master displaying his own power as a trainer, not the real power of the animals. How, the human reader asks, have these grotesques been trained to the master's will? There is, unnoticed by him but patent to us, a pathos in their fixed gaze, as they watch the whip. (307-08)

It may be that Douglas' characters are too contrived to be completely realistic, but it seems clear also that Pritchett has allowed his metaphor to get out of control. The picture of Mr. Keith or Miss Wilberforce gazing pathetically at the Cipolla-like figure of their creator and pleading for more individuality is amusing. It is just as important that characters function harmoniously and effectively in the total scheme of the novel as that they seem to live a life of their own. If all characters ran away from their authors, as Becky Sharp is supposed to have run away from Thackeray, novels would be chaotic affairs. Characters should be what their author wants them to be, or as nearly so as he can make them. Some are created with close attention to subsurface factors and hence give an impression of many dimensions. Others are intentionally and necessarily superficial.

Douglas' characters have the quality of caricature, each representing some particular tendency to an extreme degree. They thus approach the nature of symbols. E. M. Forster in *Aspects of the Novel* has written astutely about characters of this type, which he calls "flat" characters. He points out that they are built around "a single idea or quality" and can often be expressed in one sentence. He finds two principal advantages to "flat" characters. First, they are easily recognized by the reader: "It is a convenience for an author when he can strike with his full force at once, and flat characters are very useful to him, since they never need reintroducing, never run away, have not to be watched for development, and provide their own atmosphere— little luminous disks of a pre-arranged size, pushed hither and thither like counters across the void or between the stars; most satisfactory (105)."

A second advantage is that such characters are easily remembered by the reader after he has finished the book: "They remain in his mind as unalterable for the reason that they were not changed by circumstances; they moved through circumstances, which gives them in retrospect a comfortable quality, and preserves them when the book that produced them may decay. . . . All of us, even the sophisticated, yearn for permanence, and to the unsophisticated permanence is the chief excuse for a work of art. We all want books to endure, to be refuges, and their inhabitants to be always the same, and flat characters tend to justify themselves on this account."[5]

Forster cites Dickens as an example of a "big" writer who employed "flat" characters almost exclusively and produced a "wonderful feeling of human depth" through them. Although such characters as Mr. Micawber and Mr. Pickwick are, if looked at edgeways, "no thicker than a gramaphone record," Dickens presented them so ingeniously that the reader never gets "the sideway view." Moreover, Dickens' immense vitality caused his characters "to vibrate a little, so that they borrow his life and appear to live one of their own." Forster concludes that "Dickens' success with types suggests that there may be more in flatness than the severer critics admit(109)."

The interpretation of humanity produced by Douglas' characters may be, in some senses, a shallower and less adequate one than that of Dickens, even though it has in some ways, greater complexity. Yet, in the main, Forster's observations about Dickens apply to Douglas. Douglas' characters are memorable, despite their flatness; and they do embody some of their creator's intellectual vitality. The kind of world that Douglas' fiction created—and all three novels bear this out—is a stylized world. It contains, somehow, one dimension less than the worlds of Henry James, D. H. Lawrence, or James Joyce—to cite diverse examples. Douglas' characters are at home in this world, as "rounder" characters would not be. They serve his purposes. He will not "pry" into them beyond a certain depth, as he would not "pry" into himself for his reader's benefit.

It is ironic that Forster chooses to quote, as an example of critical disapproval of the kind of flat characters that he is defending, "one of our foremost writers, Mr. Norman Douglas." The passage which he quotes is from *A Plea for Better Manners*. Douglas is taking to task writers like D. H. Lawrence who, he claims, place their friends in novels and falsify them with "the novelist's touch." He defines this as follows:

It consists, I should say in a failure to realize the profundities and complexities of the ordinary human mind; it selects for literary purposes two or three facets of a man or woman, generally the most spectacular and therefore "useful" ingredients of their character, and disregards all the others. Whatever fails to fit in with these specially chosen traits is eliminated; must be eliminated, for otherwise the description would not hold water. Such and such are the data; everything incompatible with those data has to go by the board. If follows that the novelist's touch argues, often logically, from a wrong premise; it takes what it likes and leaves the rest. The facts may be correct so far as they go, but there are too few of them; what the author says may be true, and yet by no means the truth. That is the novelist's touch. It falsifies life. (224)

This is in some ways shortsighted criticism; perhaps it reflects Douglas' chagrin at Lawrence's characterization of him in *Aaron's Rod* and certainly it reflects the conviction which he often expressed that the individual's privacy should always be respected. Douglas should certainly have realized that the artist can never disclose everything but must choose the details which serve his artistic ends. A large part of the *dramatis personae* of any novel must consist of characters who are considerably less than completely developed. The novelist's art should not photograph life but epitomize it.

In violation of the principles Douglas had announced in his attack on Lawrence's methods, he seems to have put living people into his own novels. There is hardly an important character in *South Wind* who did not have a living counterpart. And, although Douglas claimed that all of them were idealized and that no one was maligned or offensively depicted, some characters, such as Malipizzo and Freddy Parker, have been construed as rancorous attacks on their models.

Mr. Heard must be considered the protagonist of *South Wind*, for it is to him that the important things happen. He is a good deal "rounder" than most of Douglas' people—as a protagonist must necessarily be—and does undergo a development. As a protagonist he has not been well received by all readers. Those critics who disapprove of Mr. Heard seem to do so on the absurd basis that if he had been another kind of bishop, instead of the kind he was, the story would have had a different outcome. Elizabeth Wheatley, for instance, calls him a "flexible dummy instead of a man." "It is child's play to knock down a dummy. Had Mr. Douglas faced a real bishop with his golden absurdities, he would have met an *impasse*. For it is the business of bishops to forgive and forget more terrible crimes than murder."[6] And Pelham Edgar in *The Art of the Novel*, complains that, by making Heard an easy target for the island's message, Douglas had stacked the cards. Edgar says that, though Heard is the only character in the book "capable of a critical reaction," he is "an unsatisfactory reagent (278)."[7] Needless to say, a better bishop would have been another story; but it would not have been written by Norman Douglas. These are actually criticisms of Douglas' values rather than of his characterization. Bishop Heard is the kind of bishop that Douglas' purpose required. A "real" bishop would be out of place in *South Wind*, or in any other satire for that matter.

Among the characters in *South Wind* is the confused student, Denis Phipps. He comes to Nepenthe unsure of his values—timorous, idealistic, and too English. The atmosphere takes its effect:

All was not well with Denis. And the worst of it was, he had no clear notion of what was the matter. He was changing. The world was changing too. It had suddenly expanded. He felt that he, also, ought to expand. There was so much to learn, to see, to know—so much, that it seemed to paralyse his initiative. Could he absorb all this? Would he ever get things into order once more, and recapture his self-possession? Would he ever again be satisfied with himself? It was an invasion of his tranquillity, from within and without. He was restless. (138)

Like the bishop, Denis too has been somewhat prepared: "The

novel impressions of Florence had helped in the disintegration. Nepenthe—its sunshine, its relentless paganism—had done the rest. It shattered his earlier outlook and gave him nothing in exchange. Nothing and yet everything (138)." Denis supplements the Bishop because, being younger, he can have a love affair and give Douglas an opportunity to comment on this aspect of things. Thus Denis falls in love with a sensuous and amoral servant girl, the essence of southern beauty; but he is crushed when the less idealistic and more aggressive Edgar Marten wins her promiscuous love. Then Denis receives advice from Mr. Keith:

"He said I made a mistake in paying attention to what human beings said and did, and that I ought to forsake mankind for a while, and art and books, and so on. You know the way he talks! He said it would give me a stronger individuality if I came into contact with nature and thought things out for myself instead of listening to other people. He advised me to sit among the rocks at midnight and in the hot afternoons, conversing with the genii of earth and air. It would correct my worldly perspective." (344)

Having followed Keith's advice, Denis, like Bishop Heard, is regenerated at the end the story.

Of the several characters who seem to represent aspects of Douglas' own point of view, Mr. Keith is the most important. He is a rationalist, a pagan, an individualist, a hedonist—and he is strikingly articulate. He also has Douglas' reverence for nature, his hunger for knowledge, and his worship of facts:

Keith was a pertinacious and omnivorous student; he sought knowledge not for a set purpose but because nothing was without interest for him. He took all learning to his province. He read for the pleasure of knowing what he did not know before; his mind was usually receptive because, he said, he respected the laws which governed his body. Facts were his prey. He threw himself into them with a kind of piratical ardour; took them by the throat, wallowed in them, worried them like a terrier, and finally assimilated them. They gave him food for what he liked best on earth: "disinterested thought." They "formed a rich loam." He had an encyclopaedic turn of mind; his head, as somebody once remarked, was a lumber-room of useless information. He could tell you how many public baths existed in Geneva in pre-Reformation days, what was the colour of Mehemet Ali's whiskers, why the manuscript of Virgil's friend Gallius had not been handed down to posterity, and in what year, and what month, the decimal system was introduced into Finland. Such aimless incursions into knowledge were a puzzle to his friends, but not to himself. They helped him to build up a harmonious scheme of life—to round himself off. (103-04)

Mr. Keith further has Douglas' liking for solitude: he contended "that no garden on earth, however spacious, was large enough for more than one man." He even shows the note of pagan melancholy which we have seen Douglas display. A kind of chorus, Mr. Keith serves to develop the moral implications of the plot. And, though his long and frequent conversations about human conduct might easily have become tedious, Douglas has made him sufficiently eloquent to avoid this danger.

Count Caloveglia is also a spokesman for the author. He is a Classicist, a Hellenist, a lover of the Mediterranean, and something of a Machiavellian: "There was sunshine in his glance—a lustrous gem-like grace; one realized from his conversation, from his every word, that he had discarded superfluities of thought and browsed for a lifetime, in leisurely fashion, upon all that purifies and exalts the spirit. Nothing one felt, would avail to ruffle that deep pagan content (67)." The crowning achievement of the Count's life is the sale of his faked antique to the American millionaire, Van Koppen; the money will secure a dowry for his daughter. But, even when this success is assured, he does not forget the "golden mean": "The cheque would be in his pocket that night. Three hundred and fifty thousand francs—or nearly. That is what made him not exactly grave, but reserved. Excess of joy, like all other excess, is not meet to be displayed before men. All excess is unseemly. Nothing overmuch. Measure in everything (401)."

Douglas had known people who sold fake antiques as Count Caloveglia did. Orioli describes a man named Martin, whom Douglas undoubtedly also knew, who made a business of such nefarious dealings (246). Douglas also knew a man who had some of the characteristics of Mr. Eames, the scholar of Nepenthe. This was John Ellington Brooks, to whom Douglas dedicated *Birds and Beasts of the Greek Anthology*. Brooks, who lived alone on Capri, never returned to the mainland. He was content to play with his cat, strum his piano, and enjoy his scholarly pursuits. Included in his pile of unpublished manuscripts were, according to Orioli, original poetry and prose as well as translations from Greek, Latin, and French. His only publication, apart from the translations Douglas used in *Birds and Beasts* was a sonnet which he once sold for a few pounds (258-

59). Brooks may have contributed to several of the characters in *South Wind*, but he was clearly a model for Mr. Eames, who is described as "this man of single aim and purpose, this monk of literature. . . . Happy mortal! Free from all superfluities and encumbrances of the flesh! Enviable mortal! He reduced earthly existence to its simplest and most effective terms; he owed no man anything; he kept alive, on a miserable income, the sacred flame of enthusiasm. To aspire, that was the secret of his life (348-49)."

Miss Wilberforce, the Englishwoman with an addiction to alcohol and a habit of disrobing in public, is an amusing, sympathetically presented character. In his introduction to the Modern Library edition of *South Wind*, Douglas said of her creation: "Miss Wilberforce has been put together out of some twelve dames of that particular alcoholic temperament whom it has been my privilege to know, and each of whom has contributed her mite; she is a synthetic lady-sot—a type I fervently pray God may never die out (iv)." Miss Wilberforce's sailor fiancé had died at sea. His death had been a "twist," and she had tried to drown herself several times.

Then, gradually, she put on a new character altogether and relapsed into queer ancestral traits, stripping off, like so many worthless rags, the layers of laboriously acquired civilization.

. . . Staggering about the lanes of Nepenthe in the silent hours before dawn, she was liable to be driven, at the bidding of some dark primeval impulse, to divest herself of her rainment—a singularity which perturbed even the hardiest of social nightbirds who had the misfortune to encounter her. Taxed with this freakish behaviour, she would refer to the example of St. Francis of Assisi who did the same, and brazenly ask whether he wasn't good enough for them? (72-74)

Douglas had an affection for this sort of gentle, ruined profligate. Miss Wilberforce provides a humorous continuity and allows an opportunity for Mr. Keith to give an exposition of his laissez-faire social attitudes when he eloquently thwarts an attempt of local "do-gooders" to put the poor lady in a private asylum.

Another character, the Duchess, is patterned after an American lady named Mrs. Snow. In referring to this lady in *Looking Back*, Douglas reiterated his view that novelists should not take their characters from life without thoroughly remodeling them:

Mrs. Snow. She finally returned to America. A vision of her helped me to portray the "Duchess" in a certain story; other ladies
contributed their share of suggestion; imagination also played its
part. I have never tried to draw a figure from life, as they say.
My creed is that a human character, however engrossing, however
convincing and true to itself, must be modelled anew before it can
become material for fiction. It must be licked into shape, otherwise its reactions in a world of fictitious characters, would be out of
focus. No authentic child of man will fit into a novel.
   History is the place for such people; history or oblivion. (26)

Freddy Parker and his lady, Douglas confessed to have intended as Mr. and Mrs. Harold Trower. Trower was the author
of *The Book of Capri* and hence a kind of rival of Douglas. Sig-
nor Malipizzo ("Ha, the animal! He has the Evil Eye. He is also
scrofulous, rachitic") was a magistrate named Capolozzi, who,
Douglas said, "very nearly had me in the lock-up once or
twice." Orioli calls Capolozzi "a horrible creature . . ., lame and
sickly and red-haired, and hated to such an extent by everybody . . . that he asked to be transferred to another post in the
nick of time to save himself from a stab in the belly. . . . (19)"
Muhlen (or Retlow), the blackmailing husband of Mrs. Meadows, was suggested by Baron Fritz Von Meltheim, who was
apparently both a blackmailer and a murderer. And Bazhakuloff
was based on Rasputin and other Russian "imposters."[8]
   A great part of Douglas' characterization and plot development
is dependent upon conversation. Many of the ideas in *South Wind*
receive their development through the dialogue of such "spokesman" characters as Mr. Keith and Count Caloveglia. And the
advancement of the plot—that is, the evolution of the Bishop's
outlook—is in part effected through the provocative conversation of these characters who insinuate ideas into his mind. Mr.
Keith is so astute in his reading of character and so articulate
in his explanations that his discussions with the Bishop form a
kind of choral commentary on the atmosphere, the incidents,
and the other characters. *South Wind* has been called a conversational novel in the tradition of Peacock.
   Douglas' dialogue has been deemed stylized, the criticism
being that all characters speak with the same voice and that
that voice is Douglas' own. Aldington writes that Douglas
". . . had a stylized dialogue which was fatal to the living word,

so that almost everyone who talks in his books is Douglas-ised into similarity, a monotony of flippantly doggish worldliness."[9] It is true that the dialogue often lacks what might be called "realism," because the characters are all somewhat too eloquent. But realism was not Douglas' object, nor would it have been especially appropriate to his novels. He was not attempting to present a "slice of life" but to produce the well-made novel in which everything contributed to his intentions. In *Looking Back*, he criticized Lawrence's dialogue, which is ordinarily praised as lifelike: "Lawrence never divined that conversations and dialogue are precious contrivances, to be built up *con amore;* that they should suggest a clue to character and carry forward the movement instead of retarding it; that they should be sparkling oases, not deserts of tiresome small-talk (282)."

Some further defense can be made against the charge that Douglas' characters are less than real and individualized in their speech. Many of the characters in *South Wind*—Mr. Keith, Caloveglia, Don Francesco—can be eloquent without being inconsistant to their characters in other respect. Others—the Bishop, Denis, the Duchess, and Mrs. Steynlin—would also be expected to speak as correctly and as well as they do. Edgar Marten, on the other hand, is depicted as somewhat coarse. His language reflects this; notice, for instance, his reaction to the Russian fanatic Bazhakuloff; "He's a beauty! Eyes like a boiled haddock. And that thing has the cheek to call itself a Messiah. Thank God I'm a Jew; it's no business of mine. But if I were a Christian, I'd bash his blooming head in. Damned if I wouldn't. The frowsy, fetid, fly-blown fraud. Or what's the matter with the Dog's Home? (123)" It must be admitted, however, that Douglas himself had several "voices," and that even this was one of them. The expression of Douglas' characters, like their ideas, is usually recognizable as that of the author. The differentiating features are too superficial to hide Douglas' mannerisms, his liking for epigram, and even some of his favorite words. One must be content with the fact that their conversation is usually interesting and witty and that its stylized quality is not out of keeping with the atmosphere in which it is set.

South Wind appears to have been a sort of consummation of Douglas' particular possibilities. Although there are always readers who prefer *Old Calabria, Siren Land,* or even *They Went,* most grant *South Wind* to be Douglas' best book and the most consummate display of his powers. It allowed him to present some of his eccentric Capri friends in an idealized form and to project his own personality into several characters; it permitted him to talk casually and eloquently about many of his favorite topics—geology, history, and even saints' legends. And amazingly enough, through his felicitous style and ironic wit, he was able to inform the whole with a unity of mood and purpose. Less than a decade after the publication of *South Wind,* an influential critic, writing in the *New York Times,* summarized the basis of the critical esteem in which the book had already come to be held: "The high engrossment in atmosphere delineation, the almost flawless projection of character, the steady stream of faintly ironic humor, the philosophical undercurrent, the sense of completeness and, above all, the achievement of a colorful and melodious prose that is both pleasant and fastidious, combine together in a work that has won for itself a small but vociferous body of admirers who insist upon denominating it as one of the smaller classics."

But this critic added, prophetically, that " 'South Wind' is his triumph and vindication as a writer, and somehow one suspects that it will remain so; that another such work would be impossible from him for the simple reason that he has put all of himself in it. He is not a great creative writer, but for once his powers fused at their best and the result is one that should accord him a place in the minds of those readers who love what are termed 'the delicacies of literature.' "[10]

III They Went: *Beauty Over Betterment*

They Went (1920) Douglas' second full-length novel, was written during the lean years after World War I. Begun at St. Malo, it was "interrupted owing to lack of food," and finished at Mentone after the war "when I was feeling comfortable again."[11] In *Looking Back* Douglas described the circumstances of its writing and the thoughts which prompted it:

At Mentone I was already drifting away from humanity pure and simple, with its odd little loves and hates and ambitions; into the regions beyond, and saying to myself as I actually wrote later: "How many avenues of delight are closed to the mere moralist or immoralist who knows nothing of things extra-human; who remains absorbed in mankind and its half-dozen motives of conduct, so unstable yet forever the same, which we all fathomed before we were twenty!" There is an infusion of the extra-human in *They Went,* which depicts the conflict between beauty and betterment, art and morality. Betterment wins, despite the extra-human intervention of Theophilus. It is apt to win. In the shape of priestcraft, it extinguished art and science in Egypt; in the shape of Plato and his followers, it extinguished them in Greece. That city, the thing of beauty, lies drowned under the waves, while betterment remains perched on its granite rock. (352-53)

They Went is a short, whimsical tale, set sometime in the dim past. Its pseudo-legendary form and austere style produce an effect far different from that of *South Wind*. Description is kept to a minimum; conversation plays a much less prominent part than in the earlier novel; the mood is less bright and sparkling; and despite a strong humorous element, the tone is more serious and less tolerant.

The setting is a strange, mist-shrouded city on the rugged northern coast, presumably Brittany, in the fifth or sixth century. The heroic age of the city is past; it is in a period of decadence—of splendor, luxury, and immorality. The King, now an old and doddering man, has memories of great conquests over the Vikings; but now the weapons and armor are rusting, and the old smith Lelian is reduced to making trinkets for the beautiful but cruel Princess.

The King's last great victory has been over the sea, for he has caused a mighty sea wall to be constructed by an exiled Roman engineer. The sea has been pushed back, a flooded plain drained, and a city built on a spit of reclaimed land. Now, at the King's belt hangs the key to the sluice gates which hold back the angry ocean that thunders at the city's foundation, eager to take back what was once its own.

The Princess, whom all men adore at first sight, is a lover of beauty and has rebuilt the city, transforming the plain functional buildings of the Roman engineer by adding exotic towers and porticoes. The control of the city is hers, for her personality and intellect are far stronger than those of her senile father or her innocuous mother. It is the Princess who has made the city a center of world commerce and an object of wide interest by bringing skillful craftsmen and artisans from distant lands. She toys with the city as she does with the men who make the mistake of offering her their adulation, and her private tower is known to contain rare secrets and to have been the scene of strange orgies. It has a stairway opening on the great drain; when her lovers begin to bore her, or when her favorites have been gleaned of all their knowledge, *they go.*

The Princess was not actually the child of the king. Once Aithryn, the great ruler of the north whom people thought to be a sea god, had become jealous of the city beside the sea and had sailed there in his green ship. He did not enter the city, but found the Queen seated on the sea wall embroidering and took her on his ship for a brief visit. Thus the element of discord entered the city; now, nineteen years later, Aithryn's spies carefully watch the maturing of the strong-willed young Princess who seems so unlike the King.

The religious life of the city is dominated by Manthis, a harsh old druidess and worshiper of Belen who keeps a girls' school on an island in the bay and who propagates her doctrines of betterment, social utility, and the superiority of women. The last Christian missionary had been treated tolerantly; but, when he proved to be a bigot and hacked down the sacred druidical grove, the King and Manthis decided that he had to go. He went, but in his dying malediction he had mentioned "retribution from the sea." Manthis scrutinized the missionary's entrails to read the future and promptly moved her girls to the island.

The new missionary, a handsome young man named Kenwyn with a weakness in matters of sex, proves acceptable to Manthis and attractive to the Princess. But even more appealing to this self-willed young lady is a mysterious Greek named Theophilus, who, though ugly and diabolical, has a vast knowledge of architecture and the other arts that the Princess lives for. He is able to make workmen and materials appear as if by magic, and he is the only person whose fate Manthis has been unable to read.

With Theophilus, whose resources of knowledge are unlimited, the Princess is happy for the first time in her life. Together they make the city beautiful. From him she learns not only new methods and crafts, but also new qualities of kindness and mercy that temper her former callousness; for the pragmatic Theophilus knows well that nothing is accomplished by unnecessary cruelty. But now the Princess is to learn the meaning of sacrifice as well, for Theophilus finds it necessary to ask recompense for his help. He explains to her that people like them, lovers of beauty, have dangerous enemies—, the forces of betterment and the All-Highest. He explains that Aithryn, her real father, is now leagued with the All-Highest. Suffering a kind of senility as a result of an old head wound, Aithryn has fallen under the power of the Christians, who promise him a future life in return for extensive grants of land to the Church. And now the Christians insist that Aithryn destroy the evil city by the sea, whose Princess, rumor has it, has sold her soul to the evil one. The first measures which Theophilus requires the Princess to take are the disposal of the Christian missionary and the securing of the great key from her irresponsible father.

The Princess, half in love with Kenwyn, at first refuses Theophilus' request; but, when he threatens to leave, she complies. The lovesick young missionary is easily lured to her tower at night, as others before him have been; and, like them, "he *went.*" The great drain tells no tales. Now the Princess, who has shed tears for the first time in her life, knows what it means to sacrifice for something one loves. But she has failed to secure the key to the sluice gates. The green ship comes again; Aithryn enters the palace during the nightly revelry; the Queen is so excited that she forgets to put the old King to bed when he reaches "high water mark"; and Aithryn leaves with the key.

The ocean surges over the city. Aithryn is waiting outside the tower for his daughter, but Theophilus easily destroys him. Theophilus is dejected to see his magnificant work destroyed, but he is accustomed to such disappointment. The All-Highest, who prefers a preacher to a portico, is always ready to destroy thousands of innocent people in order to accomplish his whims. But Theophilus will take the Princess to his own land, where they can rear a new city without the interference of the forces of betterment. The princess is happy and willing. "They went."

Manthis, safe with her girls on the island, realizes that her hopes of some kind of an alliance with Christianity were futile because they depended on men, and Kenwyn has proved that men are too weak for such high purposes. She is happy in the realization that the sinful city is gone and, with it all, the annoyances and frustrations. Now she will be able to develop her own ideas of betterment: "She felt like some sagacious gardener who holds in his hands a seed scarcely visible, and already contemplates, with the mind's eye, the tall and seemly growth which must inevitably spring therefrom (250)."

The loss of the city's population—and hence of all the men— disturbs Manthis' pupils, who ask, "If all the men are drowned, and even the young ones, and even the tiny little boys, how shall we ever—" But Manthis is undisturbed. "Belen will provide," she announces gravely (245). And thus "the thing of beauty lies drowned under the wave, while betterment remains perched on its granite rock."

The book received some favorable reviews. The *Athenaeum* said, "... Mr. Douglas has developed and transformed the Peacockian novel, carrying it to a point far beyond that charming if uneven writer. . . ."[12] And Rebecca West wrote in the *New Statesman* that Douglas' talent had found a more appropriate expression than in *South Wind* or in *Old Calabria*.[13] A few other critics have since echoed this preference. Raymond Mortimer considers *They Went* Douglas' best novel,[14] and Elizabeth Wheatly considers it "finer" than *South Wind* and "more severely patterned (64)."

Some reviewers were confused about the interpretation of the story. The American *Bookman* said:

Perhaps Mr. Douglas is taking a crack at family life.... perhaps it is love that annoys him. Maybe he means her [the Princess] to be woman incarnate.

Let me warn you against this novel if you are the sort of person who must know the exact meaning of your story books.[15]

And another review:

Perhaps it is the tragedy of a womanhood that is simply the will to have and to enjoy, and which so becomes in the end its own victim. Or is the princess a symbol of paganism successfully resisting the lures and the threats of a religion of sacrifice? Or do you take her (with me) as the child with the dormant soul whose interest for the cold and cruel destruction of warm things has carried her so far that the moment of possible awakening has come too late?[16]

Light is thrown upon the meaning of the novel, or at least upon the intention of its author, in the prefatory letter which Douglas prefixed to the third printing. He explained that while visiting Brittany he had discovered that the country was saturated with legends and had decided to "dissect a handful of these for a scientific purpose." His goal was to prove the theory that a myth is "the slow product of ages . . . a kind of palimpsest . . . overscored at various periods of its growth by the fresh experience of the race." Although Douglas makes no claim for the absolute originality of these views of the nature of myth, he seems to have considered them more startling than they were. He chose the *Roi d'Ys* story, the drowned city motif which had appeared in a number of plays and poems, as well as in the "melodiously saccharine opera by Lalo." Working with the Breton variant of the legend, he found "that primordial or autochtonous note—the domineering and lustful woman, as well as another aboriginal feature which I proposed, just for the sake of the theory, to attribute to the old dolichocephalous inhabitants of Brittany: the personification of wild nature forces—in this case a revengeful ocean." Next he discerned "the *brachycephalic* contribution" (in the metals, craftsmanship, and so on); then a Roman element; and last, the "Christian patina— the intervention of a saint." Thus, six thousand years of accretions, "Q.E.D. Pure guess work, you perceive (vi)."

In considering these legends, Douglas was disturbed—as might be expected—by the intrusion of saints and angels and by the admixture of Christian values: "It dulls their pristine vigour and originality and even, by appearing as *deus ex machina* at a critical moment, renders them almost *jejune*—nonsensical. . . ." He relates that he tried to strip off these "adventitious wrappings" and to reconstruct the legend in "pagan garb." But he soon lost sight of his original problem and began to wonder what version offered most artistic merit, what improvements might be made, which characters were superfluous, and what new ones might be added. And thus *They Went* came into being. Douglas called it therefore ". . . not a phantasy of my own, but an adaptation from a familiar legend which keeps alive, maybe, the memory of some actual historical occurrence, some inroad of the sea destructive to the works of man (vii)."

As to the meaning of his novel Douglas wrote:

In this little allegory of beauty *versus* betterment into which the Roi d'Ys has developed (you see what happens when I take a legend in hand for "scientific purposes") I have tried to remain aloof and to hold the balance evenly. It is true that the All-Highest wins by a rather tortuous device. He does; and not for the first time in history. For this exalted personage would be unendurable had he not likewise his curse, his tragedy, his cloven hoof. He is omnipresent and yet not invariably wise; he blunders now and then (*see* Genesis) and is streaked, moreover, by a curious little vein of senile malice. Which of us, at one time or another, has not suffered from it? Kindly note, nevertheless, that the catastrophe would not have occurred and that the All-Highest would have been delightfully outwitted, but for the refusal of the princess to ask for the key. What made her refuse? "Sheer wrongness—wrongness and pride." Pride—hybris: that unforgivable sin which brings about the downfall of mortals. (x)

Thus Douglas attempted, with indifferent success, to maintain a balance between the opposing teams. Both sides have weaknesses. The All-Highest has the incongruities characteristic of anthropomorphic deities. He has, from the human point of view, that disconcerting flaw that poor Job discovered: he is neither just nor consistent. The Princess has the flaw of humanity which the Greeks discovered: she is proud, immoderate, and shortsighted. It is obvious that Theophilus contains much of Douglas' own character and temperament. He is the lover of beauty, the Machiavellian, the gentleman of perfect taste. But he has the problem that all Satans in literature have faced: he is by definition unable to overcome his adversary.

Although the deepest conflicts of the plot are those between the antithetical cosmic forces, the little weaknesses of men play their parts in the turn of events. Without the personality of the King, the needs of the Queen, the hybris of the Princess, and the flawed mind of Aithryn, things would not have come about as they did. Thus Douglas apparently tried to keep a balance also between fate and human responsibility—the kind of balance which forms part of the achievement of Greek tragedy and epic. The people in *They Went* make their own fate to a degree, but their very nature makes it impossible for the best that is in them to win out. They get the god they deserve. Manthis is right in her perception of human weakness; but she has her own flaw, and the handling of the story makes her flaw perhaps the worst of all. She is allied with the forces of betterment which will always thwart man in his efforts to fulfill his potentialities for beauty and civilization, and these latter values are clearly the ones to which the author gives his nod of approval. Rebecca West has adroitly summed up what happens in the story and what the outcome implies:

. . . this struggle between the artist and the moralist is illusory. It comes to no decisions; it merely embellishes the pattern of life by adding to the intricacy of events, and the course of history is settled by things quite other. The city was washed away not by any machination of the devil or the missionary, but because the barbarian king, jealous of this rival kingdom and barred from any constructive belligerent policy by the effects of a crack on the skull, sent spies overseas to tamper with the embankment. It is stupidity that always finishes the argument between the artist and the saint, the cracked skull of humanity that is the decisive factor in the affairs of men.[17]

Concerning the principal characters, Douglas had something to say also. Theophilus, unlike the Princess and her parents, had no precedent in other versions of the legend. He was introduced because "the semi-savage Princess Ahes could never have reared a town surpassing Paris in splendour "without the help of the great Master-Builder of medieval days. . . (viii)." In regard to the devil Douglas had written in *Siren Land:* "And what lends the devil his charm? His quasi-human attributes; his bargainings, his ill-treatment at the hands of heaven. Beings wholly divine are inevitably endowed with qualities of good and evil identical with our own: they are mere caricatures of good or bad men (37)." Douglas made his devil in *They Went* human and appealing. Though astute and masterful, Theophilus is also tactful and sympathetic; he does not push himself in where he is not wanted. He is sensitive to beauty, kind when it is not necessary to be otherwise, and much affected by the sight of suffering. And, despite a few outbursts, he is resigned and relatively humble before the state of things—as far from the proud rebel of the earlier books of *Paradise Lost* as from the suave Voltarian of Goethe's *Faust.* A true gentleman, Theophilus has the sense of proportion that Douglas admired. Douglas' own analysis of this character emphasizes the commendable human qualities of enlightenment and creativity, but it emphasizes also the tragic dimension: "Ever to aspire and ever to be thwarted; that is the curse, the tragedy, of Theophilus and other Light-bringers. Well may they 'despair of mankind!' I grant he is not the devil of the schoolmen. He is the devil as he ought to be (ix)."

Princess Ahes was not intended to be as sympathetic a character as Theophilus: she is coarser and less self-sufficient. But she demonstrates a facet of Douglas that is sometimes overlooked; she represents an effort to show that pure intellectuality, without some tincture of warmheartedness, is objectionable. Douglas described her:

. . . a cold, earthly thinker, an egoist predestined from birth to fall under his [Theophilus'] influence, which moulds her character in singular fashion, softening it here, and hardening it there. She too has troubles, troubles that move her to tears. Yet they fail to enlist our compassion; we find it a strain to sympathize with the griefs, however acute, however sincere, of those whose head controls their heart. Many tragic figures were murderers; none has ever been a pure intellectual. (ix)

They Went has serious defects, not the least of which is the obtrusive repetition which will be discussed elsewhere. There are elements of preciousness and snideness of tone which are at times offensive to the most kindly disposed reader. But it has the saving qualities of Douglas' felicitous prose and his potent wit, as well as remarkable economy—thanks to its author's pithy style and his belief in the unities—and a bizarre and engaging mood. Its tone—a peculiar compound of sophistication, cynicism, and equanimity—is distinctively Douglas.

IV In the Beginning

In the Beginning (1927) was also based on legendary material: the tale of Ninus and Semiramis, the mythological founders of the Assyrian Empire. They are mentioned by Herodotus, and their story is discussed by Sir James Frazer in *The Golden Bough.* Douglas claimed in *Late Harvest* that he had consulted all the ancient writers and "not a few of their modern commentators . . . (24)." But the legend itself is so slight and vague that the plot of *In the Beginning* can be considered original with Douglas. It is, in fact, his most sustained and complex plot; and a detailed summary of this little-known novel is necessary to make discussion possible.

The story takes place long ago, when mankind lived naked and unashamed and the gods took their pleasures not only in their own celestial halls but among the sons of men. Young Linus, a goatherd, is in love with Ayra, the daughter of a fisherman. They know little, but both feel some mysterious need. Often Linus draws the girl to a shady forest glen and caresses her clumsily, saying to himself, "This time, yes!" But her answer is always, "Oh, Linus, another day."

Ayra's father disturbed by the boy's slowness, also wonders about his wits because Linus has often reported seeing a fish of prodigious size and splendid hue, and the old man knows of no such monster. Ayra excuses her lover as a "dreamy boy" and secretly wonders whether he has not seen some immortal.

Linus has also seen a giant figure stepping across the jagged white spires which are visible halfway up the eastern sky and which are, unknown to men, a great chain of mountains. This figure is indeed the Earth god, off to pay a visit to the distant Colocynthians, whom he likes to tease with earthquakes. The Colocynthians have an advanced culture: they cultivate their land, build tall buildings, and powder their hair. It is they who have given the Earth god the nickname "O-Boum"—the Clatterer—which he resents.

The gods live in leisurely pleasure. They are immortal and fearless—but not passionless—and thrive on the worship of mortals. There are multitudes of them, peopling earth and sky, and also many half-gods products of "tender dalliance" between gods and mortals. These half-gods live on earth. They are fair and, like their divine parents, lazy, frivolous, and mischievous. Poor human beings, subject to the divine caprices of their deities, toil, suffer, and die; but they are always trying, usually in vain, to propitiate the gods.

There is, at the moment, great merriment in the celestial halls because Menetha the Maiden, cleverest of the goddesses and favorite daughter of the Great Father of the gods, has fallen in love with the young moon, who, alone among immortals, is sterile. The Clatterer laughs especially heartily, because Menetha has often chided him about his diversions, but she claims that her love for the moon is of another kind. Some of the gods think that the clever Menetha has chosen well, for she will not have to bear the pangs of childbirth from which gods are not immune. The Great Mother is pleased; there are too many philanderings with mortals and too many half-gods about. The moon, for his part, says it is all a rumor and the fault of the gossiping wind. It is quickly agreed that the wind shall be bottled up and rolled about again—one of the favorite sports in the celestial halls. It is left to Menetha to "put the moon to rights."

The Great Father has long since lapsed into lethargy and is no longer as jovial and as inventive as he once was. He is enveloped in a starry mist from which his stainless hand occasionally emerges to grasp a cup of myut, the wondrous liquor of the gods.

Linus, who is an orphan, lives with his grandmother, a woman with a reputation for great wisdom. One day he returns to their hut to find the old woman dead and learns from the First One, eldest of the three rulers of the village, that her last instructions were for the boy to visit Neahuni, the satyr.

The satyrs were a race of semidivine creatures who once peopled the earth. They were master builders, agriculturists, and scientists; but the Great Father became jealous and fearful of them and cursed them with sterility. Although their race was long-lived, the satyrs finally died out; now only Nea-huni remains. Rather than leave the earth unpeopled, the Great Father, who loved to invent things, created the race of men, fashioning them from the dung of Hapso, the loathly fowl. They are subservient creatures, good for nothing but to be laughed at. But before the satyrs disappeared, they taught many of their arts to the Colocynthians.

Nea-huni dwells alone, having outlived his beloved companion Azdhubal, fighter of demons. For a time Nea-huni was respected as a seer and healer, but now a rumor has circulated among men that this peaceful vegetarian satyr is a cannibal, and no one dares to approach him.

Linus and the First One spend several days with the gentle satyr and learn from him that Linus is a half-god, son of the Clatterer himself, and that he will one day cultivate the desolate plains again as they were cultivated in the days of the satyrs. Nea-huni also tells them of a visit he has had from the Earth god, who asked his help in capturing the demon Aroudi, haunter of outskirts, hater of men, and maker of floods and droughts. Nea-huni gave the Clatterer a magic potion with which to drug Aroudi and in return received a promise that his old friend Azdhubal would be returned to life and that the plain would be cultivated again.

In Eskion, a dusky old village at the other end of the world, something is wrong. A terrible drought is destroying the land. Heat is radiating from the temple of Derco, the maiden fish-goddess, a moody, vindictive creature who has caused this sort of thing before. When the disquieted populace is about to burn the temple, they notice that the flame which denotes the presence of the goddess has disappeared from its place.

At this instant, far away, Linus is resting on a river bank after his visit to the sanctuary of the satyr. Once again he sees the great spangled fish, and this time there is a sudden flash of light and Derco stands before him, gloriously beautiful. She tells the youth that he alone can quench her flames. Linus, who is after all his father's son, proves an apt pupil; and Derco has never in her age-long experience known such transport. Linus awakes from a refreshing slumber no longer a dreamy boy. He sets out to find Ayra, muttering to himself, "This time, yes."

Derco returns to Eskion confident that her latest lover will soon die as do all mortals who lie with gods. Prosperity and happiness return to Eskion, and the merchant Babramolok, an old Derco-worshiper, donates money for a new temple. Then one day the flame disappears again. Derco is with child. New miseries are in store. Babramolok is exiled.

Now all the gods laugh at Derco, who has been driven from her temple because the Eskions prefer a virgin goddess and have replaced her with another protector. Neither Menetha, nor the Great Father, nor Nea-huni can help her. She pays a visit to Linus, is at first surprised to find him alive, and then is enraged to learn that he has taken a mortal in his arms after lying with a divine lover. Transforming herself into a monstrous worm, she sucks out his blood and then burns the hut of Ayra and her father. But before the soul of Linus can flit away, it is caught up by the Earth god, taken to his workshop under the earth, and there revived.

Later, in a lonely cave where Derco is awaiting the birth of her child, she receives a visit from the gossipy wind, who tells her that Linus is the son of the Clatterer, who has rescued him. In return for the information, Derco agrees to help the wind the next time the gods decide to bottle him up and roll him about.

After reviving Linus in the subterranean laboratory, the Clatterer stops a while to taunt Aroudi, where the powerful demon is chained. The desert maker, whom the gods can never kill, strains at his bonds and swears revenge. He threatens the god with what will happen if men are not held in check: "I foresee the day when you will grow out of your fondness for such groveling creatures, when every fair spot has been scarred by their hands and deformed to their mean purposes, the rivers made turbid and hills and forests leveled away and all the wild green places smothered under cities full of smoke and clanking metal; when the Sun himself, the steadiest of your inconstant breed, will refuse to peer down through their foul vapors. . . ."[18]

The Clatterer, remembering his promise to Nea-huni, returns Adzhubal to life. He also gives Linus great wisdom and sends him to the two satyrs to learn how to cultivate the plains. In two years the young man is a great king; he has cleared jungles, drained marshes, irrigated deserts, invented many new devices, and gathered great armies about him.

Derco gives birth to a daughter whom she leaves on a mountain to be found and raised in the traditional fashion by a goatherd. The girl, Symira, is much like her mother; and, growing up among lascivious goats and doves, she becomes extraordinarily hot-blooded and impulsive. When she reaches young womanhood, her foster mother gives her to Oannes, a powerful and savage chieftain of a primitive army. Symira diligently learns the arts of war from Oannes, then strangles him and declares herself chief. With her vast army of warriors, one or another of whom is brought to her tent every night only to depart in disgrace in the morning, she descends upon the lands of Linus and conquers them. But after one night in Symira's tent, Linus proves to the savage queen that he is superior to other men; thereafter, the two rule the earth together.

Derco has been able to return to Eskion, for Babramolok, back from his exile, has sent to the city an unsatisfactory god, an old woman-chaser whom the Colocynthians brought down from heaven especially to foist upon their unsuspecting enemies. The Eskions soon have enough of him and are ready to bring back Derco, who has been changed by motherhood from a capricious virgin goddess to a kindly mother goddess, full of love and joy. All is well now. The new motto of the city is "Nobody should be a virgin." The goddess has given up her sport with mortals, and the wind is known to blow strangely often within her temple.

Linus and Symira build a magnificant kingdom, vying with each other for new and fruitful ideas. Symira builds the temple of the doves to house the flocks of those birds which have followed her since her birth. In it she installs sixty-nine dancing girls known as the Doves or the Pleasant Ones. In charge of Fatutta, a pleasure-loving old harlot, their duty is to teach the art of love to the young men of the kingdom. So successful is the institution that even those who need no lessons, even Linus himself, patronize the Doves. Symira gratifies her old instincts by frequently visiting the House of the Doves and playing the part of a Pleasant One herself. But since this is not completely satisfactory, at the suggestion of Fatutta there is established a personal bodyguard for the Queen, composed of ninety-nine chosen warriors.

Then one day Linus conceives the notion of building a temple to the Great Father. The languishing old deity is so pleased that he becomes gay again. He is seen sporting about the earth in goatish disguises and is even known to be inventing things once more, producing oddities such as a star with a ring around it, a comet without a tail, and bearded women.

Once while hunting, Linus is seized by Aroudi, who has been released by the Clatterer for the sake of a little excitement. The demon warns Linus to stay out of the wilderness, which is his.

After this fright, Linus changes. He gives up hunting and begins to devote more and more time to the Pleasant Ones. Despite his godlike powers, he becomes weak from overindulgence and reduces himself to a senile spendthrift and a danger to the kingdom. Moreover, he begins to think himself a god. Taking advantage of this eccentricity, Symira, who sees that her consort will have to go, convinces him that he should have himself burned to death so that he can soar to the celestial halls and visit the other immortals.

Things go well for a time, with Symira ruling the kingdom alone; then she too begins to change, developing a dislike for men and becoming herself more mannish. The ninety-nine warriors are cast aside and Symira "begins to develop longings as ardent as they are outrageous." Fatutta tries to keep the changes secret, but this is impossible. Soon there are tales abroad "—unpleasant tales about dwarfs, and apes, and horses, and other abominations . . . (257-58)."

It is just at this time that the Great Father looks down, sees what is happening, and loses his temper. He straightway lets loose upon the earth a terrible dust or powder which taints the wits of mortals. It infects them with prepostrous ideas about good and evil, which have hitherto been none of their business, and with a passion for quarreling. People are sick for only a few days, but they are left sadly altered: "They called themselves good, and forthwith began to act in accordance with frantic notions engendered by the disease (264)." They cease to cultivate the fields and spend all their time arguing about the welfare of their souls, "as though it were something quite apart from the welfare of their bodies . . . (265)."

A new race of men grows up from among those who have not contracted the disease. These call themselves "dreamers" and love to think about old times and about the future, searching for some more reasonable way of life. They look to Aroudi as their savior. And the haunter of outskirts, enemy of toilers and quarrelers but friend to solitaries like these, is not asleep. Oblitering the vestiges of human folly, he gladdens the dreamers by charming the world once more into desert.

Meanwhile the malady rages. Men lose their capacity for joy and learn what it means to fear. A band of prophets and lawgivers arises who capitalize on men's fear and promulgate thousands of laws concerning good and evil which no one could possibly abide by. "All delight fled from earth, and mortals, for the most part, grew to be the fools and cowards they have since remained (269)."

Symira herself takes the infection and becomes "better" than anyone else. It is plain that any subjects who wish to retain their lives must contract the disease. The Pleasant Ones and the ninety-nine warriors are condemned to death, but Fatutta saves them and herself by reporting erroneously that they have all taken the illness.

Symira gives up worldly pursuits and retires to rule the House of Doves. She enforces strict rules requiring that the sixty-nine Pleasant Ones, now known as the Good Ones, wear only sack cloth and eat only the most meager of rations. In effect, she establishes the first convent.

In a few years the kingdom has gone to pieces; the few remaining sane people escape to Eskion, where pleasure can still be had. The Queen dies one night, a bitter and abstenious old woman. In a final feverish wakefulness, she cries out: "Such horrible dreams, Fatutta! About horses . . . (287)" She leaves a sack of rubies, which are to be used to build a monument to her memory. But Fatutta spends the money on a tremendous banquet for the sixty-nine Good Ones, for old time's sake. She even invites the ninety-nine guards, who do their duty nobly.

The novel ends with a conversation between Nea-huni and Adzhubal. Nea-huni has given men up as a complete loss and both express their views concerning men and gods: "To the crocodiles, with both of them! (309)"

The reviewers of *In the Beginning* were not kind to the book. They were disturbed by what seemed to them pornographic passages. The English *Saturday Review* said, "dull, spiritless impropriety."[19] The American *New Republic* said, "Professional salaciousness." Regretting that Douglas' "refreshing paganism" had given way to "shrill impatience," the reviewer found that "The sexual debaucheries of his characters are drawn into the narrative so gratuitously and so often that they end by attracting our attention for their own sake instead of contributing to a satirical picture."[20] The most severe attack came from the *Saturday Review of Literature:*

In the Beginning is a feeble specimen of that chirping pornography that passes for strength among the weak. . . . A sort of cancerous proud-flesh has been forced to attach itself to the dry bones of the legend. If Herodotus, or Ctesius . . . alludes to some amiable sexual aberration, Mr. Douglas enlarges, envelops and expatiates. He seems completely unaware of the beauty and dignity and wonder that once were the attributes of the principle of generation. And his tone as he narrates the procreant exploits of his gods and heros and heroines is a vulgar cross between the hysterical smirking of an ill-bred fifth former and the gross crackle of a worn-out boulevardier. . . . It will bore anyone it could conceivably hurt.[21]

It is difficult to defend Douglas against accusations that the disturbing passages in the book were there for their own sake. Indeed, he would no doubt have rejected such defense just as Aristophanes or Rabelais would have done. Moreover, from the perspective of a different cultural climate, and in light of the kinds of literary themes and scenes that are now accepted as a matter of course, an elaborate defense of Douglas' practice would be pointless. Douglas himself had an explanation for the critics' disapproval of *In the Beginning*. He wrote of the book in *Looking Back:*

It lacks the admixture of saccharine which is prescribed by the taste of today. Its anti-democratic and uncompromising outlook is disquieting: "Too awful to contemplate," writes one of them, "especially the last chapter." How seriously these humans take themselves and their affairs! I do not find it awful; I find it good fun, especially the last chapter. But I understand his state of mind. I know what he wants. He wants his comforter, his treacle, his dose of irrationalism. He would have liked me to insert a touch of that "hopefulness" with which the present generation likes to delude itself, in defiance of the teaching of all history. (354-55)

Late Harvest contained a few comments concerning the composition of *In the Beginning*: "The book was a strain on my inventive faculties. Some twenty new words were coined, and a fresh heaven had to be created with eight major deities, as well as half-gods and demons and a brace of gentle satyrs, not to speak of hitherto unknown races of men. Lucian was of some help in regard to the divine members of this community, while the Great Father himself is modelled upon my conception of that old Javeh of the Jews (24)." There is also the suggestion that part of the "moral" of *In the Beginning* is that "Nothing on earth is permanent save only change, unless, of course, we include the changeless race of Gods, the Great Father and his more or less disreputable brood of children—call him Jupiter if you like—those phantasms whom we create in our own image, and endow with our own facets of good or bad humour, of lust and wisdom and inconstancy (25)."

The book presents no great problems of interpretation. Douglas hated the Jewish God, who was a spying, "upstairs" God created by the proletariat which "loves to humiliate itself." He preferred the Classical "downstairs" gods who "were invented by intellectuals who felt themselves capable of maintaining a kind of comradeship with their deities."[22] Hence the happier days of *In the Beginning* are of the period when unconcerned and pleasure-loving anthropomorphic gods roamed the world.

The important aspects of the theme are the exaltation of amoral individualism and free sensuous living, the condemnation of the practice of separating body and soul, and the satire of humanity's practice of making gods. There is also present the primitivistic strain which caused Douglas to seek the refreshment of lonely places. In his essay on Doughty's *Arabia Deserta*, Douglas had made significant remarks concerning the Great Red Desert:

We learn . . . that the so-called *Empty Quarter*, the Great Red Desert, has not yet been seen by western eyes. Long may it remain invisible, a solace for future generations! Deserts have their uses, and the *Empty Quarter*, let us hope, will sooner or later demonstrate its *raison d'être* by stirring that first intrepid beholder as he gazes down upon its trackless ocean of billowing dunes, into some rare utterance—a paragraph or two, a sonnet, or some poignant little epigram: an epigram that shall justify the existence of a million leagues of useless sand, and the non-existence of several myriad useful cultivators.[23]

Thus we find Aroudi, the maker of deserts, presented as a cleansing savior to a world which has been corrupted by the fanatical practices of men.

In its largest effect *In the Beginning* is a satirical history of human folly as Douglas saw it. It is unreasonable and uncompromising as is most satire. Presenting all sides of the story is not the job of the satirist; if it were, Douglas could never have been one. There is, indeed, a note of bitterness. Perhaps the aging libertine, losing his ability to enjoy the sensuous life, found gratification in indulging his hedonism by presenting it written large in these prodigious and carefree gods and half-gods, and in aiming some spiteful shafts at the dullards who so stubbornly refused to exploit life as he no longer could.

Not all critics have deplored the book. Edward Garnett liked it and wrote to Douglas, "I am glad you have nailed our colours to the mast." He called the supper party of the harlots "pure gorgonzola," "which," said Douglas, "was exactly what I intended it to be."[24] Rachel Taylor, reviewing the book for the *Spectator*, praised the "limpid, iridescent prose," which Douglas himself considered among his best writing, and called it the nearest thing in the language to the manner of Anatole France.[25] Edward McDonald, a staunch Douglas admirer, found Linus a character who touches the heart more than any character in *South Wind*. But his final judgment of the book echoed the consensus of critics: "Perhaps a travesty designed on so huge a scale must inevitably fall of its own weight. In any event, fall it certainly does, and in the midst of its scaffolding.[26]

CHAPTER 5

Style

D OUGLAS' prose style and descriptive techniques, which are here considered together, almost unquestionably form his major achievement. Although critics have often been disappointed by various aspects of Douglas as writer and as thinker— by his cynicism, his lack of creativity, his crankiness—they have seldom had occasion to offer anything other than praise for his prose style. His descriptive ability has seldom received an evaluation in print which was not of the nature of approval. His style has in its cadences, its diction, and its tone a certain dignity which is achieved without sacrifice of lightness and ease. Richard Aldington calls this quality "that decent *propreté* which always distinguished his linen and comely white hair," and adds, "it is quite truly a classical prose, as far from the finicky elegance of Walter Pater's writing as from banal neatness. . . ."[1] Douglas' writing is grammatically and syntactically correct and proper, without stiffness or pedantic heaviness. His sentences are cleanly phrased, structurally clear, and pleasing in their variety. In short, he had the ability, far rarer than it may seem to be, of saying exactly what he wanted to say, vigorously, economically, and clearly.

I *Une Belle Tonalité*

The outstanding quality of Douglas' prose is its precision. When he is striving to render detail precisely, each word and each phrase seem to be the right ones. Everything contributes to the meaning, and the picture produced is strikingly clear of line and sharply defined in mass and color. His style was seldom slovenly, and the pictures evoked are consequently seldom fuzzy or amorphous. This precision and lucidity are probably connected with his scientific bent and his disciplined experience with scientific description and Foreign-Office reports. The prose styles of such nineteenth-century scientific writers as Huxley and Darwin may also have been contributing influences. This careful clarity of expression—along with Douglas' wit, perception, and sensitivity to natural beauty—produced in his writing the quality which Joseph Conrad called *une belle tonalité*.[2]

For all Douglas' exactness of vocabulary and syntax, he nevertheless avoids the heaviness and slowness that one might expect from such scientifically informed material and such determined precision. He can be colloquial without slanginess; his wit and the flowing facility of his expression save his prose from any effect of strain. He apparently wrote carefully, and yet with the same ease and naturalness that marked his conversation. H. M. Tomlinson writes: "... you think he is the best talker you have ever heard. All his books of travel give the impression of a low-toned fireside discourse of an extraordinary quality, sparingly shot with flickering wit which keeps a listener in suspense, aware of both danger and enjoyment, forgetful of the clock (73)."

There is something of an old-fashioned note to Douglas' prose. Richard Curle found in it the "exquisite finish and irony of an eighteenth-century Frenchman,"[3] and another reviewer noted "that elaborate simplicity, that slow lucidity which is a relic of the nineties."[4] His cadences are rather more dignified than is common in contemporary writing. Many sentences are longer than the modern reader is accustomed to expect, although these are varied with sentences that are so short as to be again unusual. The punctuation is heavy with commas, and there are frequent semicolons and colons. The vocabulary makes more demands on the reader than is customary, and there is the aristocratic tone which has been discussed.

But Douglas had no need to adapt his style to current tastes and practices, for old-fashioned and meticulous though it may have been it served him well, lending itself as a versatile instrument to such varied uses as scientifically clear descriptions of rich external beauty, delicate nuances of irony and cynicism, brutal statements of cold fact, and various degrees of invective ranging from condescension to excoriation.

II *Mastery of a Defect*

The peculiar quality of Douglas' descriptive passages is something more than what is ordinarily described as clarity or exactness. It is a kind of crispness and sheen which seems to glitter before the mind's eye, a metallic luster as in this description from *Siren Land*: "Citrella, poised like a swallow's nest upon its windswept limestone crag; far below, the Titanic grandeur of South

Capri and the dimpled ocean strewn with submarine boulders that make it look, from such aerial heights, like a map of the moon enamelled in the blues and greens of a Damascus vase (118)."

He often seems to have divided his canvas and composed with careful attention to contrasts of color and texture, placing bright details where they will best serve his purpose. For example, Bishop Heard's first sight of Nepenthe: "... the mainland slowly receded. Morning wore on, and under the fierce attraction of the sun the fogs were drawn upwards. Nepenthe became tangible—an authentic island. It gleamed with golden rocks and emerald patches of culture. A cluster of white houses, some town or village, lay perched on the middle heights where a playful sunbeam had struck a path way through the vapours. The curtain was lifted. Half lifted; for the volcanic peaks and ravines overhead were still shrouded in pearly mystery (6)." The sense of movement which his scenes give is often the result of Douglas' awareness of the mists characteristic of the Mediterranean lands, especially in the early morning: "At this height the sea's horizon soars into the firmament smooth as a sheet of sapphire, and the eye never wearies of watching those pearly lines and spirals that crawl upon its surface, the paths of silver-footed Thetis. . . ."[5] The effect is seldom what one would call misty. It is more often, as in this passage in *South Wind*, an effect of clearly defined lines and masses moving across mosaics of bright color: "Sirocco mists rose upwards, clustering thickly overhead and rolling in billowy formations among the dales. Sometimes a breath of wind would convulse their ranks, causing them to trail in long silvery pennants across the sky and, opening a rift in their gossamer texture, would reveal, far down below, a glimmer of olives shining in the sunlight or a patch of blue sea, framed in an aureole of peacock hues (90)."

There is a note of unreality in these scenes—an artificial glow. The colors are a little too pure and the textures a little too glossy. There is perhaps too much dependence upon jewel and metal metaphors. But, if this descriptive technique is a trifle stylized, its effects are undeniably pleasing, perfectly suited to give the reader of a travel book the sort of heightened view he wishes to imagine or remember, and ideal for the artificial atmosphere of Nepenthe.

One of the few critics to attempt to analyze concretely the nature of Douglas' descriptive method is V. S. Pritchett. In his all-too-brief comments on Douglas' style in the *New Statesman* article, he made several significant points:

Very rarely does the poetic image appear in Douglas' descriptions; if it does it seems false, as when, for example, the precipices of Nepenthe are suddenly, in some unguarded personal note of excess, called "bastions of flame." If the sunset is described, as it is on Mr. Heard's memorable last evening on the island, Mr. Douglas obtains his results by dividing the experiment into three. First he observes the effect on the sea; then, when the sun goes down, the sudden colourlessness of the sky; at last he notes the transfer of colour to the sky. There is no messy literary palette here, nor is there anything like that personal, contemporary attempt to take the sunset on and off. Scientific observation, impersonal comment, are the means. This was Douglas' very original contribution to landscape in literature, and it comes from the mastery of a defect in temperament, a defect of heart. (307)

The poetic image does indeed often ring false in Douglas, and unfortunately instances are not quite so rare as Pritchett indicates. But there is a distinction to be made. Some of Douglas' best effects are obtained by metaphor; but these are concrete metaphors to which he turns for the exact rendering of some color or other specific detail when adjectives have failed him. However, when he attempts what might be called loosely a poetic effect, with a more complex image, perhaps a conceit or an allusion, it is often quite ordinary and sometimes even trite. He had a sharp eye and a fine facility with the language, but he was not a poet. Pritchett's point that Douglas' contribution—the impersonal note—is the result of his "mastery of a defect in temperament" is well taken.

We have already given some consideration to Douglas' ability to create atmosphere; but, since this matter is so closely connected with style, further comment is in order here. The creation of atmosphere is mainly a matter of choosing details which support the dominant feeling involved and of delineating these details with precision and immediacy so that a sense of reality is produced. As has been mentioned, the best travel writers seems to be those who are honest to their responses as they feel or remember them and are able to include in their descriptions those details which actually produced the impression. An example of a successful atmospheric effect is Douglas' impression of a favorite cellar cafe in Tunisia:

. . . within that windowless chamber, all is peace. Eternal twilight reigns, and your eyes must become accustomed to the gloom ere you can perceive the cobwebby ceiling of palm-rafters, smoke-begrimed and upheld by two stone columns that glisten with the dirt of ages. Here is the hearth, overhung by a few ancient pots, where the server, his head enveloped in a greasy towel, officiates like some high priest at the altar. You may have milk, or the mixture known as coffee, or tea flavoured in Moroccan style with mint, or with cinnamon, or pepper. The water-vessels stew everlastingly upon a slow fire fed with the residue of pressed olives. Or, if too poor, you may take a drink of water out of the large clay tub that stands by the door. Often a beggar will step within for that purpose, and then the chubby serving-lad gives a scowl of displeasure and makes pretence to take away the cup; but the mendicant will not be gainsaid— water is the gift of Allah! And, if so please you, you may drink nothing at all, but simply converse with your neighbour, or sit still and dream away the days, the weeks, the year. . . .

A spirit of immemorial eld pervades this tavern. Silently the shrouded figures come and go. They have lighted the lamp yonder, and it glimmers through the haze like some distant star.[6]

This description is made up largely of concrete detail, deftly chosen and simply but carefully described: the cobwebby and smoke-begrimed ceiling; the ancient pots on the hearth; the greasy towel around the server's head; the various drinks with specific tastes details; the serving lad and the beggar, along with their attitudes; and the silent moving figures. There are only a few metaphors, and these are neither remarkably fresh nor remarkably exact—the server is likened to a high priest at his altar, and the lamp is compared to a "distant star." There are likewise few abstract statements. The noting of a spirit of "immemorial eld," expressed with Douglas' note of quaintness, is a sort of keynote to the atmosphere; but it would be unsuccessful if that spirit were not evoked by the concrete details.

Another passage, a description of a Roman fountain, demonstrates the fact that rhythm and sound values can also play their part in Douglas' atmospheres:

That hoary, trickling structure—that fountain which has forgotten to be a fountain, so dreamily does the water ooze through obstructive mosses and emerald growths that dangle in dreamy pendants, like wet beards from its venerable lips—that fountain, untrimmed, harmonious, overhung by ancient ilexes: where shall a more reposeful spot be found? Doubly delicious after the turmoil and glistening sheen by the river bank. For the foliage of the oaks is such that it creates a kind of twilight, and all around lies the tranquillity of noon.[7]

The fountain is made to become a drowsy oasis amid the hot and bright tumult of Rome at midday, and the effect is produced again mainly with concrete detail. But also the slowed cadences of a rather ponderous sentence and the interplay of dentals, spirants, and nasals ("dangle in drowsy pendants") contribute in their mysterious way in effecting the desired mood, as do the onomatopoetic words ("trickle," "ooze"). The *t*'s, and *s*'s in "turmoil and glistening sheen" help make the outside world unpleasant. The passage ends with a falling away from the concrete, a practice common with Douglas.

It has been suggested that Douglas' style was adaptable to the various regions about which he wrote—that it took color from its setting. One feels that the style of *Together,* for instance, is subtly different from that of the other books—warmer and more intimate—perhaps because of the boyhood memories, but also because the Tyrol is not Italy. The colors in *Together* are still bright, but somehow they are more mingled than in the Italian books. Some of the iridescent quality which has been noted in Douglas' rendering of southern landscapes is missing. The gem metaphors are less frequent; form and line, less sharp; and the canvas, less orderly. There is a new luxuriance and fullness, a greater attention to odors, and a miasmic denseness of atmosphere. Here, for example, is a forest scene: "... the rank vegetation with its pungent odors, sweet and savage, has not yet been mowed down—a maze of tall blue gentians and mint and mare's-tale, and flame-like pyramids of ruby color, and meadowsweet, and the two yellows, the lusty and the frail, all tenderly confused among the mauve mist of flowering reeds (44-45)."

Similar qualities are to be found in the style of his English descriptions. When describing an English countryside—and he did this only incidentally—he seems to have incorporated into his prose some of the sense of oppression which he felt in England; the lushness, the dampness, and the smothering atmosphere: "England, with its dense vegetation, exhales a steamy heat after a shower at this season, and the sodden fields, with their sleek round trees, make the wanderer feel more than ever as though he were some caterpillar crawling about an interminable bed of lettuces. Yes, English nature is too green, and that green too monotonous in shade and outline; it is (*entre nous*) a salad landscape. . . ."[8] The preponderance of *s* sounds with which the passage opens establishes the attitude. Douglas' dislike of English scenery was another of the prejudices which he cantankerously exaggerated into a humorous effect. The salad metaphor was one of his favorites.

The style employed in the descriptions of Tunisian scenery in *Fountains in the Sand* gives the impression of being barer and more austere, in keeping with the nature of the region. As we have noted, Douglas' clear, dry style lent itself to the scenery of the barren lands. Here is a description of a palm grove which he contrasts with European woodlands:

Here are no quaint details to attract the eye; no gorgeous colour-patterns or pleasing irregularities of form; the frosted beauty of the scene appeals rather to the intelligence. Contrasted with the wanton blaze of green, the contorted trunks and labrinthine shadow-meanderings of our woodlands, these palm groves, despite their frenzied exuberance, figure forth the idea of reserve and chastity; an impression which is heightened by the ethereal striving of those branchless columns, by their joyous and effective rupture of the horizontal, so different from the careworn tread of our oaks and beeches. (213-14)

To be entirely accurate, one should realize that what appears to be an alteration of style is in the main simply Douglas' usual accuracy of observation and honesty of delineation. It is not the prose of this passage which "figures forth the idea of reserve and chastity" but the scene depicted. Details are fewer in this region and hence he includes fewer; colors and lines are unbroken, and he depicts them as such. Thus the impression of barrenness and austerity in the prose is created.

The riven cliffs of the Sorrentine coast and the nearby islands were the epitome of the romantic for Douglas. When he describes the sheer headlands of this region and the myriad color effects which changing light and shadow work upon them, he is more prone to the use of poetic imagery than elsewhere; and he strives, sometimes too hard, to reproduce the awe and mystery which these scenes held for him. He particularly liked to catch them silvered by moonlight, tinted by a setting sun, or shrouded in morning mists:

Have you never sailed under one of these precipices by moonlight? It is a picture that you see, not a palpable cliff of limestone; a picture that floats past you; some enormous, silver-tinted cartoon

conceived by William Blake, in the mad moments betwixt sleep and
waking. Those ancient, seared rocks, so familiar at noontide, have
put on strange faces since the moon rose. Their complexion has
waned to a livid splendour, and their wrinkles and bosses resolve
themselves into unsuspected designs—designs of spears and shields
and bastions and all the pomp of heraldry that melt away, under
incessant showers of gentle light from above, into other combinations
of form, ever new and so convincing, that at last the mind, weary of
riddles, surrenders to the stony enchantment and drifts along in a
calm disdain of reality.[9]

To Douglas' perceptive eye, natural scenes, even familiar ones,
were always undergoing kaleidoscopic changes of color and
light. Thus he seldom described merely a particular scene, but
rather a particular one at a certain time of day, lighted in a
particular way. The play of light and the subtle variations of
line and color which it produces are almost always present and
help lend to his pictures that effect of exactness which readers
find in them. For instance, a desert caravan may always be
in some ways picturesque, but for the most effective lighting
Douglas recommends that it be viewed at sunrise:

. . . whoever wishes for a rare impression of Oriental life must go
there [to Tozeur] before sunrise, and wait for the slow-coming dawn.
It is all dark at first, but presently a sunny beam flashes through the
distant palms, followed by another, and yet another—long shafts of
yellow light travelling through the murk; then you begin to perceive that the air is heavy with the smoke of extinguished camp-
fires and suspended particles of dust; the ground, heaving, gives birth
to dusty shapes; there are weird groans and gurglings of silhouetted
apparitions; and still you cannot distinguish earth from air—it is as
if one watched the creation of a new world out of Chaos.
    But even before the sun has topped the crowns of the palms, the
element of mystery is eliminated; the vision resolves itself into a
common plain of sand, authentic camels and everyday Arabs moving
about their business—another caravan, in short. . . .[10]

The shady recesses of a palm grove are most striking at midday:

Go . . . to the thickest part of the grove; then is the time; it must
be the prick of noon, for the slanting lights of morning and eve are
quite another concern; only at noon can one appreciate the incom-
parable effects of palm-leaf shadows. The whole garden is permeated
with light that streams down from some undiscoverable source, and its
rigid trunks, painted in a warm, lustreless grey, are splashed with
an infinity of keen lines of darker tint, since the sunshine, percolating

through myriads of sharp leaves, etches a filigree pattern upon all that lies below. You look into endless depths of forest, but there is no change in decorative design; the identical sword-pattern is for ever repeated on the identical background, fading away, at last, in a silvery haze.[11]

Sunsets and sunrises are a forte with Douglas. A fine, detailed rendition of a desert sunrise is the following:

After about five miles of comfortable wading through soft sand, I became aware of a ghostly radiance that hovered over the pallid expanse of the Chott. Abruptly, with the splendour of a meteor, the morning star shot up. Then the sun's disk rose, more sedately, at the exact spot where Lucifer had shown the way; and climbing upwards, produced a spectacle for which I was not prepared. For as it left the horizon, a counterfeit sun began to unroll itself from the true, as one might detach a pedal from a rose; at first they clung together, but soon, with a wrench, parted company, and while the one soared aloft, the image remained below, weltering on the treacherous mere. For a short while the flaming phantasma lingered firm and orblike, while the space between itself and reality grew to a hand's breadth; then slowly deliquesced. It gave a prolonged shiver and sank, convulsed, into the earth.

Light was diffused; the colour of daytime invaded the ground at our feet, flitting like some arterial rill through the dun spaces. Wonderful, this magic touch of awakening! It is the same swiftness of change as at sunset, when the desert folds itself to sleep, like some gorgeously palpitating flower, in the chill of nightfall; or rather, to use a metaphor which has often occurred to me, it hardens its features, crystallizing them into a stony mask, even as some face, once friendly, grows strangely indifferent in death.[12]

This description should be compared with the following picture of a sunset viewed from Blumenegg castle in Douglas' native Vorarlberg for the difference in atmosphere:

. . . the mossy floor has ceased to glow. Slanting sunbeams come filtered, lemon-tinted, through the beech-leaves out there; they spatter the fir-trunks with moon-like discs and crescents. . . . A soft tinkle of cow-bells, inaudible by day, floats up from the valley; even as we look on, those silvery patches begin to fade from the trees, and everything trembles in the witchery of dusk. Interplay of light and shade is ended. We feel no change, while darkness creeps up stealthily: only the voice of the torrent has grown louder and hoarser.[13]

Obviously one of the principal strengths of Douglas' descrip-

tion is the preciseness of his rendering of colors. Here his vocabulary, supplemented as it was by terminology from the natural
sciences, was helpful; and his metaphors, when kept restrained and concrete, were often apt and effective. His scientific
training is in evidence in his careful depiction of the hues of
vegetation. For example, in *Siren Land* there are these scrupu-
lous renderings of the color variations in the ilex and the eup-
horbia:

A few hectic tints there are, but one must know where to look for
them. If, in the early days of December, you happen to glance down
some of the gullies clothed in ilex, you will be surprised to see the
uniform green surface flecked with alien markings. This is the
flowering ash, companion of the ilex, about to cast its leaves; each
tree has a particular tint which it reproduces year after year at
this season; some are spectral grey, others straw-coloured, but the
most beautiful are the deep crimson whose effect, among the somber
holm-oaks, is exactly that of the red spots upon a blood stone.
(123-24)

. . . the tree-euphorbia . . . green all through the winter, it now
takes on every shade of colour in its annual deathagony. No two
bushes are tinted alike, not even when their roots are intertwined;
earthy and ghostly white, orange and brown and vermillion, from
coral pink to a rich burnished copper, from palest saffron to tawny
gold. The red kinds are visible from afar and often shine with a
lustrous iridescence, a rare freak of coquetry, like the *reflet métallique*
of Oriental pottery. (127)

Douglas' close observation of colors makes rivers seem like living things:

There is a dreary monotony in Italian rivers, once they have reached
the plain. They are livelier in their upper reaches. At Florence—where
those citron-tinted houses are mirrored in the stream—you may study
the Arno in all its ever-changing moods. The hue of rusty iron in
full spate, it shifts at other times between apple-green and jade,
between celadon and chrysolite and eau-de-nil. In the weariness of
summer the tints are prone to fade altogether out of the waves.
They grow bleached, devitalized; they are spent, withering away
like grass that has lain in the sun. Yet with every thunder storm on
yonder hills the colour sprite leaps back into the waters.[14]

The descriptions of sunsets are *tours de force* in the matter of
colors. This comparison of a north African sunset with a London

one demonstrates the part that colors play in the atmospheres Douglas creates.

I thought of the sunset this afternoon, as viewed from Sidi Mansur. They are fine, these moments of conflagration, of mineral incandescence, when the sober [sic] limestone rocks take on the tints of molten copper, their convulsed strata standing out like the ribs of some agonized Prometheus, while the plain, where every little stone casts an inordinate shadow behind it, clothes itself in demure shades of pearl. Fine, and all too brief. For even before the descending sun has touched the rim of the world the colours fade away; only overhead the play of blues and greens continues—freezing, at last, to pale indigo. . . .

And I remembered London at this sunset hour, a medley of tender grey-in-grey, save where a glory of many-coloured light hovers about some street-lantern, or where a carriage, splashing through the river of mud, leaves a momentary track of silver in its rear. There are the nights, of course, with their bustle and flare, but nights in a city are apt to grow wearisome; they fall into two or three categories, whose novelty soon wears off. How different from the starlit ones of the south, each with its peculiar moods and aspirations![15]

Douglas' proficiency as an amateur geologist was put to use in the depiction of cliff scenery: the closeness of his observations was born of genuine interest and is probably without parallel in popular literature. Here is a view of the cliffs of Ponza:

Improbale is the only word that expresses the effect upon the mind of its caverns opening upon the waves in pillared stateliness, like some dimly-lighted cathedral; of its precipices of lava and softer material that glow in the brightest hues of white, blood-red, and green; of pearl-grey and black and yellow. The singular thing is that these tints do not melt into one another by any gradations—they are as sharply defined as the various countries upon a coloured map. Improbable; dream-like; too strange, maybe, to please the imagination of everyday artists and poets. I had almost forgotten to mention the chief feature of this phantasmagoria—those stainless sheets of mauve and heliotrope, pure as a curtain of silk, which decend from vine-clad uplands down to the beach where fishermen sit mending their nets for the coming night's work.[16]

Ponza was, according to Douglas, the geological model for Nepenthe, and we may profitably compare the relatively objective picture of Ponza's cliffs just quoted with a passage from *South Wind,* where the materials are somewhat exaggerated and the effect is intensified. Here Douglas' virtuosity in the creation of atmosphere through tints, textures, and lines is shown at its unrestrained height:

He saw the bluffs of feathery pumice, the lava precipices—frozen cataracts of white, black, bloodred, pale grey and sombre brown, smeared over with a vitreous enamel of obsidian or pierced by oily, writhing dykes that blazed with metallic scintillations. Anon came some yawning cleft or an assemblage of dizzy rock-needles, fused into whimsical tints and attitudes, spiky, distorted, overtoppling; then a bold tufa rampart, immaculate in its beauty, stainless as a curtain of silk. And as the boat moved on, he looked into horrid dells which the rains had torn out of the loose scoriae. Gaping wounds, they wore the bright hues of corruption. Their flanks were blotched with a livid nitrous efflorescence, with flaring sulphur, unhealthy verdure of pitchstone, streaks of arsenical vermilion; their beds—a frantic maze of boulders.
He beheld this crazy stratification, this chaos of incandescent nature, met in a frame of deep blue sky and sea. It lay there calmly, like some phantasmagoric flower, some monstrous rose that swoons away, with upturned face, in a solar caress. (216-17)

The cliffs are not only made to seem alive; they are made to seem sensual, desirably evil, and somehow diseased.

In his description of natural scenery Douglas is given to the use of the rhetorical device known as the "pathetic fallacy"—attributing life to inanimate objects. This is, of course, a kind of implied metaphor; and, like any other metaphor, its success depends upon the appropriateness of the comparison and upon the amount and nature of the supplementary association that it brings to bear upon the object described. A large percentage of the examples that one might glean from Douglas' books would be perfunctory, often trite—the sun *leaps* into the sky, sunbeams *play* upon the heights, the river *catches* swimmers in its tawny coils, etc. Although uninteresting, these are unobtrusive and probably contribute to the general impression of vitality which Douglas seems to have given landscapes. But occasionally such figures rise above the ordinary to produce strong atmospheric effects. We have just seen an example in the description of the cliffs of Nepenthe. As a contrast to that passage, we may see how a description of waterspouts is given an unusually light touch by the use of the same device: "...for when the delirium is at its height, the clouds often descend and join the fun, tempting the waves to meet them halfway. When these waterspouts, careering distractedly over the waste, break, the clouds cling to what they can of the nether element and bear it away with them on their aerial voyages."[17] The individual touch and the atmospheric effect in this description of olive trees are obtained through the same device: "These trees are small in size, mere pigmies beside the writhing monsters of Spain and Greece and Apulia; their upper limbs are stretched in a nervous tension which is the despair of artists, but in those tumid roots there sits—to all appearances—a deep repose. Yet who can tell what passionate alchemy is astir in that subterranean laboratory, sustaining life and fashioning fruit through those scorching summer months, among stones that are often too hot to handle."[18]

III *Devices Exploited*

One of the most noticeable characteristics of Douglas' style is his use of epigrams. These are especially frequent in the fiction: *South Wind,* for instance, abounds in them. But they are to be found in the travel books as well, and *Good-bye to Western Culture* contains a great many, usually in the form of barbs aimed at the complacent middle class. Douglas' epigrams naturally reflect his points of view and his particular prejudices: "Leisure is the curse of the poor in spirit";[19] "... the profoundly divine is . . . profoundy uninteresting."[20] They are often ironic, sometimes with the irony of obviousness: "One should never pass for an imbecile, if one can help it,"[21] Sometimes there is bitter exaggeration: "Our Statute Book is growing into a sinister contrivance for the protection and conservation of fools."[22] Frequently they are paradoxical: ". . . to find a friend one must close one eye: to keep him—two";[23] "One may (or may not) respect people for their virtues, one loves them only for their faults."[24] Often they contain a homey sort of insight: "Justice is too good for some people, and not good enough for the rest;"[25] "Friends will share our joys, but every man is a solitary in his griefs."[26]

Richard Aldington considers Douglas' epigrams to be imitations of Oscar Wilde. He puts this criticism into the mouth of a French critic who, when challenged, points out specific examples from *South Wind.* The specific models from Wilde are not given.

"How many imitation Oscar swallows from *South Wind* do you want? Two? There is so much goodness in real life. Do let us keep it out of our books.' Three? 'To want a wife, Duchess, is better than to need one. Especially if it happens to be our neighbour's.' Four? 'Is it true that you used to say, in your London days, that no season was complete without a ruined home?' Five? 'When people cease to reflect they become idealists.' Six? 'I find everything useful and nothing indispensable. I find everything wonderful and nothing miraculous.' Seven? 'You are thinking of your own mother. You forget that you never see her. Any son can live with any mother under those circumstances.' Eight? 'Nothing ages a man like living always with the same woman.' Nine? 'Altogether the question that confronts me is not whether morality is worth talking about, but whether it's worth laughing at.' Ten? 'To feel self-righteous, or to feel sinful, is quite an innocent form of self-indulgence.' "[27]

It is difficult to establish the degree of indebtedness. Both writers flourished their wit and both were fond of paradox, and it is true that one cannot read the two simultaneously without being struck by similarities of thought and expression. However, that two writers who were close to being contemporaries should have had these characteristics in common should not seem strange. As has been pointed out, the ideas—the cynical hedonism and exaggerated individualism—were in the air; and paradox has always been a useful tool for outraging the Philistine. When Aldington says of Douglas, "even his best sayings lack the profundity of Wilde,"[28] he provokes one to wonder how the profundity of a witty paradox can be judged to so fine a degree. All things considered, Wilde's mind was probably superior to Douglas' in its scope—in ranges of sensitivity and insight that were closed to Douglas—but one could hardly establish this or any other sort of superiority on the basis of the comparative merit of their epigrams, especially when one is dealing with men who made a refined technique of affectation and pose. But an exhaustive comparison would no doubt disclose that, so far as epigrams are concerned, Wilde had higher polish and greater sophistication, as well as more inventiveness and ingenuity.

Douglas made a statement in *Siren Land* concerning the value of the epigram, and it tends to support an argument that the epigram was for him more an amusing and commercial stylistic device than a vehicle of wisdom: "Most of us have learned to distrust apophthegms [sic]. You may cram a truth into an epigram: the truth, never. Did not the stoics and epicureans, for example, rebuild the old striving under the title of 'virtue';

have not sane men lived sane lives from the beginning of the
world, despite their teachers? Thus every epigram requires a
foot-note (195)."

Douglas' most effective epigrams are ones that are not de-
tachable from their contexts. They are usually short, witty un-
derstatements, pregnant with implications that are obvious enough
from what precedes; but out of context they seem pointless.
The "they went" formula is an example in the book of that name,
as is "She was a good girl. She gratified her parents whenever
she could." And in *In the Beginning,* such simple phrases as
"They rose to the occasion," "trust Linus for that," or "O, Linus,
I like your way best" take on meaning only in relation to their
context.

Brief sentences often appear as paragraphs and often end in
ellipses (presumably to indicate an incompleted or interrupted
thought), a punctuation mark which Douglas overuses. Such
phrases also appear, sometimes very effectively, as clinching
sentences ending chapters. Thus in *They Went,* several chapters end with the title phrase. One chapter ends, "Queer
tales. . . . (132)" Another ends, "A portico was worth a preacher (212)."

There are idiosyncrasies in Douglas' style as there are in his
thought. Some of these are artistically effective, but most prove
tiring—at least to one who reads a good deal of his work within a short period. The two features which fall most clearly under
this heading are his use of archaisms and his habit of repetition.
Both are undoubtedly employed consciously with an eye to the
effect they will produce; both are, nevertheless, frequently over-
done. The archaisms are very definitely a mannerism, and for
the most part a harmless one. They contribute to the antique
and aristocratic flavor which Douglas liked. Such phrases as "I'
faith," "there's an end on't," and "hither he was wont to repair" are frequent. And many words are employed which are
no longer in common use except as conscious poeticisms: *yon,
ere, athwart, betwixt, anon,* and others. One chapter in *Siren
Land,* "On Leisure," exploits this sort of thing and proves amusing. In the pseudomythological novels it is not inappropriate;
and in *Paneros,* the collection of antique aphrodisiacs, it is perhaps almost demanded by the subject. In *Paneros* the style,
pseudoantique throughout, is reminiscent of Burton and of Sir
Thomas Browne.

Douglas' repetition is, at its best, successfully humorous. In

South Wind the repetition of certain catch phrases in connection with particular characters provides a part of the fun. It is a sort of *leitmotif* system. Bishop Heard's motif is his often repeated observation, "things were happening," a sort of periodic reiteration of the novel's theme. Freddy Parker's favorite comment, characterizing the futility of his existence, is "Something ought to be done." A mention of Miss Wilberforce often provokes the statement, "The dear lady was becoming quite a problem." There are also more extensive repetitions. For instance, in Chapter 3 there is a list of false reasons why Eames left England:

It was not true to say of this gentleman that he fled from England to Nepenthe because he forged his mother's will, because he was arrested while picking the pockets of a lady at Tottenham Court Road Station, because he refused to pay for the upkeep of his seven illegitimate children, because he was involved in a flamboyant scandal of unmentionable nature and unprecedented dimensions, because he was detected while trying to poison the rhinocerous at the Zoo with an arsenical bun, because he strangled his mistress, because he addressed an almost disrespectful letter to the Primate of England beginning "My good Owl"—or for any suchlike reason; and that he now remained on the island only because nobody was fool enough to lend him the ten pounds requisite for a ticket home again. (26)

In Chapter IX, when Eames once again becomes the focus of attention, another list occurs:

It was not true to say of Mr. Eames that he lived on Nepenthe because he was wanted by the London police for something that happened in Richmond Park, that his real name was not Eames at all but Daniels—the notorious Hodgson Daniels, you know, who was mixed up in the Lotus Club scandal, that he was the local representative of an international gang of white-slave traffickers who had affliliated offices in every part of the world, that he was not a man at all but an old boarding-house keeper who had very good reasons for assuming the male disguise, that he was a morphinomaniac, a disfrocked Baptist minister, a pawnbroker out of work, a fire-worshipper, a Transylvanian, a bank clerk who had had a fall, a decayed jockey who disgraced himself at a subsequent period in connection with some East-End mission for reforming the boys of Bermondsey and then, after pawning his mother's jewelry, writing anonymous threatening letters to society ladies about their husbands and vice-versa, trying to blackmail three Cabinet Ministers and tricking poor servant-girls out of their hard-earned wages by the sale of sham

Bibles, was luckily run to earth in Picadilly Circus, after an exciting chase, with a forty-pound salmon under his arm which he had been seen to lift from the window of a Bond-street fishmonger. (99)

The other novels also employ repetition in the form of formulas, but the practice is not adequately restrained. It often serves no purpose other than to produce monotony. The gods of *In the Beginning* are always saying, "We must know the truth. Call up the sun! Where may he now be wandering?" And when they catch the wind, they always cry: "Now for the fun. Catch him! Bottle him up! Roll him about! Where is he? . . . Oh, there he is!" *They Went* also suffers somewhat from the overuse of repetition. The great gong is always said to "shout when smitten." Everyone has "a reputation to keep up." Each time one of the Princess' lovers is doomed, the same formula appears: the Princess' boy announces the person and the Princess answers, "Indeed? Go to bed Harré."

> The devoted blue innocent, as usual, tripped off.
> As usual—ah, well!
> He went.

The formula "they went" appears more than a dozen times in the short book. One situation treated by a formula is given a different twist. Each evening, when the King reaches "high-water mark," he rises and calls out: " 'Bring hither a trumpet, straight or curved. This is music to make the world tremble. Let us blow a blast and see whether it sounds as of yore, when I used to summon my enemies—' " He then blows a blast, looks around, and asks gravely: " 'Now where is the enemy?' No enemy was ever to be seen. 'Skulking, as usual?' " This passage is repeated verbatim several times throughout the novel; but at the climax of the story, with the tension high and with Aithryn nearing the palace to obtain the key and destroy the city, the Queen inadvertently allows the King to drink too much, and he suddenly arises and announces: "Bring hither a strumpet—trumpet, straight or curved." When he says "Where is the enemy? Skulking as usual?" the door opens and the red-haired stranger enters.

Hardly a page of *They Went* is without some repetition, and long before one finishes the book, the formulas which were at first amusing have become tedious. Several critics have found this mannerism disturbing. Sherard Vines, finding the novel to contain too little substance to support such affected presentation, wrote: "Without a jewel to bite on, the machine that cuts lapidary wit, grinds the empty air (248)."

Among Douglas' other mannerisms are certain locutions, some of them old-fashioned, which appear again and again in his writings. "It stands to reason that. . . ." (followed by some strange idea which does not stand to reason at all); "Uphill work!"; "What next!"; and something "is worth" something—applied to things of ostensibly far different values ("A portico is worth a preacher").

Douglas had a few grammatical idiosyncrasies as well. He disliked the conjunction "but," which he called in *Late Harvest* "the most misused and debilitating mono-syllable in our language (42)," and he favored the use of *like* as a conjunction: "Nobody can manage it like she can" (*South Wind* [14]). His publishers tried to make changes, once changing "They cannot stand alone, like we could" to "They cannot stand alone, like us." Douglas was righteously indignant: "Who perpetrates these imbecilities, and why? Do they want to teach me English?"[29]

Something should be added to what has already been said about the style of *Good-bye to Western Culture*. This book is, as we have seen, ill-conceived and ill-tempered. The tone is one of shallow superiority and egotistical narrowness, and the invective which makes up a large part of the book is often blatant and trite. Constantine Fitzgibbon writes of *Good-bye to Western Culture*: "It seems to me the least satisfactory of his books, for the violence of the tone . . . (33)." And a typical review said, "The invective, utilizing such terms as 'stupidity,' 'vulgarity' . . . has little force behind it, and somehow neither bites nor stings."[30] The following passage is, unfortunately, typical: "Get out of Europe! Rectify your values while there is still flexibility in your mind, and learn to laugh at the flabby gibberings of our cultured classes and the comical bestiality of their inferiors, our nauseating politics and childish social ideals, our moral hypocrisy that breeds liars, the inquisitorial tyranny of our laws that breeds cowards, and certain absurd newspapers whose function consists in persuading us to attach importance to what is not worth thinking about. Get out of it (20-21)."

Nancy Cunard discloses the prejudiced admiration which flaws her book about Douglas when she describes *Good-bye to Western Culture* as "perceptive and exact, with never a trace of vagueness or looseness in thought or expression (7)."

CHAPTER 6

Conclusion: The Reputation

THE strangely varied and unusual body of writing which Douglas produced presents a challenge to anyone attempting to generalize concerning it. As a writer he defies being placed in a category, and certainly no general evaluation of his achievement is likely to meet with anything like complete agreement from his readers and critics. His reputation has undergone a decline since the 1930's; and, though it appears to remain substantial in England, it is at present a good deal less than assured in the United States, where he is known only for *South Wind*. During the 1920's and 1930's, he was a favorite with young intellectuals who were not much concerned to understand fully his personality or his thought. In America the young men who posed as Fitzgerald heroes and the young women who aspired to be Lady Brett Ashleys knew *South Wind* as a classical statement of the carefree amorality which they affected, often to hide genuine inner confusion. It has been said that, to Americans on the way to Europe, *South Wind* was the traveling companion that *Ulysses* was on the return trip.[1]

I *Influence*

The influence of *South Wind* in subject, technique, and attitude upon the younger writers of Douglas' day is well known. The sharply contrasted and specialized characters, the witty erudition, the lucid paganism, and the derisive attitude all appeared with some frequency. The practice of bringing together a group of characters with distinctive ideas in order to have them converse in a learned and satirical fashion became a familiar device. Aldous Huxley's *Crome Yellow*, which appeared in 1921, shows the influence clearly. Pelham Edgar writes of *Crome Yellow*: "It is inconceivable that its tone and movement would have been quite the same without its predecessor (227)." *Point Counter Point*, a more important novel, also has the clearly distin ishable types and the intellectual discussions, as well as the c al tone. The sardonic, brutal humor is to be found in

Evelyn Waugh, and the moral deliquesence appears in the work of a number of novelists. Compton Mackenzie wrote of the Capri group in *Vestal Fire,* and Rose Macaulay adopted important aspects of the tone and method of *South Wind.* One historian of the modern novel describes Rose Macaulay's work during the 1930's as containing "a broad sanity and a tendency to *épater le bourgeois,* witty observations, a sympathy with pagan values, and the realistic portrayal of a lost generation of doubting and diffident young people who were discovering a world in which there was no meaning, no order, no sense"[2]—all qualities which owe much of their popularity to *South Wind.* In some novels—*Staying With Relations, Going Abroad, I Would Be Private*—she included the tropical setting as well. Some of Douglas' views concerning the importance of the body and the inviolability of the individual may have influenced D. H. Lawrence, who once told Aldington that "his own father and Norman Douglas had been the two figures who seemed most to live out a natural joy in life."[3] So much did Douglas, the hearty pagan expatriate, catch the imagination of the younger generation of writers that he appeared as a character in several novels—as Scrogan in Huxley's *Chrome Yellow* and as Argyle in Lawrence's *Aaron's Rod.*

II *The Decline*

That Douglas' popularity did not persist is in great part due to the fact that he refused or was unable to give his readers another *South Wind.* Moreover, his ideas became less attractive as the period of disillusionment and skepticism of the 1920's and early 1930's gave way to a period of political ideologies. Douglas' views were antipathetic to the political left and also to the American social and political heritage. No writer of Douglas' persuasions is likely to find much popularity in times of emotionally considered ideologies, and Douglas' career covered a period which included two world wars and the inflamed patriotisms consequent upon them. Joseph Conrad had written him as early as 1905: "Don't forget, my dear fellow, that your point of view in general is the unpopular one. It is intellectual and uncompromising. This does not make things easier."[4]

Another factor in the decline of Douglas' reputation was the change that his writing underwent beginning in the late 1920's when the new note of bad temper entered his work. It is true that to see him as transformed suddenly from a carefree bohe-

mian to a cranky misanthrope is to exaggerate the change, for
the later books present no ideas or complaints that had not
been present all along. *Good-bye to Western Culture* merely
contained an oversized dose of his old venom unattenuated by
the features which made his travel books and novels palatable.
Likewise *They Went* and *In the Beginning* had thematic ideas
which had been present in *South Wind*, but these novels did
not have the sparkling atmosphere that provided the palliative
and indeed the center of interest in that book. Nor were they as
funny. Douglas' humor had become more sardonic and more
cruel: rather than laughing along with his audience, at society,
and at himself, he now tended to sneer at the world. Elizabeth
Wheatley noticed this change in 1932:

His last works indicate that he has reached a point of cold sanity
which borders perilously on insanity. I [sic] fact, one might, not un-
reasonably, think on reading *In the Beginning*, that the leaf had
fallen which turns the scale. In time past Douglas had a thousand
Protean shapes both terrible and sweet. He has become by the
stricture [sic] of time, and, one fears, of neglect, a stiffening figure,
sometimes negatively and peevishly ferocious. He is hardening into a grinning garden god, a battered Priapus. And still he stands alone,
superior in golden, Hellenic vitality. It is as if Priapus stood in a
glade of eternal sunshine.[5]

The Priapean aspect of Douglas' later work is an unhappy
subject. He had always attempted to demonstrate that sex was
one of the natural pleasures which life offers and as such should
be cultivated and exploited without undue concern for moralistic
restraints. But some of the passages in *In the Beginning*, like
many of the limericks which he collected, could have no possible
effect except to produce disgust. Several explanations suggest
themselves: the old desire to shock the puritanical had grown,
with Douglas' increasingly antagonistic attitude, less subtle
and less restrained. He was slashing out at his pious enemies.
Then too Douglas had apparently undergone a certain amount
of moral degeneration in the search for new sensations. Richard
Aldington implies that if the whole truth were known Douglas'
career would be seen as not unlike that of Huysman's Des Es-
seintes.

The increased bitterness and pessimism of Douglas' viewpoint, while it was not a qualitative change, was a perceptible
one. The same factors which produced the elegiac note we have

discussed are no doubt responsible for what some critics called a note of despair in his later books. The man who urges "consider your neighbor, what an imbecile he is," will probably always come to such an end unless he is able to continue enjoying this imbecility by never expecting anything more.[6] Cervantes and Dickens had such a perspective; and, if over-ripening brought discouragement, they were able to move in the direction of nostalgia or even of sentimentality. Their work has a greater degree of universality because of this accommodation. But Douglas, like Swift, had an uncompromising mind. He had the deep-seated strain of Humanism which few writers of the Western tradition are without and which persists whatever the contradictions taught by experience and reason. No one who really cared as little about humanity as Douglas claimed to care would bother making people laugh at their own foibles; and no one who cared so little would become so bitter.

Douglas saw man as essentially masochistic and, in part at least, hated him for it. His preoccupation with the physical, which began in a healthy humility before nature, made it difficult for him to conceive of purposes or goals beyond the tangible. It is impossible to determine the degree to which his early experiences with religion were responsible for these attitudes; but, whatever the cause, he apparently could not believe that human happiness was compatible with Christian morality. The kinds of·spiritual aspirations which are universal among civilized men at first amused him, then disgusted him; and the expedients and consolations with which he tried to "shore up the ruins" were at last not quite adequate. His sympathetic friend H. M. Tomlinson wrote: "Only in Ultima Thule is there escape for one who can see no health in us, and nothing to be done for us that we would not reject, his only solace an old memory of fellowship and goodwill, and the thought of the Grecian Urn.(78)

But Douglas' diminished reputation is not merely the result of a changed climate of opinion or of wounded public sensibilities; the books of his last few decades not only had the objectionable qualities already discussed, but were also less valuable artistically. His readers grew tired of reworked material, and it became evident that his reputation would have to stand on the early travel books and on the outdated *South Wind*. The result is that most of his books are now out of print, and he receives very little critical attention. Samuel Chew allots him an eighteen-line footnote in the comprehensive *Literary History of the English People,* edited by Albert Baugh. Louis Cazamian gives him a sentence in the Legouis and Cazamian *History of English Literature.* The historians of the novel do little more, and books on the modern novel ordinarily concern themselves more with Douglas' influence on other writers than with his books.

III *Satirist*

It has been suggested that this critical silence may be due to the fact that Douglas is difficult to fit into a category. Although some people regard him, probably correctly, as mainly a travel writer, it is inevitable in an age in which the novel is paramount that most of the reading public should remember him as a novelist. But *South Wind,* his principle contribution, is not in the mainstream of the tradition of the English novel and is difficult to discuss as a novel. It is, to be sure, in the tradition of the modern satire, one which includes such figures as Voltaire, Byron, Peacock, Butler, and Anatole France. And Douglas has been specificially compared to most of these writers. He has the Byronic scorn of middle-class hypocrisy; in *South Wind* he is strongly reminiscent of Peacock in his use of the conversational method, of erudition satirically presented, and of characters who are specialized intellectual types; some of his attitudes resemble those of Samuel Butler, who also attacked narrow Victorian religious and educational practices and feared the effects of modern technology; and Douglas' witty style and cynical tone invite comparison with Anatole France.

Satire is, in essence, a matter of attitude. The satirist measures humanity against an implicit ideal and finds it lacking. This statement would seem to be as true of Butler or Douglas as of Mandeville or Swift. Although the ideal may differ from writer to writer, it has usually—for the satirists of the tradition—involved reason and nature. These are large, vague terms which cannot be defined here—indeed the men who have employed them would not agree entirely on definitions—but it should serve our purpose to point out that the point of view from which satirists have traditionally considered life has been rationalistic, naturalistic (if we may use the term in a sense broad enough to include Deism), Humanistic, and Neoclassical. These writers have been disturbed at the Yahoo in man, and they have particularly deplored the hypocrisy and pretense with which he is inclined to regard himself—the way in which he pretends to live according to ideal standards but in reality lives according to selfish and superstitious ones. They have pleaded for honesty and realism, asking that men consider themselves for what they are. They have attacked "hybris" in its countless forms and have attempted to demonstrate that this is not, whatever the self-deluders may say, *"le meilleur des mondes possible."*

The platform upon which Douglas stood to view society and to strike at it—that is, the set of values according to which he judged man and found him lacking—I have attempted to establish in Chapter 2. It is an amalgam of naturalism, hedonism, and Epicureanism and is not readily reducible to a label. But it is sufficiently close to the general attitudes of the satiric tradition to allow the conclusion that Douglas is, in his thought at least, in that tradition. And in our age, when just as in the eighteenth century or any other great period of satire, men live for their own ends, the idealistic moral system of the Christian tradition seems to the unsympathetic eye entirely outmoded and absurd. With the X-ray vision of the satirist, which sees so readily through pretense and cant, Douglas reacted; and his reaction ranged at various times from Epicurean indifference to Swiftian bitterness. Between the two extremes lay derisive but not ill-humored laughter; and when this moderate response prevailed, he was at his satiric best.

IV *Thinker*

As a philosophical and critical thinker Douglas' contribution is slight. His ideas are neither original nor profound. However, they have their use as correctives and will probably continue to have. In an age of "Packaged answers"—Lawrence's sex and instinct, Hemingway's blood and courage, Eliot's Church and state—Douglas' frank acceptance of the tangible world and of the implications of empirical science may have helped open-minded readers to find a balance. Even his Nietzschean caste, as antithetical as it may be to some of the best in modern thought, should not be entirely wasted at a time when a sentimental cult of "the common man" is damaging educational and cultural standards. A modicum of intellectual flexibility should be proof against Douglas' eccentricities and extremes, and a little perspicacity cannot fail to find the germ of common sense that almost invariably informs his thinking. E. M. Forster's tribute may be overly kind, but is not entirely fallacious: ". . . he has done the human race an immense amount of good, and done it as a pleasure. That is his life's work."[7]

It is a mistake to think of Douglas as uncompromisingly intellectual. True, he disliked sentimentality; but he deplored metaphysical conjecture even more seriously and profoundly. The somewhat unexpected primitivism which he often displays is a protest against the intellectualization of humanity. What he stood for was *the fact*, and its immediate and sensitive apprehension and acceptance. The kind of thinking that he approved was the kind for which there is no more satisfactory term than "common sense." As an abstract thinker he had no very great strength. The best qualities of his writing are the result of clear feeling and are the qualities usually found in those writers who are called "Classical." He had the broad effect as against the subtle and illusive one, and he had the predominance of intellect over emotion. This last observation need not be considered contradictory to what has been said about Douglas' weakness as an abstract thinker. The intellectual quality which one associates with Neoclassical art, and hence with many satirists, need not imply depth of insight; it refers rather to keen critical wit, whether entirely sound or not, and to unity and consistency of conception. Thus, Douglas, although quick enough to apprehend facts and their relationships, was impatient with philosophical systems.

V *Modernist*

Norman Douglas also had little use for the kind of "feeling" involved in most modern poetry, in which he apparently often mistook complexity for poorly defined emotion or intentional obscurity. A passage in *Siren Land* about Greek sculpture throws light upon this attitude:

The Greek sculptor . . . demanded an instantaneous flash of comprehension. . . . For Greek art remained objective long after philosophy had gone the way of Plato, as we know from late masterpieces like the Nike of Samothrace and the Venus of Milo, which speak in clearest language to the beholder. The artist feels: the philosopher reasons, and reasoning, the latest and most delicately etched pencilling on the mind's surface, is the first to become blurred. Clear feeling will outlast clear argument, because it is older: the drunkard, who strips off the various layers in the order in which he has put them on, is an admirable illustration of this. Gorgias might grow grey in discussing problems of immortality; he might interpret them this way and that and never solve the knot; but if the Greek citizen remained for a moment in doubt as to the significance of a work of art, its purport was missed.

And nowadays?

Nowdays we are become somewhat metaphysical and subjective to these matters. The meaning of a picture or statue may not thrust itself upon us in this crude straightforward fashion; the morsel must be chewed before swallowed and relished only of the elect; prayer and fasting are requisite to initiate us into the mysteries which the master sought to express. It is all for the best, no doubt. Times are changed. The Greeks liked garlic. (228-29)

Despite Douglas' fundamental antipathy to modern literary practices, he had also an important affinity. He practiced an inclusiveness in his choice of subject and detail and in his ironically qualfied responses. The kind of compartmentalizing of life that modern critics complain of in the Victorian poets and that T. S. Eliot considers to have set in after the decline of Metaphysical poetry was unknown to Douglas. Nothing was "antipoetic" to him: his books contain colloquialisms, cliché, sterile technical terms, academic arguments, self-contradictions, ironies, realism, artificiality, burlesque—all somehow given unity by the tone and style. Indeed, he complained that the modern critical thinker too often fails to realize

that with the torrential inrush of new notions a contrary tendency has asserted itself—a tendency towards unity and simplification. His training has been too medieval to compass the elementary state of enlightenment which would enable him to perceive that an ichthyosaurus, and socialism, and an *etude* by Chopin—incongruous entities, once upon a time—are now seen to be emanations of a common principle, reducible to quite familiar and cognate laws of growth. Therefore he hates facts and allusions to them; they give him sensations of dyspepsia, because they refuse to fit into his distorted and incomplete little universe.[8]

Although Douglas' sensibility was doubtless limited, it was not dissociated. He recognized the kind of splintering that exists in modern thought, but he was too well satisfied with contemporary conceptions of physical reality and natural law to approve the sort of synthesis which is the resort of modern neo-orthodoxies. The road of an Eliot, an Auden, a Waugh, or a Huxley was closed to him. He blamed religion rather than looked to it for a synthesis.

Douglas must ultimately be thought of as part of the reaction against Victorian values which included the Pre-Raphaelites and the Aesthetes of the 1890's. Here, especially with such people as Oscar Wilde and George Moore, his closest affinities probably lay, in the cult of beauty and pleasure, and in exaggerated individualism. He formed, as has been suggested, a kind of link between the rebels of the 1890's and those of the twentieth century, bringing to the reaction a Hellenism which harked back to Matthew Arnold; and he gave it direction with a fearlessness and candor that others had not shown. He offered the Anglo-Saxon literary world an introduction to the Mediterranean point of view which was reminiscent of what Madame De Stael and Stendhal had offered the French or Goethe the Germans, and which bore fruits in the work of E. M. Forster, D. H. Lawrence, and Aldous Huxley.

VI *Humorist*

Douglas' erudition and his unorthodoxy have perhaps caused reader and critic alike to underemphasize a factor in *South Wind,* (and not in it alone) which Douglas considered central to its purpose and value—its comedy. When time has dulled the significance of *South Wind* as an influence on ideas and technique, critics may well come to feel that the important thing about the book is that it is funny. Many of the characters are humorous in the fashion of the Dickensian burlesque character, and the situations have the humor of the absurdly incongruous presented with straight face and in a pseudoserious scholarly tone. Douglas' comedy of erudition belongs with the finest. It is less obscure than, for instance, that of Rabelais or Sterne; and the warmth of a real affection for learning shines through the satire. His humor, while apparently subtle enough to elude the eye of the unsuspecting, is nevertheless as robust as that of *The Pickwick Papers* or of restoration comedy; and it is as daring, if not quite so frank, as that of *Gargantua* and *Pantagruel.* In our day Kingsley Amis might be thought of as, in this sense, in Douglas' tradition.

They Went and *In the Beginning* are in that unusual tradition of exotic, pseudolegendary prose which began with the Greek romance and includes such widely different books as *The Golden Ass, Rasselas, Candide,* and *Vathek.* Of course Douglas' mythological novels are both in a degree humorous, unlike many novels of this tradition. The closest parallels are in the writings of

Anatole France and James Branch Cabell, although Douglas' touch is somewhat heavier than theirs.

VII *Travel Writer*

Although *South Wind* is better known than anything else Douglas wrote, his travel books must be given consideration in any attempt to evaluate his contribution to letters. Fitzgibbon says of his major travel books: "Had he written nothing else, these five books would assure his fame as one of the great writers of English prose (24)." Among the important reputations for travel writing of our day, Douglas' stands high. His book on the desert regions is eclipsed only by the works of T. E. Lawrence and of Charles Doughty. While Douglas lacks what Naomi Lewis calls the "noble intensity" of his friend Doughty, his style and descriptive power are usually considered comparable and in fact rather similar. And although Douglas' book necessarily lacks the narrative interest found in the writings of T. E. Lawrence, his evocation of the atmospheres of the barren lands has as much to recommend it. In Italy he had illustrious predecessors and contemporaries, for English writers have been interested in Italy since the Renaissance. The list of Englishmen who have written descriptions of that country includes such names as Leigh Hunt, Mary Shelley, Charles Dickens, J. A. Symonds, George Gissing, and D. H. Lawrence. Douglas' advantages over these writers lay in his wider knowledge of the region, in the greater depth and versatility of his learning, and in his humor. D. H. Lawrence's work on Italy is highly regarded at present and the felicitous style and the poetic sensitivity which informs it will probably give it permanence. But Lawrence, who worked in a different dimension from Douglas, tended to interpret what he saw in terms of his distinctive beliefs and even to handle descriptive passages in such a way that the impression seems to have been imposed upon the scene rather than derived from it. Most reminiscent of Douglas' methods in the travel writings—and one feels that there must be a direct influence—are certain books of Lawrence Durrell, such as *Prospero's Cell* and *Reflections on a Marine Venus*.

VIII *Personality*

One factor that distinguishes Douglas' travel writing is the infusion of his strong and singular personality, and it is this presence more than any other factor that gives unity to his unusually diversified body of writing. Whatever the subject or the form, a book by Norman Douglas always contains the familiar Douglas approach—the leisurely pace, the gratuitous erudition, the disdainful sarcasm, the lush but precise descriptions. What the reader receives is not a photograph from life, nor is it merely vicarious experience of the places concerned. For Douglas' art is, as all art should be, a subtle refinement on life—a refinement accomplished to some extent through selection of detail and topic, but more significantly through the informing presence of his personality, through the application of his particular attitude toward existence. When the reader experiences reality filtered through Norman Douglas, he undergoes a Mediterraneanizing process similar to what Bishop Heard underwent on Nepenthe; and, if the effect is successful, he may achieve something of the sense of accommodation which the Bishop found—the "opening of moral pores." In any event, he is almost certain to have his sensibility modified in some direction.

The characteristics of Douglas' personality which gave the peculiar charm to his best writings infected a certain susceptible portion of his reading audience and apparently caused them to collect his books with a remarkable interest and loyalty. His first editions have a value more than commensurate to his fame and in many instances to the literary value of the books involved. These followers like the unusual lights that Douglas played upon any subject which fell to his hand, and they seem to have awaited eagerly the experience of finding some new subject so illuminated. But it was often the man they followed rather than the subject.

The magnetism of Douglas' personality caused critics and friends to compare him to Samuel Johnson, whose fame with some who admire him rests more upon his personality than upon his literary achievement. But Douglas had no Boswell to whom we might give credit. He provided his own commentary on his life and mind through the autobiographical element in his books, and there is little of his work, apart from the three novels, in which interest in the material is not shared with interest in the writer himself. But the autobiographical material is presented in such a way that Douglas' personality was in a sense a thing of his own creation and had something of the artificiality and refinement of the actual that he gave to other subjects. We see him as he chose to be seen. And, egotist that he was, he enjoyed this kind of carefully controlled public introspection. In *Late Harvest* he wrote:

... there is this advantage in the writing of books when they are in some measure autobiographical, describing events from early childhood onwards: instead of being confused memories they are authentic documents which allow a man to live his life over again and cast his thoughts backwards with assurance. There is nothing vague about a written record. Such an author, reading once again what he has written and revisiting with some twinges of melancholy certain scenes of the past, is in position to come to a definite understanding with himself whenever so disposed; he can praise or blame to his heart's content. (10)

Thus Douglas was not willing to allow vagueness in his own conception of himself or in his readers' conception. The personality which he created, while it is neither complete nor very deep, is not vague. It may be idealized, but—and this is probably fortunate—it is idealized in terms of his own values rather than in those of the general reading public.

Had it not been for Douglas' egocentrism, his writing would have been different—doubtless more systematic in approach, more qualified in tone, and considerably more objective. As Frank Swinnerton suggests, "Perhaps a greater and less self-sufficient man could have brought scholarship less desultorily and more universally to book (142)." But, on the other hand, we should not have had the personality, which in the last analysis may be of more interest to literature-loving posterity than a number of the more detached studies which Douglas might have produced.

IX *Stylist*

As has been frequently pointed out, Douglas' greatest power lay in his prose style and in his descriptive power. Nothing needs to be added to what has already been said, concerning these matters, except to point out that, if Douglas' prose had not been the lucid and balanced instrument that it was, his other achievements would have been negligible. It won a place in English letters for a man who was otherwise only an erudite dilettante and pleasure lover with a keen but rather rigid mind. With his gift of expression Douglas remains a fascinating anachronism, an "amateur" *par excellence,* a literary figure who looks both backward and forward from an age which he never dominated but which he in many ways defined.

Notes and References

The following abbreviations will be used throughout the notes, and the editions shown are those referred to by the page numbers in the text and in the notes. Bibliographical data not included in the notes can be found in the bibliography.

FITS *Fountains in the Sand.* London: Martin Secker, 1921.
GTWC *Good-bye to Western Culture.* New York: Harper and Brothers, 1930.
LH *Late Harvest.* London: Lindsay Drummond, 1946.
LB *Looking Back.* New York: Harcourt, Brace, 1933.
OC *Old Calabria.* New York: Harcourt, Brace, 1956.
SL *Siren Land.* London: Penguin, 1948.
SW *South Wind.* New York: Dodd, Mead, 1925.

Preface

1. Introduction to *Venus in the Kitchen,* p. viii.

Chapter One

1. "Profile in Sunlight," p. 164.
2. *Pinorman* (London, 1954), *passim.*
3. *Together* (New York, 1923), p. 83. Subsequent references will be to this edition.
4. *Ibid.,* p. 130.
5. *Ibid.,* p. 57.
6. *LB,* p. 41.
7. Quoted in Edward McDonald, "The Early Works of Norman Douglas," *Bookman* (American), LXVI (September, 1927), 43.
8. *Pinorman,* p. 63.
9. *LB,* p. 168.
10. Quoted in Edward McDonald, *A Bibliography of Norman Douglas* (Philadelphia, 1927), p. 27.
11. *Ibid.,* p. 25.
12. Constantine Fitzgibbon, *Norman Douglas: A Pictorial Record* (London, 1953), pp. 17-18. It is difficult for the layman to judge the scientific value of these early writings, but McDonald is probably correct in his judgment that they "bespeak the en-

thusiastic neophyte rather than the regularly ordained priest of science." (*Bookman*, p. 44.)

13. *Pinorman*, pp. 60-61.
14. *Bookman*, pp. 44-45.
15. In Nancy Cunard, *Grand Man* (London, 1954), p. 268.
16. Muriel Draper, "Buffetings in a South Wind: Some Memories," *Harper's Magazine*, CLVI (April, 1924), 568.
17. *Pinorman*, pp. 59-60.
18. *New Statesman and Nation*, XLXIII, 69.
19. *LB*, p. 19.
20. *Ibid.*, p. 45.
21. *Pinorman*, p. 67.
22. Giuseppi Orioli, *Adventures of a Bookseller* (New York, 1938), p. 264.
23. *LH*, pp. 74-75.
24. Quoted in McDonald, *Bibliography*, p. 68.
25. *LH*, p. 73.
26. McDonald, *Bookman*, p. 42.
27. Quoted in McDonald, *Bibliography*, p. 24.
28. J. H. Retinger, *Joseph Conrad and His Contemporaries* (London 1943), p. 77.
29. Letter of April 25, 1905, in *Joseph Conrad: Life and Letters,* edited by G. Jean-Aubry (New York, 1927), II, 16.
30. Robin Douglas, "Ah, There You Are," *Virginia Quarterly Review*, XVI (October, 1940), 575.
31. R. W. Flint, "Norman Douglas," *Kenyon Review*, XIV (Autumn, 1952), 663.
32. Quoted in McDonald, *Bibliography*, p. 29.
33. Letter of August, 1911, in *Life and Letters*, II, 133.
34. *Pinorman*, p. 148.
35. *LB*, p. 256.
36. A correspondence regarding this matter appeared in *The Bookseller* in 1943. A short article called "International Copyrights: the Case of *South Wind*" appeared in the issue of February 18 (p. 84), quoting the last paragraphs of Douglas' introduction to the 1942 edition in which he complained about having received no royalties on the popular Modern Library edition. A reply by Bennett Cerf was printed later (April 29, 1943, pp. 340-42), pointing out that Douglas had sold Random House the publishing rights for *Summer Islands* in 1931 for a hundred pounds but had also sold them to an English publisher who intended to produce a cheap edition. Random House complained to Douglas, who answered that it was "none of their business." They then stopped paying courtesy royalties on *South Wind*, which fell under the old copyright laws and was actually in the public domain in the United States. An eighteen-line letter from Douglas in answer to Cerf's also appears, along with editorial remarks

Notes and References

which support Douglas and claim that his act of reselling was a common practice countenanced by other publishers.

37. William Alexander Percy, introduction to *Birds and Beasts of the Greek Anthology* (New York, 1929), p. ix.
38. *Joseph Conrad and His Circle* (New York, 1935), p. 97.
39. *Alone* (London, 1921), p. 46. Subsequent references will be to this edition.
40. *Pinorman*, p. 48.
41. Orioli, p. 238.
42. D. H. Lawrence, "The Portrait of M. M.," in Alexander Woollcott, *Woollcott's Second Reader* (New York, 1937), pp. 156-57.
43. *Ibid.*, p. 161.
44. *Ibid.*, p. 225.
45. *LH*, p. 4.
46. *Pinorman*, p. 179.
47. In *Experiments* (New York, 1925), p. 253. Subsequent references will be to this edition.
48. "The Late Mr. Maurice Magnus," *New Statesman*, XXVI (February 20, 1926), 579.
49. "Norman Douglas and Calabria," *Atlantic Monthly*, CLXIII (June, 1939), 757.
50. *Outlook*, CXLIII (January 6, 1926), 34.
51. *LH*, p. 17.
52. *GTWC*, p. 4.
53. Benjamin Stolberg, "Au Revoir, Mr. Douglas!" *Nation* (American), CXXXI (October, 1930), 351.
54. John Davenport, "Norman Douglas," *Atlantic Monthly*, CXCIV (September, 1954), 74.
55. *Pinorman*, p. 72.
56. Kenneth Macpherson, "A Day," in *Grand Man*, p. 261.

Chapter Two

1. R. M. Dawkins, *Norman Douglas* (London, 1952), p. 9.
2. Cunard, p. 8.
3. *Alone*, p. 221.
4. Introduction to *Norman Douglas: A Selection from his Works* (London, 1955), p. 15.
5. *SL*, p. 31.
6. *Selections*, p. 323.
7. "Cold Comfort," *English Review*, XIII (February, 1913), 455.
8. *Ibid.*, pp. 455-56.
9. *OC*, p. 277.
10. *GTWC*, p. 110-11.
11. *Ibid.*, p. 108.
12. "Aspects of Russia," *English Review*, XX (January, 1915), 245.
13. *SL*, p. 120.
14. *OC*, p. 328.

15. *Ibid.*, p. 327.
16. *SL*, note to p. 176.
17. Dawkins, p. 17.
18. *Three Philosophical Poets* (Garden City, New York, 1953) pp. 36-37.
19. Dawkins, p. 51.
20. *LH*, p. 41.
21. *OC*, note to p. 131.
22. "Going South in Italy," *Living Age*, CCCII (September 13, 1919), 684.
23. Quoted in Dawkins, p. 32.
24. *Twentieth Century*, CLI, 364.
25. *SL*, p. 63.
26. *Atlantic Monthly*, CXCIV, 72.
27. "Portrait," p. 155.
28. *London Times Literary Supplement*, August 27, 1954, p. 545.
29. *SL*, p. 206.
30. *GTWC*, p. 160.
31. Quoted in Davenport, *Twentieth Century*, CLI, 367.
32. *LH*, author's note to the second impression.
33. *Ibid.*, p. 57.
34. *SL*, p. 201.
35. *New Statesman and Nation*, XLVIII, 164.
36. Pritchett, p. 308.
37. "Portrait," pp. 158-59.
38. *Alone*, p. 119.
39. *OC*, p. 130-31.
40. *LB*, p. 197.
41. *New Statesman and Nation*, LXVIII, 164.
42. *The Georgian Literary Scene: 1910-1935* (New York, n.d.), p. 138.
43. *GTWC*, p. 24.
44. *Together*, p. 175-76.
45. *Ibid.*, p. 57.
46. "A Spasm of Lucidity," *Saturday Review of Literature*, VII (November 22, 1930), 359.
47. Douglas' position on the matter of *work* was not entirely consistent. Apparently *work* was desirable for some elements of society, but not for others. He once said, "The man who speaks to me of work is my enemy." His allegiance to Turkey Rhubarb, however, was unwavering.
48. *Together*, p. 231.
49. Cited in Dawkins, p. 32.
50. "Aspects of Russia," pp. 245-46.
51. "Cold Comfort," p. 460.
52. Saxon Salgood, *New York Times Book Review*, September 7, 1930, p. 1.

53. *LH,* p. 71
54. Translated by Helen Zimmer, in *The Philosophy of Nietzsche* (New York, 1927), pp. 429-30.
55. Discussed in Edouard Roditi, "The Ethics of the Dandy," in *Oscar Wilde* (New York, 1947).
56. *Pinorman,* p. 135.
57. *New Republic,* October 22, 1930. Reprinted in *Shores of Light* (New York, 1952), p. 485-91.
58. *SL,* p. 55.
59. Cunard, p. 108.
60. "Judaism and Paganism: An Imaginary Conversation with Norman Douglas," *Menorah Journal,* X (August, 1924), 327-32. See also Louis Golding, "Mr. Douglas and Mr. Golding." *Menorah Journal,* XII (December, 1926), 635-39.
61. *OC,* p. 48.
62. *Alone,* p. 48.
63. *SW,* p. 400.
64. *SL,* p. 194.
65. *SW,* pp. 322-23.
66. Cited in Cunard, p. 41.
67. *The Greeks and Their Gods* (Boston, 1950), p. 132.
68. *SL,* p. 125.
69. Davenport, *Twentieth Century,* CLI, 364.
70. In *Three of Them* (London, 1930), p. 22. Subsequent references will be to this edition.
71. *SL,* p. 16.
72. *Ibid.,* p. 194.
73. *OC,* p. 131.
74. *Three of Them,* p. 33.
75. *Norman Douglas,* (New York and London, 1931, revised 1952), p. 30.
76. *Paneros* (London, 1931).
77. *Pinorman,* p. 209.
78. *Forces in Modern British Literature* (New York, 1947), p. 373.
79. Review of *A Boy's Will* in *English Review,* XIV (June, 1913), p. 373. Reprinted in *Experiments.*
80. *Experiments,* p. 114.
81. Harold Acton, *Memoirs of an Aesthete* (London, 1948), p. 385.
82. *Three of Them,* p. 82.
83. *OC,* p. 176
84. *Alone,* p. 95.
85. *Ibid.,* p. 113.
86. Introduction to *Selections,* pp. 19-20.
87. *Experiments,* p. 225.
88. Charles Duff, "A Letter About Norman Douglas," in Cunard, p. 247.
89. Muriel Draper, *Harper's,* CLVI, 565.

90. (1927).
91. *Experiments,* p. 19.
92. *Ibid.,* p. 115.

Chapter Three

1. Quoted in *LB,* p. 350.
2. *OC,* p. 1.
3. Ferninand Gregorovius (1821-91) was a German historian whose principal work was his *Geschichte der Stadt Rom im Mittelalter* (1859-72). The travel book to which Douglas refers is probably *Wanderjahre in Italien* (1853), Vol. III, which treats southern Italy.
4. Cited and discussed in Dawkins, pp. 62-63.
5. *Pinorman,* p. 149.
6. *A Century of the English Novel* (New York, 1925), p. 462.
7. "Vintage: 1912," *English Review,* XIII (December, 1912), 121.
8. July 4, 1952, p. 430.
9. "Modern Minstrelsy," *English Review,* IX (January, 1913), 263.
10. *English Review,* XIV (June, 1913), 505.
11. *SL,* p. 176.
12. *FITS,* pp. 169-71.
13. *Atlantic Monthly,* CLXIII, 759.
14. London, 1921, prefatory letter to third impression. Subsequent references will be to this edition.
15. *Pinorman,* p. 200.
16. *Ibid.,* p. 61.
17. *Alone,* pp. 233-34.
18. "An Unconventional Traveler," *New York Times Book Review,* December 24, 1922, p. 9.
19. *OC,* p. 356.
20. *Experiments,* pp. 124-25.
21. Quoted in Swinnerton, p. 139.
22. Percy, p. xiii.
23. Quoted in Cecil Woolf, "A Bibliographical Note," in Cunard, p. 268.
24. *Pinorman,* pp. 159-60.
25. Quoted in McDonald, *Bibliography,* pp. 28-29.
26. Woolf, in Cunard, p. 268.
27. *Pinorman,* p. 53.
28. "Modern Minstrelsy," pp. 259-60.

Chapter Four

1. Letter of February 29, 1908, in *Life and Letters,* II, 68.
2. Arthur Eckersley, *English Review,* XXV (August, 1917), 189.
3. *Pinorman,* pp. 139-40.
4. This view of the structure of *South Wind* is in part suggested by Herbert Gorman, *New York Times Book Review,* February

8, 1925, p. 2.
5. New York, 1927.
6. "Norman Douglas," *Sewanee Review*, XL (January, 1932), 64.
7. New York, 1933.
8. Douglas discussed the models for these characters in *Looking Back* (p. 121 and pp. 342-43) and in the introduction to the Modern Library edition of *South Wind* (p. vi).
9. *Pinorman*, p. 109.
10. Gorman, p. 2.
11. *LH*, p. 43.
12. II (October 8, 1920), 471.
13. XV (October 2, 1920), 706.
14. *Nation and Athenaeum*, XLIII (September 22, 1928), 795.
15. LIII (May 21, 1921), 249.
16. H. W. Boynton, *Weekly Review*, IV (April 30, 1921), 121.
17. *New Statesman*, XV, 706.
18. *In the Beginning* (New York, 1929), p. 152. Subsequent references will be to this edition.
19. L. P. Harley, *Saturday Review* (London), CXLVI (September 22, 1928), 365.
20. LV (June 6, 1928), 945.
21. Leonard Bacon, "Norman Douglas' Latest," *Saturday Review of Literature*, IV (June, 1928), 945.
22. *SW*, p. 218.
23. In *Experiments*, pp. 20-21.
24. *LH*, p. 22.
25. CXLI (September 18, 1928), 340.
26. *Bookman*, p. 378.

Chapter Five

1. *Pinorman*, p. 62.
2. Quoted in *London Times Literary Supplement*, July 4, 1952, p. 429.
3. *English Review*, XII (November, 1912), 665.
4. *Nation and Athenaeum*, XXXVIII (December 5, 1912), Supplement, p. 38.
5. *SL*, p. 29.
6. *FITS*, pp. 57-60.
7. "Roman Incidents and Impressions," *Travel*, XXXVIII (October, 1922), 25-26.
8. *SL*, p. 123.
9. *Ibid.*, p. 122.
10. *FITS*, pp. 212-13.
11. *Ibid.*, p. 213.
12. *Ibid.*, pp. 220-21.
13. *Together*, pp. 80-81.
14. "Going South in Italy," p. 686.

15. *FITS*, pp. 59-60.
16. "Islands of Oblivion," in *LH*, 95.
17. *SL*, pp. 49-50.
18. *Ibid.*, p. 28.
19. *SL*, p. 207.
20. *Ibid.*, p. 37.
21. *Alone*, p. 198.
22. *GTWC*, p. 177.
23. *SW*, p. 131.
24. "Going South in Italy," p. 684.
25. *GTWC*, p. 180.
26. *SW*, p. 153.
27. *Pinorman*, pp. 132-33.
28. *Ibid.*, p. 145.
29. *LH*, p. 24.
30. Charner Perry, *International Journal of Ethics*, XLI (January, 1931), p. 272.

Chapter Six

1. H. T. Webster, "Norman Douglas: A Reconsideration," *South Atlantic Quarterly*, XLIX (April, 1950), 226.
2. William C. Frierson, *The English Novel in Transition: 1885-1940* (Norman, Oklahoma, 1942), p. 256.
3. Quoted in Flint, p. 665.
4. Letter of October 18, 1905, in *Life and Letters*, II, 24.
5. P. 57.
6. Robert Lynd, *Books and Authors* (New York, 1923), p. 292.
7. *New Statesman and Nation*, V (May 27, 1933), 692.
8. "Vintage: 1912," p. 130.

Selected Bibliography

PRIMARY SOURCES

1. Books. Only first editions, English and American, are shown except when subsequent editions include revisions or new introductions by the author.

Contribution to an Avifauna of Baden. Privately printed in London, 1894. An essay reprinted from the *Zoologist* (May, 1894).

Report on the Pumice Stone Industry of the Lipari Islands. London: The Foreign Office, 1895. An official report to Parliament.

On the Darwinian Hypothesis of Sexual Selection. Privately printed in London, 1895. An essay reprinted from *Natural Science* (November and December, 1895).

Unprofessional Tales by "Normyx" (pseudonym). Privately printed in London, 1901. Short stories written in collaboration with his wife Elsa Fitzgibbon.

Capri studies (1904-15). Privately printed, parts 1, 2, 7, 9, and 10 in London, parts 3-6, and 8 in Naples.

1. *The Blue Grotto and Its Literature* (1904)
2. *The Forestal Conditions of Capri* (1904)
3. *Fabio Giordano's Relation of Capri* (1906)
4. *The Lost Literature of Capri* (1906)
5. *Tiberius* (1906)
6. *Saracens and Corsairs in Capri* (1906)
7. *The Life of the Venerable Suor Serafina di Dio* (1907)
8. *Some Antiquarian Notes* (1907)
9. *Disiecta Membra* (1915)
10. *Index* (1915)

Collected and reprinted as *Capri: Materials for a Description of the Island.* Florence: G. Orioli, 1930.

Siren Land. London: J. M. Dent, 1911; New York: E. P. Dutton, 1911; revised edition, London: Martin Secker, 1923. Travel (southern Italy).

Fountains in the Sand: Rambles Among the Oases of Tunisia. London: Martin Secker, 1912; New York: Dodd, Mead, 1921; 3rd edition, revised, Harmondsworth: Penguin, 1944. Travel.

Old Calabria. London: Martin Secker, 1915; New York: Houghton Mifflin, 1915; New York: Modern Library, 1927; with a new introduction, New York: Oxford, 1938. Travel.

London Street Games. London: The St. Catherine Press, 1916; revised, Chatto and Windus, 1931. Catalog with descriptions, comments, and digressions.

South Wind. London: Martin Secker, 1917; New York: Dodd,

Mead, 1918; with new introduction, New York: Modern Library, 1925; revised with introduction, London: Secker and Warburg, 1946. Novel.

They Went. London: Chapman and Hall, 1920; New York: Dodd, Mead, 1921. The third impression (1921) has a discussion of the novel by Douglas in the form of a prefatory letter. Pseudolegendary novel.

Alone. London: Chapman and Hall, 1921; New York, R. M. McBride, 1922. Travel (Italy).

Together. London: Chapman and Hall, 1923; New York: R. M. McBride, 1923. Travel (the Tyrol).

Experiments. London: Chapman and Hall, 1925; New York: R. M. McBride, 1925. Also privately printed in Florence, 1925. Essays and reviews, largely from the *English Review.* Includes, among others, "Arabia Deserta" (on Doughty), "Intellectual Nomadism" (on Isabella Eberhardt and Marie Bashkirtseff), "A Mad Englishman" (on Charles Waterton), and *D. H. Lawrence and Maurice Magnus* (a reply to Lawrence's introduction to *Memoirs of the Foreign Legion* by Maurice Magnus).

In the Beginning. London: Chatto and Windus, 1928; New York: John Day, 1928. Privately printed in Florence, 1927. Pseudomythological novel.

Birds and Beasts of the Greek Anthology. London: Chapman and Hall, 1928: New York: Jonathan Cape and Harrison Smith, 1928. Privately printed in Florence, 1927. Catalog and commentary.

Some Limericks. Privately printed in Florence, 1928, and often pirated. There were, apparently, some authorized editions, but the question is complex.

How About Europe? Some Footnotes on East and West. London: Chatto and Windus, 1930; New York: Harper and Brothers, 1930. (American edition was called *Good-bye to Western Culture.*) Privately printed in Florence, 1929. A commentary and polemic prompted by Katherine Mayo's *Mother India* (1927).

Three of Them. London: Chatto and Windus, 1930. Includes *One Day* (a travel piece about Greece originally published in France, Chapelle Réanville, 1929), *Nerinda* (a short story from *Unprofessional Tales*), and *On the Herpetology of the Grand Duchy of Baden* (a monograph previously published in London, 1894, reprinted from the *Zoologist of* 1891).

Paneros: Some Words on Aphrodisiacs and the Like. London: Chatto and Windus, 1931; New York: R. M. McBride, 1931. Privately printed in Florence, 1930. Essay in pseudoarchaic style.

Summer Islands: Ischia and Ponza. London: Desmond Harmsworth, 1931; New York: Colophon, 1931. Travel.

Selected Bibliography

Looking Back: An Autobiographical Excursion. London: Chatto and Windus, 1933; New York: Harcourt, Brace, 1933. Autobiographical notes and comments with vignettes of various personalities.

An Almanac. London: Chatto and Windus; Secker and Warburg, 1945. Privately printed in Lisbon, 1941. Quotations from his works selected for each day of the year.

Late Harvest. London: Lindsay Drummond, 1946. Comments on his books—autobiographical and bibliographical.

Footnote on Capri. London: Sidgwick and Jackson, 1952. Comments on photographs by Islay Lyons.

Venus in the Kitchen or Love's Cookery Book by Pilaff Bey (pseudonym), with an introduction by Graham Greene. London: Heinemann, 1952; New York: Viking, 1953. A collection of exotic aphrodisiac recipes, partially the work of Orioli.

Norman Douglas: A Selection from his Works. Selected and introduced by D. M. Low. London: Chatto and Windus; Secker and Warburg, 1955. A full and useful selection with a valuable introduction.

2. Periodical publications. Most of Douglas' important periodical publications were incorporated into one or another of his books, where they are more readily accessible. But several of the more significant essays from the *English Review* were never collected and these are listed here.

"Vintage: 1912," XIII (December, 1912), 121-33.
"Modern Minstrelsy," XIII (January, 1913), 255-64.
"Cold Comfort," XIII (February, 1913), 454-63.
"Aspects of Russia," XX (January, 1915), 235-49.

SECONDARY SOURCES

1. Bibliographies.

McDonald, Edward D. *A Bibliography of Norman Douglas.* Philadelphia: The Centaur Book Shop, 1927. Contains valuable notes by Douglas.

Woolf, Cecil. *A Bibliography of Norman Douglas.* London: Rupert Hart-Davis, 1954.

2. Studies.

Aldington, Richard. *Pinorman: Personal Recollections of Norman Douglas, Pino Orioli, and Charles Prentice.* London: Heinemann, 1954. Personal reminiscences and criticism, mainly unsympathetic. The title is a portmanteau of Norman and Pino.

Cunard, Nancy. *Grand Man: Memories of Norman Douglas.* London: Secker and Warburg, 1954. Personal reminiscences and criticism, adulatory in tone. Includes appreciations by Victor Cunard, Harold Acton, Charles Duff, Arthur Johnson, and Kenneth Macpherson, and a bibliographical note by Cecil Woolf.

Davenport, John. Introduction to *Old Calabria*. New York: Harcourt, Brace, 1956. A valuable biographical and critical essay.

Dawkins, R. M. *Norman Douglas*. London: Rupert Hart-Davis, 1952. First edition, Florence, 1933, under the pseudonym R. MacGillivray. A brief (88 pages) critical study with one of the more thorough studies of Douglas' thought. Sympathetic.

Fitzgibbon, Constantine. *Norman Douglas: A Pictorial Record*. London: The Richards Press, 1953. A brief general study (35 pages) with seventeen plates. Sympathetic.

Greenlees, Ian. *Norman Douglas*. London: Longmans, Green, for the British Council and the National Book League, 1957. A useful general study with a selected bibliography.

Low, D. M. Introduction to *Norman Douglas: A Selection from His Works*. London: Chatto and Windus; Secker and Warburg, 1955. A critical study (16 pages) notable for its objectivity and insight.

Macpherson, Kenneth. *Omnes Eodem Cogimur*. Privately printed, 1953. A memorial tribute.

Tomlinson, H. M. *Norman Douglas*. London and New York: Harper and Brothers, 1931. Revised, 1952. A brief general study, personal and sympathetic.

3. Articles:

Among the numerous periodical articles, mostly reviews, the following are suggested as the most general and most useful.

Davenport, John. "Norman Douglas," *Twentieth Century*, CLI (April, 1952), 359.

——. "Profile in Sunlight," *New Statesman: and Nation*, XLVIII (August 7, 1954), 164.

——. "Norman Douglas," *Atlantic Monthly*, CXCIV (September, 1954), 69.

Flint, R. W. "Norman Douglas," *Kenyon Review*, XIV (Autumn, 1952), 660.

Gorman, Herbert. "Norman Douglas, Novelist and Master of Prose," *New York Times Book Review*, February 8, 1925, p. 12.

London Times Literary Supplement, July 4, 1952, p. 429.

Pritchett, V. S. *New Statesman and Nation*, XLIII (March 15, 1952), 307.

Webster, H. T. "Norman Douglas: A Reconsideration," *South Atlantic Quarterly*, XLIX (April, 1950), 226.

Wheatley, Elizabeth D. "Norman Douglas," *Sewanee Review*, XL (January, 1932), 55.

Index

Index